Mikhail Bakhtin and Walter Benjamin

Mikhail Bakhtin and Walter Benjamin

Experience and Form

Tim Beasley-Murray

First published 2007 by
PALGRAVE MACMILLAN
Houndmills, Basingstoke, Hampshire RG21 6XS and
175 Fifth Avenue, New York, N.Y. 10010
Companies and representatives throughout the world

PALGRAVE MACMILLAN is the global academic imprint of the Palgrave Macmillan division of St. Martin's Press, LLC and of Palgrave Macmillan Ltd. Macmillan® is a registered trademark in the United States, United Kingdom and other countries. Palgrave is a registered trademark in the European Union and other countries.

ISBN-13: 978–0–230–53535–0 hardback
ISBN-10: 0–230–53535–6 hardback

This book is printed on paper suitable for recycling and made from fully managed and sustained forest sources. Logging, pulping and manufacturing processes are expected to conform to the environmental regulations of the country of origin.

A catalogue record for this book is available from the British Library.

A catalog record for this book is available from the Library of Congress.

10   9   8   7   6   5   4   3   2   1
16   15   14   13   12   11   10   09   08   07

Printed and bound in Great Britain by
Antony Rowe Ltd, Chippenham and Eastbourne

For Charlotte and Felix

Contents

Note on Abbreviations and References   viii

Introduction   1
1 Habit and Tradition   19
2 Experience   48
3 Language   88
4 Totalities   122

Notes   153
Bibliography   196
Index   209

Note on Abbreviations and References

References to most texts by Bakhtin and Voloshinov are to the English translations of their works and are included in parentheses in the text. The following system of abbreviations is used:

AH Bakhtin, M. M., 'Author and Hero in Aesthetic Activity', in *Art and Answerability: Early Philosophical Essays by M. M. Bakhtin*, ed. Michael Holquist and Vadim Liapunov, trans. Vadim Liapunov, Austin TX, 1990.

DI Bakhtin, M. M., *The Dialogic Imagination: Four Essays by M. M. Bakhtin*, ed. Michael Holquist, trans. Caryl Emerson and Michael Holquist, Austin TX, 1981.

DP Bakhtin, M. M., *Problems of Dostoevsky's Poetics*, ed. and trans. Caryl Emerson, Manchester, 1984.

MPL Vološinov, V. N., *Marxism and the Philosophy of Language*, ed. and trans. Ladislav Matejka and I. R. Titunik, London, 1973.

Rabelais Bakhtin, M. M., *Rabelais and his World*, trans. Hélène Iswolsky, Bloomington IN, 1984.

SG Bakhtin, M. M., *Speech Genres and Other Late Essays*, ed. Caryl Emerson and Michael Holquist, trans. Vern W. McGee, Austin TX, 1986.

TPA Bakhtin, M. M., *Toward a Philosophy of the Act*, ed. Vadim Liapunov and Michael Holquist, trans. Vadim Liapunov, Austin TX, 1993.

Other works by Bakhtin and the Bakhtin Circle are referred to in the normal fashion.

References to Benjamin are to the German edition of his writings as well as to English translations, except in the few cases where no published translation exists. Most references are also given in parentheses in the text and are abbreviated as follows:

GS Benjamin, W., *Gesammelte Schriften*, 7 vols, ed. Rolf Tiedemann and Hermann Schweppenhäuser, Frankfurt/ Main, 1974.

Briefe	Benjamin, W., *Briefe*, 2 vols, ed. Gershom Scholem and Theodor W. Adorno, Frankfurt/Main, 1993.
SW	Benjamin, W., *Selected Writings*, 4 vols, ed. Michael W. Jennings and others, trans. Howard Eiland, Rodney Livingstone and others, Cambridge MA, 1996–2003.
OGTD	Benjamin, W., *The Origin of German Tragic Drama*, trans. John Osborne, London, 1977.
AP	Benjamin, W., *The Arcades Project*, trans. Howard Eiland and Kevin McLaughlin, Cambridge MA, 1999.

Whilst the translations given follow the published versions for the most part, occasionally I have made slight modifications. I indicate where such modifications have taken place.

Introduction

Experience and Form: the actuality of Bakhtin and Benjamin

The question of the relation of experience to form is the question of the extent to which human beings are able to recognize themselves in the forms that the historical and social moment in which they live makes available to them. It is the question of the way that my experience is reflected in the formally organized world that surrounds me. The relationship between experience and form is necessarily historically located. For Mikhail Bakhtin and Walter Benjamin, born in Orel, Russia, in 1895, and in Berlin, in 1892, respectively, and entering adult life at the close of the First World War, their historical experience is the experience of a rapidly and radically modernizing world. Though neither saw service in that conflict, they both were only a little younger than the generation of young men who returned shattered and transformed from the battlefields of Europe. In 'The Storyteller', his essay of 1936 that notes the decay of the power of traditional narrative forms, caused in part by the experience of mechanized warfare, Benjamin describes the experience of this generation as follows:

> A generation that had gone to school on horse-drawn streetcars now stood under the open sky in a landscape where nothing remained unchanged but the clouds and, beneath those clouds, in a force field of destructive torrents and explosions, the tiny, fragile human body.
>
> (*GS II* 439; *SW III* 144)

Bakhtin and Benjamin's thoughts are similarly marked by a sense of the fractured nature of specifically modern experience. This fracturing

1

arises from an historical dislocation of experience from the forms that are designed to enable human beings to make sense of that experience (the forms of habitualized social behaviour, tradition, cognition, language, artistic genres, and art *per se*). Thus, for example, Bakhtin and Benjamin, in their thinking on the epic and the story, respectively, are heirs to a sense similar to Hegel's sense of the falling into oblivion of the practice of forms through transformations in concrete social life.[1] Nevertheless, both thinkers seek the seeds of new, productive, and emancipatory experience in the new forms that those transformations bring into being.

Bakhtin and Benjamin write of a modernity that may not seem so modern to readers to whom horse-drawn trams are familiar only from jerky images of silent newsreels and for whom, in the post-Auschwitz nuclear age, trench warfare is, by a distance, no longer the most technologically advanced way of killing. Nevertheless, the thematic centre of this study, the question of experience and form, has continuing relevance today. Unlike affirmative theorists of postmodernity, such as Jean-François Lyotard and Jean Baudrillard, I do not believe that we have entirely left Bakhtin and Benjamin's era – a modernity of flux, characterized, one might argue, by anxiety – and entered a postmodernity of possibility, characterized by play. The dislocation of form and experience continues and has become, if anything, accentuated by the ever-increasing intensity of centrifugal and centripetal forces that operate in processes of globalization and social fragmentation. Never have Bakhtin's and Benjamin's insights been more pertinent in their radical deconstruction of hegemonic and authoritarian hierarchies, combined with a relentless attention to possibilities – not empty possibilities, but possibilities for the intervention of human subjects, possibilities that are tensely coiled in the midst of the new.

The age in which we live is not characterized by the official seriousness of medieval culture that Bakhtin saw undermined by Rabelaisian carnival, nor is it characterized by quite the same alliance of a cult of primal experience with technology that Benjamin saw in fascism and to which he opposed his own brand of disjunctive critical thinking and disjunctive artistic practice. Nonetheless, it might be argued that the Straussian neo-conservatism, currently dominant in the United States, constitutes a qualitatively similar entwinement of myth and technology, and that the promotion of fear and orthodoxy by the proclamation of a 'war on terror' constitutes a new form of official seriousness and fear.[2] Bakhtin's and Benjamin's critiques of such phenomena, then, retain their actuality.

In similar fashion, the sense of an 'end of politics', of the 'third way', of the absolute and universal necessity of liberal democracy, as expressed, in different forms, by thinkers such as Anthony Giddens, Jürgen Habermas and Ulrich Beck, has become the hegemonic discourse of our post-1989 world. It has become (taking a Bakhtinian standpoint) the monologic discourse which brooks no answering back. It has become (taking a Benjaminian standpoint) an uncritical hypostatization of the concept of progress which can conceive of no possible alternative state of affairs other than the present. Frustration at this situation has led some on the left to run into the embrace of some dangerous comrades: Chantal Mouffe into the arms of Carl Schmitt;[3] Slavoj Žižek into the arms of Lenin.[4] An alliance of Bakhtin and Benjamin may provide a more effective theoretical resource in breaking out of the *Denkverbot* of late capitalism – for the emancipatory forms that challenge authority need not be the by-now dusty pages of Dostoevsky or the by-now familiar stage-tricks of Brecht.[5] Both thinkers exhibit a lucid ability to see potentialities in the nascent, in the still-coming-into-being. It may take a perspective that draws on both Bakhtin and Benjamin to engage with such nascent forms. Furthermore, the alliance of politics and ethics, of political commitment and loving attention, that is formed when we bring Bakhtin's and Benjamin's thought alongside each other is valuable and powerful.

Angles of comparison

As far as comparative studies of Bakhtin and Benjamin are concerned, despite many assertions of affinities and many comments in passing, very little has been written. Sandywell's essay offers suggestions (such as possible affinities between Benjamin's concept of translation and Bakhtin's concept of dialogue or between Benjamin's concept of messianic redemption and Bakhtin's concept of 'great time') but operates at such a level of generality and abstraction that his contribution is minimal.[6] Eagleton's treatment of Bakhtin in the context of his study of Benjamin (he devotes in total about 13 pages of his 179-page study to Bakhtin) is typically provocative but an also typical predominance of rhetorical élan over analytical content limits its usefulness. Nevertheless, his work on Benjamin is suggestive in its use of Bakhtin's conception of carnival to supplement Benjamin's messianic Marxism and in the concomitant insight that Bakhtin and Benjamin might be brought together on the territory of both Marxism and theology.[7] Perhaps the most perspicacious study of Bakhtin and Benjamin is the essay by Zima which fastens onto the central similarity between Benjamin's concept of the shock of montage and Bakhtin's concept of carnival laughter. For Zima, both phenomena, shock and laughter, are 'liberatory elements of critique whose ambivalence (the joining of incompatible values) constitutes the motor of a discourse both dialectic and dialogic'.[8] Nevertheless, Zima's emphasis on the eternally unfinalizable nature of what he terms Bakhtin's and Benjamin's ambivalence is something that I take issue with in my final chapter.[9] Despite these and other contributions, then, this study represents, to the best of my knowledge, the most complete attempt at a comparative study of these two thinkers to date.[10]

There are good reasons for this situation. A comparative study of Bakhtin and Benjamin cannot proceed along straight lines. It would be wrong to ignore the elements of incommensurability in a desire to focus on commensurability and comparison. An awareness of such incommensurabilities has led me along a crooked path through Bakhtin's and Benjamin's thought. This produces images of the two thinkers that diverge fundamentally from the images that one might construct when picturing any one of the thinkers independently. Thus, the image of Bakhtin presented here is one of the Bakhtin who appears in conjunction with Benjamin, and is a product of the oblique angle of comparison – and *vice versa*.[11] My aim is to show that the oblique angle of comparison highlights aspects of both thinkers that otherwise remain in the shadows. Thus, for example, in Chapter 3 that deals with Bakhtin's and Benjamin's philosophy of language, a Bakhtinian position on the primacy of intersubjectivity over the fixed antinomy of subject and object has led me to a reading of Benjamin's conceptions of translation and montage as articulations of an intersubjective relationship between the human subject and the world. Similarly, in the final chapter on totality, a Benjaminian standpoint on the temporal relationship between provisional brokenness and future completion has led me to emphasize the provisional nature of dialogue, rather than what some critics see as its eternal open-endedness. Furthermore, my thematic focus on the nexus between experience, form and modernity aims at more than the simple intersection of the two thinkers' ideas: it constitutes an attempt to uncover enduring insights that Bakhtin and Benjamin may have into how to make sense of our own modernity.

Connections

Mikhail Bakhtin and Walter Benjamin inhabited worlds that seem, at first glance, to have few points of contact. The two months that

Benjamin spent in Moscow in the winter of 1926–27 were marked by the failure of his love affair with the Latvian communist Asja Lacis and, despite the outwardly enthusiastic tone of his 'Moscow Diary', Benjamin found life in the city alienating and exhausting. Benjamin knew no more than a few words of Russian, and whilst his interest in Russian and, especially, Soviet culture was, at times, passionate, it remained second-hand and somewhat naive. It seems improbable that he could have come into contact with the Bakhtin Circle at all. Likewise, Bakhtin, who never left his native Russia and the Soviet Union, despite being rooted in the German-orientated *Bildungskultur* of his time, shows no evidence of having been acquainted with Benjamin or his work. Benjamin's publications, in either book or magazine form, would have been unlikely to be accessible to Bakhtin, although one might speculate that Bakhtin was familiar with the entry on Goethe that was commissioned from Benjamin for the *Great Soviet Encyclopaedia*. Nevertheless, as Kassack points out in the editorial apparatus to the *Gesammelte Schriften*, the published text only contains 12 per cent of Benjamin's original from which everything of substance has been eliminated.[12] The points of connection, then, between the two subjects of comparison are necessarily mediated obliquely.

First and most straightforwardly, one may speak of the two thinkers' similar backgrounds in the European philosophical tradition. These might be considered diachronic contexts. In Chapter 2, I deal with Bakhtin's and Benjamin's engagement with the philosophical opposition of the late nineteenth and the early twentieth century between (neo-)Kantianism and *Lebensphilosophie*. I argue that these parallel engagements create structures that persist throughout the careers of the two thinkers and result in parallel emphases on the question of the relationship between life and culture, experience and form. Yet, as Chapter 2 and the book as a whole demonstrate, a reconstruction of diachronic context is itself not straightforward given the far from straightforward ways in which the two thinkers relate to and represent their intellectual inheritances.[13]

Second, one may speak of the connections provided by intermediary figures on the synchronic axis. One figure who stands out here is Georg Lukács, another thinker whose concern is the relationship between form and experience. Lukács's early work *The Theory of the Novel* (1914) exerted a profound influence on both thinkers. Similarly, just as his later work *History and Class Consciousness* (1923) provides a formative subterranean strand in Benjamin's thought from the *Trauerspiel* book onwards, so Tihanov, in his book on the subject, demonstrates in great detail the extent of Bakhtin's complex debt to both the early and later Lukács. One may also include in these synchronic connections the link between Benjamin and Brecht, on the one hand, and Bakhtin and Russian Formalism, on the other. Formalism and Brecht provide a rare moment where the contemporary intellectual worlds of Bakhtin and Benjamin come into direct contact and the former has an influence on the latter – for it seems that Brecht, on his trip to Russia in 1935, drew directly on the Formalist concept of *ostranenie* in his formulation of the notion of *Verfremdung*.[14] Moreover, more generally, the radical avant-garde aesthetics of both Brecht and Formalism present a disruptive relationship between experience and form, a relationship conceived of as the automatization and deautomatization of life and art, that exerts a continuing influence on both thinkers.[15]

Third, it is possible to talk of a form of connection that is posthumous. As I argue in Chapter 1, both Bakhtin and Benjamin hold that the meanings contained in a work, and a work of philosophy as much as a work of art, are revealed in time in the process of criticism. The ideas of Bakhtin and Benjamin are brought together not just on the territory of this study but also in the intellectual developments that have followed them. By way of example, both thinkers have, to greater or lesser extents, been co-opted into varied discourses of post-Structuralism: Bakhtin, initially through Kristeva's development of a post-Bakhtinian theory of intertextuality and later by thinkers who found in Bakhtin a gesture of perpetual openness, analogous to Derrida's notion of the perpetual deferring of signification, which nevertheless did not jettison the notion of the individual subject;[16] and Benjamin, whose focus on the hidden resources of writing have proved an inspiration to those who have also been inspired by Derrida's theory of grammatology and whose conception of reading 'against the grain' has likewise drawn the attention of proponents of Deconstruction.[17] In both instances I contend that Bakhtin and Benjamin have lent themselves to such an appropriation because of their insistence that what seems at first to be a secondary phenomenon (dialogue, writing) might fruitfully be understood as being of primary importance. Another case is that of Bakhtin's collaborators, Voloshinov and Medvedev, whose work has, like that of Benjamin, provided some commentators on the left with a more Marx-based critique of Structuralism than the ideologically ambiguous approach of post-Structuralism.[18]

Finally, as I have already suggested, the most important connection between the two thinkers lies at the level of their different but analogous engagements with a world that is distinctively modern. This connection is more than a question of the three years that separate their births and is based on more than an empty notion such as *Zeitgeist*. It is a commonplace to say that Benjamin is a thinker of modernity. His entire work is preoccupied with finding ways of negotiating and making sense of a rapidly changing modern world. As one of his biographers puts it:

> His life's work [...] is basically a reflection on his own city origins. It amounts to a meditation on the experience of the individual's altering needs and possibilities within the labyrinth of constantly and rapidly changing impressions, on whether he can still perceive or grasp his historical and social environment in some sort of context, or indeed make any kind of picture of it. In a nutshell: how to cope, how to find one's way around.[19]

This is the question of experience and form. How can one find forms that allow the subject to grasp, yet do not distort, an experience that is post-traditional, located in the heart of modernity? Benjamin's writing has as its backdrop the traffic of the boulevard and the flickering of neon. The forms that he promotes, such as Baudelaire's poetry of shock and allegorical *correspondances*, Proust's prose that is convulsed by *mémoires involuntaires*, or Brecht's epic theatre of interruption, articulate and preserve the rhythm of modern life. Even when Benjamin looks back to the Baroque, one eye is firmly fixed on his own present.

An engagement with the modern world is less obvious in Bakhtin. For all his emphasis on the dynamic flow of life and the burning need for its preservation and not ossification as it takes on linguistic form, and for all his emphasis on the diversity of the social world, his own world can seem remarkably bookish and rooted in the nineteenth century.[20] It is to the chagrin of many Bakhtin scholars that the most modern of Bakhtin's line of heroes is Dostoevsky and not, say, Joyce.[21] Nevertheless, Bakhtin's commitment to the novel, the genre of emancipation that receives its form from modernity itself (as recognized by thinkers from Schlegel, through Hegel and Lukács, to Ian Watt and Lucien Goldmann), demonstrates his analogous search for formal models by which a specifically modern experience may be understood and in which it may justly find expression. The novel, the 'only genre born of this new world and in total affinity with it' (*DI* 7), is, in Bakhtin's analysis, the anti-genre of becoming (in so far as genre may be defined as a congealed set of norms) through which the experience of modernity and the giving of form come into dynamic resolution.

Nevertheless, if the Bakhtin that appears here is more obviously a participant in his modernity than might be the case of a stand-alone Bakhtin, then the comparison with Benjamin throws certain absences and blank spots into relief. Despite his insistence on the social, at times Bakhtin's modernity seems to consist in a form of historical dynamism that is curiously devoid of content: a modernity of flux without a clear image of the technological and social developments that bring that flux into being. His indestructibly modern novelness may, at times, seem to be little more than an expression of Hegelian delight in a new expression of *Geist*.[22] From early on in his career, Benjamin is alive to the threat of the violence that emerges from what Adorno and Horkheimer will later analyse as the entanglement of enlightenment and myth. This crystallizes in the impassioned and concrete analysis of and defence against fascism that occupies him from the late 1920s until his death. As I show in Chapter 2, Benjamin's critique of fascism rests on his understanding of the relationship between experience and form: fascism, for Benjamin, consists in the fatal bringing together of a cult of mythic, pure experience with the abstract formal workings of capitalist technology. In this context, the case of Bakhtin is problematic: Bakhtin's philosophy has proved so attractive to his readers exactly because his conception of form is one in which the experience of otherness can be negotiated without violence. And yet a comparison with Benjamin throws into sharp relief the question of Bakhtin's disquieting silence in the face of Stalinist violence.[23] Here, Benjamin's more thorough-going and more responsible political engagement may be used to supplement Bakhtin. Similarly, Bakhtin's more concrete model of benign relations between self and other may be used to supplement Benjamin's sometimes frustratingly vague pleas for cultural activity to engage in political combat with violence itself.

Incommensurabilities and commensurabilities

Melancholy and laughter

A key difference between Bakhtin and Benjamin, and a difference that makes them seem, at times, incommensurable, is that of temperament. If Bakhtin is a theorist of laughter and celebration, Benjamin comes across as resolutely melancholy and sober. The image of Benjamin the melancholic is fixed most firmly in the writings of his friend, Gershom Scholem. Scholem's biographical *Walter Benjamin: The Story of a Friendship* portrays Benjamin primarily in terms of melancholy.[24]

Likewise, in his speech given in 1972 to commemorate what would have been Benjamin's eightieth birthday, Scholem reads Benjamin's 'On the Concept of History' as the expression of his return to his 'true' theological roots following the disillusion caused by the Molotov–Ribbentrop pact. This return to theology is the result of deep melancholy and, for Scholem, Benjamin's angel of history is a harbinger of melancholy:

> If one may speak of Walter Benjamin's genius, then it was concentrated in this angel. In the latter's Saturnine light Benjamin's life itself ran its course, also consisting only of 'small-scale victories' and 'large-scale defeats,' as he described it from a deeply melancholy point of view in a letter which he addressed to me on July 26, 1932, one day before his intended, but at the time not executed suicide.[25]

The effect of Scholem's melancholic picture is a depoliticization of Benjamin's thought. This is part of a deliberate strategy on the part of Scholem, who wishes to disentangle Benjamin in a posthumous fashion from the clutches of materialism and draw him back to the Jewish mystical tradition. In addition, however, one sees here the outlines of what has now developed into a full-blown cult: the cult of Benjamin's suicide which casts him as the first victim of Nazism and the victim of history *par excellence*. Benjamin becomes the victim of his comments in 'The Storyteller', which I discuss later and loosely paraphrase here: a man who, in memory, is destined all his life to die by his own hand, if not at the age of 35, then at the age of 48. Such a melancholic view of the specificity of Nazi brutality, however, robs that brutality of historical meaning and transforms it into the mere object of pathos.

Just as Scholem, in the speech referred to above, accuses his audience of *marxisants* post-*soixante-huitards* of canonizing Benjamin as a saint of the revolutionary cause, so the fascination of critics (and even of those outside the academy to whom the name Walter Benjamin means something) with his death has made Benjamin a martyr to the cause of universal victimhood. Contemplating Benjamin in this muddled-headedly meta-Benjaminian way results in a melancholic gaze into the past that, once again, depoliticizes.[26] Benjamin himself, rather, was concerned with attempts to turn melancholy against itself in the cause of action. Thus, in his review of Erich Kästner's poetry, Benjamin venomously rejects 'left-wing melancholia', defined as 'self-indulgence and passivity tricked out as social criticism' (*GS III* 283; *SW II* 426). Rather, Benjamin sought genuinely critical forms of melancholy, such as *Trauerspiel*, that can be transformed into its active opposite.[27]

In opposition to the image of Benjamin, the melancholic, a comparison with Bakhtin and his apparently contrary emphasis on laughter has led me to look again at Benjamin and recognize in his work a theory of laughter.[28] This theory first appears in Benjamin's dissertation *The Concept of Criticism in German Romanticism* (1920). Here, Benjamin marks out an opposition between ironic scorn and sobriety. The serious and prosaic mode of reflection is the mode in which the truth content of the work of art is revealed as the 'eternal sober continuance of the work' (*GS I* 109; *SW I* 178). Nevertheless, withering, ironic, scornful satire that reveals the absurdity in the bad work of art (which, hence, for the Romantics, is not art at all) is a necessary clearing of the ground that establishes what is criticizable and hence what is art:

> The Romantic *terminus technicus* for the posture that corresponds to the axiom of the uncriticizability of the bad – not only in art, but in all realms of intellectual life – is 'annihilate'. It designates the indirect refutation of the nugatory through silence, through ironic praise, or through the high praise of the good. The mediacy of irony is, in Schlegel's mind, the only mode in which criticism can directly confront the nugatory.
>
> (*GS I* 79–80; *SW I* 160)

The cruel laughter of irony is necessary as the destruction of illusion. Laughter (here as scorn) and sobriety exist in dialectical interdependence.

Benjamin's theory of laughter reappears later in his work, particularly in his analysis of Brecht's epic theatre. In 'The Author as Producer' (1934), he writes: 'there is no better trigger for thinking than laughter. In particular, convulsion of the diaphragm usually provides better opportunities for thought than convulsion of the soul. Epic theatre is lavish only in occasions for laughter' (*GS II* 699; *SW II* 779). This liberating laughter is akin both to the withering scorn of Romantic irony and to what one critic terms the 'scornful, ruinous laughter of Surrealism which humiliates the obsolete and absurd'.[29] Once again, laughter is a critical debunking, a clearing of ground, akin to Bakhtin's concept of 'parodic destruction'.[30] But it is more than mere debunking; it is a deconstructive prerequisite, the starting point for something else: sober reflection, in Romantic criticism, and now, in his treatment of Brecht, political action. Laughter and seriousness in Benjamin's thought must be comprehended as dialectically intertwined. The result of this comprehension is, unlike the effect of pathological melancholization of Benjamin, his repoliticization.[31]

Turning back to Bakhtin from Benjamin's theory of laughter that only came to the fore in the light of Bakhtin, the Bakhtin who now reappears has likewise been transformed. It is easy to find a Bakhtin who stands firmly on the side of laughter in an opposition between laughter and melancholy. According to Bakhtin in the Rabelais book (1965),[32] on feast days, medieval students were:

> freed from the heavy chains of devout seriousness, from the 'continual ferment of piety and the fear of God.' They were freed from the oppression of such gloomy categories as 'eternal,' 'immovable,' 'absolute,' 'unchangeable' and instead were exposed to the gay and free laughing aspect of the world, with its open and unfinished character, with the joy of change and renewal.
>
> (*Rabelais* 83)

Nevertheless, if certain strands in the critical literature on Benjamin have subjected him to a thorough melancholization that renders him politically immobile, so, too, some critics of Bakhtin have emphasized this theory of laughter to the extent of emptying his thought of any substance. The theory of decrowning, debunking laughter in Bakhtin's writings raises the serious matter of how far such laughter acquiesces with, even participates in, violence.[33] Furthermore, Bakhtin's emphasis on carnival laughter is used by some critics to paint him as a post-ideological liberal. Thus, for example, Clark and Holquist contend that Bakhtin's laughing Rabelais is a champion of unbridled relativism:

> Rabelais's importance lies not in his own particular ideology but in his awareness of the limits, the incompleteness of any ideology. No matter how serious Rabelais appears to be at any point in a text, he makes sure to leave a gap, to provide what Bakhtin calls a 'merry loophole' – a loophole that opens on the distant future and that lends an aspect of ridicule to the present or to the immediate future [...].[34]

The Rabelais that results may have a 'key place in the history of freedom', as Clark and Holquist put it,[35] but, through a denial of the possibility of seriousness, such a freedom becomes purely negative: it is the empty, reactive, if not passive phenomenon of liberation, rather than positive and concrete freedom.[36] What emerges is a depoliticized Bakhtin.

It is necessary to reassess the relationship between laughter and seriousness in Bakhtin's thought. In part, this reassessment has already taken place as a result of the critical discovery of Bakhtin's early works, the tone of which is unquestionably serious. Furthermore, religious readings of Bakhtin have helped to rebalance the issue. The focus of Coates's book, for example, on the central theme of the Fall produces a far more serious, if not melancholy, image of Bakhtin's thought. Independently of a necessarily religious frame of reference, however, Coates's technique also involves an inversion of the standard reading of Bakhtin. Where other critics see in Bakhtin's theory of the polyphonic novel the joyful arrival and coming-to-voice of liberated subjects, Coates sees the melancholy exile and falling silent of the author. She traces progressive narratives of exile in Bakhtin's work, which comprise the exile of 'God Himself, whose supremely authoritative discourse has been squeezed out of the world of culture as a result of the same paradigmatic shift which, if Bakhtin is correct, forced the writer of prose fiction to hide his or her true self'.[37] This view of Bakhtin, as will become clear in Chapter 3, bears marked similarities to the position of Benjamin in 'On Language as Such and on the Language of Man' that likewise describes a post-lapsarian world of silence and melancholy. One can also draw attention to the distinction in Bakhtin's thought (emerging most clearly in the notes towards a revision of the Rabelais book) between official seriousness, the legitimate target of laughter, and its unofficial counterpart that Bakhtin describes in very Benjaminian, melancholic tones: 'the unofficial seriousness of suffering, of fear, of fright, of weakness, the seriousness of the slave and the seriousness of the sacrificial victim' which expresses 'the ultimate protest of individuality (bodily and spiritual) yearning for immortality, against change and absolute renewal, the protest of the part against its dissolution in the whole'.[38]

Benjamin, I have argued, sees laughter as the dialectical precondition for a genuine seriousness. It is the agent of clearing and cleansing new territory. It is possible to see a similar dialectic at work in Bakhtin. Bakhtin writes in the Dostoevsky book:[39]

Carnivalization is not an eternal and immobile schema which is imposed upon ready-made content; it is, rather, an extraordinarily flexible form of artistic visualization, a peculiar sort of heuristic principle making possible the discovery of new and as yet unseen things. By relativizing all that was externally stable, set and ready-made, carnivalization with its pathos of change and renewal permitted Dostoevsky to penetrate into the darkest layers of man and human relationships. It proved remarkably productive as a means for capturing in art the developing relationships under capitalism, at a time when previous forms of life, moral principles and beliefs were being turned into 'rotten cords' and the previously concealed, ambivalent and unfinalized nature of man and human *thought* was being nakedly exposed.

(*DP* 165–66)

I suggest that this passage is subtly double-voiced. The passage with which it polemicizes is a passage from the Communist Manifesto:

Constant revolutionizing of production, uninterrupted disturbance of all social conditions, everlasting uncertainty and agitation distinguish the bourgeois epoch from all earlier ones. All fixed, fast-frozen relations, with their train of ancient and venerable prejudices and opinions, are swept away, all new formed ones become antiquated before they can ossify. All that is solid melts into air, all that is holy is profaned, and man is at last compelled to face with sober sense his real conditions of life, and his relations with his kind.[40]

Bakhtin appears to be implying a structural analogy between the relativizing dynamism of carnival and the revolutionizing dynamism of capital. Both forces invert previous hierarchies. Both forces transform all that they touch ('moral principles' and 'venerable prejudices and opinions'). Carnival blasphemy finds its counterpart in the profaning of all that is holy; 'fixed, fast frozen relations' find their counterpart in what is 'externally stable, set and ready-made'; carnival overturning of the hierarchies of courtly culture finds its counterpart in the bourgeois revolutionizing of feudal social and economic relations of production. Here is not the place to dwell on what sort of testimony this double-voiced passage bears to Bakhtin's relationship with Marxism. My concern is with the parallel that I have established in so far as it affects the last part of these two passages. The intoxication of Marx's description of capitalism finds its terminus in sobriety: man's compulsion to face with sobriety the real conditions of his existence. So, too, with Bakhtin: the terminus is not the laughter of the carnival mask but the nakedness that follows. The historical and philosophical significance of laughter is not laughter itself but the new form of seriousness that laughter brings into being. As Bakhtin comments of Rabelais: 'while breaking up the false seriousness, false historic pathos, he prepared the soil for a new seriousness and for a new historic pathos' (*Rabelais* 439). Laughter, then, far from being the inaction and irresponsibility of eternal relativization,

clears the ground, as in Benjamin's thought, for a new form of seriousness that makes responsible action possible.

Laughter, for Bakhtin and Benjamin, is an instrument of reconfigured,
anti-Aristotelian catharsis. Bakhtin comments on this in the Dostoevsky book:

> Certain scholars [...] apply to Dostoevsky's works the ancient
> (Aristotelian) term 'catharsis' (purification). If this term is understood
> in a very broad sense, then one can agree with it [...]. But tragic cath-
> arsis (in the Aristotelian sense) is not applicable to Dostoevsky. The
> catharsis that finalizes Dostoevsky's novels might be [...] expressed
> in this way: *nothing conclusive has yet taken place in the world, the
> ultimate word of the world has not yet been spoken, the world is open
> and free, everything is still in the future and will always be in the
> future.* But this is, after all, also the purifying sense of ambivalent
> laughter.
>
> (*DP* 165–66)

It is necessary to reassess this passage, the second part of which might
well be used in support of a conception of Bakhtin as a propagandist
of an empty relativism. For both Bakhtin and Benjamin, laughter clears
the ground and purifies. This is an inversion of the Aristotelian view.
According to Aristotle: 'Tragedy, then, is a representation of an action
that is serious, complete, and of a certain magnitude [...] and through
the arousal of pity and fear effecting the *katharsis* of such emotions.'[41]
Pity and fear move the spectator; he or she is intoxicated by wonder
(*rhaumaston*). Bakhtin's and Benjamin's unserious mimesis, not of the
great and complete, but of the everyday and incomplete, consists of a
laughter that knows no pity and fear and results not in intoxication
but in sobriety. According to Benjamin's analysis of Brecht's theory of
epic theatre, Aristotelian theatre, which works through tragic catharsis,
is politically affirmative of the status quo, paralysing human beings
and shutting out opportunities for genuine change. An anti-Aristotelian
catharsis through laughter that results in a new seriousness, such as
is visible in Bakhtin's and Benjamin's theory of laughter, may equip
human beings for real change and action.

Politics and theology

Benjamin and Bakhtin scholars are divided by the differing stand-
points that critics take on Bakhtin's or Benjamin's commitment either
to radical politics or to theology. It is, however, at the level of the

commensurability between these two modes of thinking that a comparison of Bakhtin and Benjamin is most productive.[42] Let us turn to Benjamin's most striking image of the relationship between theology and Marxism from 'On the Concept of History' (1940):

> There was once, we know, an automaton constructed in such a way that it could respond to every move by a chess player with a countermove that would ensure the winning of a game. A puppet wearing Turkish attire and with a hookah in its mouth sat before a chessboard placed on a large table. A system of mirrors created the illusion that this table was transparent on all sides. Actually, a hunchbacked dwarf – a master at chess – sat inside and guided the puppet's hand by means of strings. One can imagine a philosophic counterpart to this apparatus. The puppet, called 'historical materialism', is to win all the time. It can easily be a match for anyone if it enlists the services of theology, which today, as we know, is small and ugly and has to keep out of sight.
>
> *(GS I 693; SW IV 389)*

In Bakhtin and Benjamin scholarship that emerges from an engagement with Marxism, theology, on the one hand, is often the dwarf who must keep out of sight.[43] On the other hand, studies of the two thinkers that deal with theological themes in their work frequently display a disquieting silence with respect to politics, such that legitimate political concerns are neutralized and transferred to a distant religious plane.[44]

My approach is to see theological and political themes in Bakhtin and Benjamin not in terms of their mutual exclusivity but in terms of their possible alliance. (One might also remember here the argument of thinkers such as Carl Schmitt that religion and politics have only recently parted company and that our political thinking might still be structured by theological concepts – this might be especially true from a Jewish standpoint.)[45] In the terms of Benjamin's image above, whether Marx is to come to the aid of religion, or religion to the aid of Marx (albeit with the confusing but tactically necessary obfuscation of smoke and mirrors), the automaton of historical materialism and the ugly dwarf of theology are both engaged in combat with the same opponent. Both thinkers are concerned with religion and politics as a matter of human experience. For both Bakhtin and Benjamin, the emphasis is on the divine as the sphere of the (possible) fulfilment of strictly human needs, hopes and calls for justice. They seek to win the game of chess for the sake of the integrity of the human being within history, not for the sake of abstract and eternal theological truth. As I show in the final chapter, in their view, both politics and theology should aim at the redemption of human beings and the restoration of a totality of their experience in the here and now.[46] In the service of these ends, Bakhtin and Benjamin use theological and political strategies, where appropriate, as flexible tools of intensification.

An insistence on the irreducible theological and political double-voicedness of Bakhtin and Benjamin might appear to evince an unwillingness to take a decision; it might constitute a form of what Bakhtin terms alibi. Leslie writes forcefully and originally on this issue:

> Filtered through the refracting lenses of Scholem, of Heidegger, of the postmodern and of poststructuralism, Benjamin returns to us now as either fractured or multiplied. [...] He is torn between the messianic and the material [...]. Angelic Benjamin floats in theory as a half-figure – half-Marxist, half-Jew – and the partiality of his identifications makes it impossible to locate his theory, and it places him on a border that cuts through all his work, and even (deconstructively? actually?) killed him.[47]

In opposition to Leslie, one might assert that partisans of either the theological or Marxist position are far more guilty of seeing only half of their subjects: either merely Bakhtin/Benjamin the Marxist or merely Bakhtin/Benjamin the theologian. Ultimately, however, it must be conceded that my approach runs into certain buffers: the evidence seems overwhelming that Benjamin does indeed 'break with esotericism' in favour of materialism, as Habermas puts it, and all Scholem's patient argumentation will not win him back.[48] Similarly, the evidence against certainly a Marxist Bakhtin, if not against a political Bakhtin, will not refuse to stack up.[49] In this sense, though their strategies are similar, the nature of the alliances the two thinkers forge are different: in the end, on the one hand, Benjamin's wizened dwarf is indisputably in the service of historical materialism; on the other hand, the voice of Marxism in Bakhtin's discourse is not the final and organizing voice. Nevertheless, the differing combinations of theological and political tactics are an important element of commensurability between the two thinkers in their battles for the integrity of earthly, human experience.

Chapter outlines

In Chapter 1, 'Habit and Tradition', I examine Bakhtin's and Benjamin's conception of habit and habitualized patterns of behaviour such as ritual and tradition. The question of this chapter is the question of whether such habitual forms represent media for the subject's free self-actualization, rescuing her or him from the mere flux of existence; or whether, on the contrary, these forms represent authoritarian media of alienation in which the subject finds him or herself objectified.

In Chapter 2, 'Experience', I take an intellectual-historical approach to the relation between experience and form. Taking the ideas of Kant and Hegel as a starting point and ending in the confrontation of the late nineteenth- and early twentieth-century movements of neo-Kantianism and *Lebensphilosophie*, I investigate the development of two opposing conceptions of experience in the philosophical tradition: on the one hand, the concrete, subjective and vital experience, opposed to formal regularity, which this tradition terms *Erlebnis*; and, on the other hand, the abstract, objective and intrinsically formal experience which this tradition terms *Erfahrung*. The chapter then proceeds to chart both thinkers' articulations of the inadequacy of either conception of experience and their attempts to formulate ways beyond this bifurcation of experience.

Chapter 3, 'Language', examines Bakhtin's and Benjamin's conceptions of language as a possible site of unity of the subjective and objective aspects of experience. Here, I examine the particular varieties of language that Bakhtin and Benjamin suggest might be forms that do not violate the integrity of experience: double-voiced discourse, the polyphony of the novel, translation, montage and, perhaps paradoxically, silence.

Chapter 4, 'Totalities', is devoted to an examination of the place of theories of totality in Bakhtin's and Benjamin's aesthetic theory. In this chapter, I expand on the argument of the study as a whole that Bakhtin's and Benjamin's central concern is the question of the closedness or openness of form. Closed forms (epic and monologue, for example, in the case of Bakhtin; the traditional auratic work of art or the Romantic symbol, for example, in the case of Benjamin) provide a completion of experience which fixes experience within the flux of life. Nevertheless, both thinkers argue that closed forms such as these are intimately tied up in social and political hierarchies and result in an objectification of human beings and the world that they inhabit. Bakhtin and Benjamin develop theories of open forms that challenge closedness: dialogue and the novel, in the case of Bakhtin, and translation, allegory and montage, in the case of Benjamin. These forms promote the preservation of (inter)subjectivity, the dismantling of authoritarian hierarchies and a responsible relationship between the conferring of form and the integrity of experience. This final chapter examines the negatively constructed images of totality contained in these theories. In the context of a discussion of the two thinkers' theology and their politics, this chapter also deals with the temporal orientation of the thinkers' work and the extent to which Bakhtin's and Benjamin's promotion of the openness of form might be provisional positions predicated on a future completion that will come on either the messianic-theological or the political-revolutionary plane.

1
Habit and Tradition

Habit

Bakhtin and habit

Habit is activity that has been subjected to a process of formal ordering whereby it is made repeatable. In this chapter, I discuss habit in conjunction with a range of other cognate phenomena such as custom, rhythm, ritual, collecting and tradition. In these phenomena (which may operate at either the individual or the societal level) the experience of the world receives form: it acquires, to a greater or lesser extent, the attributes of order and repeatability. A concrete example of this is the dirty habit of smoking. The legend according to which Bakhtin smoked away the only manuscript of his work on the *Bildungsroman* has been countered by Hirschkop on the grounds that the work itself never existed in any more than the fragmentary form that we possess today.[1] Hirschkop's secondary argument, however, casts scorn on the notion that Bakhtin, 'this most ascetic of scholars was [...] in equal measure casual as regards his texts and passionate about one of life's more suspect pleasures'.[2] Although he notes Bakhtin's passion for smoking, Hirschkop's labelling of smoking as nothing but a pleasurable vice underrates the seriousness of Bakhtin's smoking.

Bakhtin was a serious smoker and a serious drinker of tea. These habits were, for Bakhtin, at least as much a ritual as a pleasure in the usual sense. These habits caused difficulties for Bakhtin's friends when they attempted to move the invalid Bakhtin and his wife from Saransk to Moscow. As his biographers put it:

On the one hand, the Bakhtins had always led a simple and ascetic life, but on the other, their habits were so fixed at this point that there was very little flexibility [...]. Bakhtin drank tea all day which [Elena] insisted on both making and serving herself. She would not agree to using an electrical kettle, so that whatever new accommodations were found would have to provide a stove on which she could boil water.[3]

Aspects of Bakhtin's life were ruled by habit that had become binding ritual in the midst of his outward asceticism.

In opposition to the role of habit in his life, however, Bakhtin's work displays a 'preoccupation with variety, nonrecurrence, and discorrespondence'.[4] A revolt against habitualizing modes of thought and behaviour forms a major theme in Bakhtin's work that spans the different incarnations of his thought.[5] Thus, *Toward a Philosophy of the Act* stresses the unrepeatable act in the face of the habitualized and repeatable transcription of theoreticism; Voloshinov's work on language argues for the dynamic and unrepeatable nature of 'theme' against the static and habitualized nature of 'meaning'; Bakhtin repeatedly contrasts the open-ended nature of the novel with the habitual nature of the epic, the end of which is always known in advance. Likewise, Bakhtin shares with the Russian Formalists a sense of the vital and disruptive function of genuine art that resists automatization. Keeping an eye on Bakhtin the smoker and Bakhtin the tea-drinker as well as on Bakhtin the champion of the unrepeatable essence of human activity may help to keep in focus an essential ambivalence of Bakhtin's thought.

A way of approaching Bakhtin's ambivalence towards habit is to examine his treatment of the concept of rhythm. The creation of rhythm is the drawing of the irregular and unpredictable activity of the world into regular and more predictable patterns. One need only think of, for example, the role that rhythm plays in the tradition of oral poetry, making verse memorable and habitual to both singers and listeners. In the extensive fragment written in the years 1920–24, 'Author and Hero in Aesthetic Activity', Bakhtin develops a complex notion of rhythm. Here, in so far as the author rhythmicizes the hero's life, he rescues that life from existential contingency:

In the interior being of another person, when I experience that being actively in the category of *otherness*, 'is' and 'ought' (being and obligation) are not severed and are not hostile to each other, but are organically interconnected and exist on one and the same axiological plane; the *other* grows organically in meaning. His self-activity is heroic for me and is graciously cherished by rhythm (for the whole of him may be in the past for me, and I can justifiably free him from the ought-to-be, which confronts only myself, within me myself, as a categorical imperative) [...]. Rhythm is an embrace and a kiss bestowed upon the axiologically consolidated or 'bodied' time of another's mortal life. Where there is rhythm, there are two souls (or rather a soul and a spirit) – two self-activities; one of these lives and experiences its own life and has become passive for the other, which actively shapes and sings the first.

(AH 121)

Bakhtin is making grand claims for the gift of rhythm here that need elucidation.

By rhythmicizing the hero, the author bestows the gift of form on a life, setting it free from the demands of ethical activity. The reference here is to Kant's moral theory. Kant, unlike Hume from whom the distinction between 'is' and 'ought' is derived, holds that in our use of reason we unite the spheres of *is* and *ought* through obedience to the categorical imperative. This is the permanent task (*Aufgabe*) of our existence from which we are never absolved. It is, nevertheless, a task that we perform in freedom, since we divine the demands of the categorical imperative by means of our faculty of reason which is the sign of our free will and, in obeying those demands, we obey ourselves. According to Bakhtin, however, the loving gift of rhythm absolves the hero of this task. It should, however, be clear that this gift comes at the price of his freedom, returning him to the heteronomous sphere of necessity.[6] The kiss of rhythm sets us free from freedom:

Free will and self-activity are incompatible with rhythm. A life (lived experience, striving, performed action, thought) that is lived and experienced in the categories of moral freedom and of self-activity cannot be rhythmicized. Freedom and self-activity create rhythm for an existence that is (ethically) unfree and passive. [...] To be sure, the unfreedom, the necessity of a life shaped by rhythm is not a *cruel* necessity [...] rather, it is a necessity bestowed as a gift, bestowed by love: it is a beautiful necessity. A rhythmicized existence is 'purposive without purpose'.

(AH 119)

This necessity, however, is not the sphere of natural necessity. Rather, rhythmicization raises the hero into the aesthetic sphere of 'purposiveness without purpose'.[7] Nevertheless, despite the fact that beauty has a symbolic and propaedeutic connection to morality, the beautiful does not lie within the scope of morality and hence is unfree.[8] The rhythmicized life, then, acquires an ambivalent status as an other transfixed in beloved unfreedom.

In the later essay 'Discourse in the Novel' (1934–35), Bakhtin returns to the theme of rhythm:

> Rhythm, by creating an unmediated involvement between every aspect of the accentual system of the whole (via the most immediate rhythmic unities), destroys in embryo those social worlds of speech and of persons that are potentially embedded in the word: in any case, rhythm puts definite limits on them, does not let them unfold or materialize.
>
> (*DI* 298)

Bakhtin has revised his conception of rhythm here. Rhythm is death to the plurality of social worlds embedded in language: it 'destroys them in embryo'. This deadening has the effect of reification, reducing these worlds with their manifold speaking subjects to an inert thing. One might understand this passage in terms of an image: the image of a bud or a seed. The bud is not able to unfold into the multiplicity of the living flower; the seed is unable to germinate into a growing plant. Rather it remains a dead seed-head or, indeed, a stone, the same for all eternity in its unproductiveness. Here, then, the habit of rhythm is the mark of a total deadening of the world. Taken as a whole, one can discern a crucial ambivalence towards habit in both Bakhtin's life and his work.

Benjamin and habit

It is perhaps strange to associate Benjamin with habit. His was a life of continued interruption, an itinerant life of in part chosen and in part enforced exile and movement. Van Reijen and van Doorn have vividly chronicled the moves between hotel rooms and rented flats in Berlin, Frankfurt, Ibiza, Paris and Moscow, and elsewhere, where Benjamin rarely remained for more than six months at a time.[9] Nevertheless, Benjamin's life was governed by habitual rituals no less strict than those that governed Bakhtin. As Adorno writes in an essay reminiscing about his friend:

> [Benjamin's] private demeanour at times approached the ritualistic. In the letters this ritual element extends to the graphic image, indeed

even to the selection of writing paper; during the period of emigration his friend Alfred Cohn continued a longstanding practice of presenting him with a specific grade of paper. Benjamin's ritual behaviour was most pronounced in his youth, and only towards the end of his life did it begin to relax.[10]

Benjamin's obsessive nature and his preoccupation with habit are to be seen in both life and work.[11]

Benjamin's practice of and philosophical interest in collecting bears witness to his tendency for habit. Collecting is a matter of obsession and a ritualized form of habit, just like smoking and tea-drinking. Collecting grew into a passion during his preparatory work for the *Trauerspiel book* as Benjamin bought from antiquarian booksellers, often at ruinous cost, the seventeenth-century allegory books that were to form the core material of that work. The concern with collecting as a phenomenon to be studied runs throughout Benjamin's work from his interest in the Baroque preoccupation with collecting symbols and allegories, through the passage on stamp-collecting in *One-Way Street*, through the essays 'Eduard Fuchs, Collector and Historian' and 'On Unpacking my Library', to the *Arcades Project*, the sprawling notes for a work on nineteenth-century Paris that Benjamin began in 1927 and never completed. In the *Arcades Project*, the reader confronts a document that is a disquisition on collecting: the mania for collecting that is exhibited in the nineteenth-century bourgeois interior and in the seductive piling of commodity upon commodity in the Paris arcade. But it is simultaneously a monument of collecting itself: a store of quotations and sources, laboriously copied out by hand into vast lists during long hours in the *Bibliothèque nationale*.

With Benjamin's concern with ritual and habit, however, coexists an ever-present emphasis on their other: shock and disruption. Habit, for Benjamin, deadens experience. In his 'Berlin Chronicle' (1932), Benjamin, reminiscing about his childhood experience of the city, writes: 'Let no one think we were talking of a *Markt-Halle*. No: it was pronounced "*Mark-Talle*", and just as these words were eroded by the habit of speech until none retained its original sense, so by the habit of this walk all the images it offered were worn away' (*GS VI* 475; *SW II* 603). Benjamin champions childhood experience for its capacity to see everything as new, for its pre-habitual nature. He similarly champions Surrealism for its potential, through the 'profane illumination' of chance and unconscious energies, to disrupt the habitualized experience of modern life. It is the power of cinema to jolt the viewer into new ways of experiencing the world and to destroy, through shock, the aura that Benjamin celebrates in 'The Work of Art in the Age of its Technological Reproducibility'.[12] It is the power of montage to bring deadened objects into new and revitalized constellations.

Benjamin's attitude to habit, like Bakhtin's, contains a high degree of ambivalence. Caygill notes that, in 'On the Programme of the Coming Philosophy', Benjamin warns of the conflation of the notions of freedom and experience:

> This confusion [of freedom and experience] can occur in two ways, both of which threaten to qualify the concept of freedom to the point of abolishing it. The first reduces freedom to empirical experience by stripping it of any transcendental qualities while the second removes freedom from experience by making it purely ideal and far removed from the spatio-temporal world. [...] Benjamin's adumbrated speculative concept of freedom/experience discerns freedom in the rhythms and patterns as well as the warps and distortions of experience.[13]

I read this as arguing that, for Benjamin, the habit of rhythm and patterns and the disruption of life must be arranged in ways that preserve the continuum of freedom and experience. Neither habit (Caygill's 'rhythms and patterns') nor its opposite (the 'warps and distortions of experience') is sufficient alone. As far as collecting is concerned, it is worth noting that the figures of the collector and the destructive character in Benjamin's writings stand in antinomical relation to each other. In 'The Destructive Character' (1931), Benjamin notes that the collector finds solace in the apparent order that habit discovers in the midst of disorder: 'for what else is this collection but a disorder to which habit has accommodated itself to such an extent that it can appear as order?' (*GS IV* 388; *SW II* 486–87). The destructive character, however, represents the antithesis of habituation and exists in an environment that is the opposite of the collector's book-lined interior: 'The destructive character knows only one watchword: make room. And only one activity: clearing away. His need for fresh air and open space is stronger than any hatred' (*GS IV* 396; *SW II* 541). Thus habit and destruction, the collector and the destructive character, are dialectically dependent on each other.

Bakhtin's and Benjamin's conceptions of habit are ambivalent. Yet only an awareness of these forms of ambivalence can accomplish what proves otherwise to be a difficult task: the reconciliation of two seemingly incompatible models in the thought of both thinkers. In the case of Bakhtin, these are the championing of consummation in the early texts and the championing of dialogic dynamism in later texts.[14] In the case of Benjamin, these are the celebration of auratic, traditional experience in texts such as 'The Storyteller' and the celebration of the destruction of the aura in 'The Work of Art'.

The major difference between Bakhtin's and Benjamin's approach to habitualization lies in the differing development of their thinking. In the case of Benjamin, it is possible to discern positive and negative evaluations of different forms of habit simultaneously throughout his career. Most strikingly, 'The Storyteller' (published October 1936) and the second version of 'The Work of Art' (written December 1935–February 1936), essays that seem to present absolutely divergent evaluations of habit, are composed more or less simultaneously.[15] In the case of Bakhtin, one finds a shift from a qualifiedly positive evaluation of certain forms of habit or rhythm in the early texts to a far greater emphasis on the breaking of habitualization in the later work, and finally a guarded rehabilitation of habit in the late notes. This assessment is, however, merely a general assessment of the shape of Bakhtin's thought. It is clear that the early concern with the power of habitual form to provide a refuge from existential flux leaves its trace in the later writing. These traces are visible, above all, in Bakhtin's seemingly paradoxical contention that the novel whilst being the antithesis of all other genres, an anti-genre, is nevertheless a genre, that is to say a form-giving gesture, rather than a principle of formlessness.[16]

One way to understand Bakhtin's and Benjamin's thinking on the relation between habit and disruption is to understand their positions as historically situated in a specific modernity, and hence provisional and tactical. Hirschkop thinks along these lines in his discussion of the question of relativism in Bakhtin. Arguing that to see the essence of all language in Bakhtin's theory of novelizing discourse leads to a conception of Bakhtin as a proponent of pure relativism, Hirschkop contends that

> What [such a view] misses is the political meaning of a historicizing and relativizing discourse when it opposes a discourse that presents itself as timeless, natural, and self-evident; dialogism, in its novelistic form, is itself defined by its opposition to monologism. Bertolt Brecht's strategy was roughly similar: to dismantle a naturalizing ideology, one opposed it with a discourse which historicized life, revealing it as something produced and therefore changeable.[17]

This passage usefully reveals Bakhtin's affinities with Brecht, Benjamin's political and intellectual ally, and thus, by association, accords with my arguments for affinities between Bakhtin and Benjamin. It also points out, however, that Bakhtin's celebration of the disruption of the novel is the result of the nature of that disruption's historically located target. This corresponds to Buck-Morss's suggestion that Benjamin evaluates the loss of the aura in different ways according to what it affects: positively in regard of the work of art; negatively in regard of people. Buck-Morss thus implies that Benjamin's evaluation of this phenomenon is not absolute but tactical and provisional.[18] If this understanding of Bakhtin and Benjamin as tactical and flexible thinkers is correct, it follows that an examination of the different targets is needed.

Different forms of habit: tradition and modernity

It is possible to distinguish two different forms of habitualized and habitualizing behaviour that coexist and contend with each other in modern society. The first, one might term the tyranny of custom and authority. This applies to received, hierarchically valorized cultural forms that naturalize certain ways of viewing the world. In the face of these static and closed practices, Bakhtin and Benjamin seek out resources of resistance: what one can describe as dynamic openness, in the case of Bakhtin, and shock, in the case of Benjamin. In Bakhtin, the tyrannical force of custom is represented by the suffocation of dialogue in traditional genres or courtly culture. In Benjamin, it is to be seen in the authority of aura, for example, or the *Schein* of the symbol in the book on *Trauerspiel*.[19]

The second form of habitualization is brought into being by the abstracting and rationalizing modes of thought and behaviour associated with modernity and with the mode of calculation engendered by a capitalist society geared towards exchange-value. This universalizing approach to the world abstracts from the particular its particularity, thereby erasing the differentiated nature of experience and reducing experience to an endlessly repeated series of repeatable phenomena. In both the early Bakhtin and the early Benjamin, this form of habitualization is often associated with Kantianism. It is at the heart of Voloshinov's critique of Saussure. In the later Benjamin it is associated with the 'eternally the same' (*das Immer-gleiche*) of commodity production; in the later Bakhtin, with modern monologism.

Bakhtin's awareness of these two possible sources of habit reveals a profound ambivalence towards modernity. The novel draws its essential dynamism and open-endedness from its relation to modernity. In 'Epic and Novel' (1941), Bakhtin speaks of the novel as 'the vanguard of change' (*DI* 33), whose modernity is 'indestructible, and verges on an unjust evaluation of the times' and which develops its full potential only in the modern world (*DI* 31). Nevertheless, in the Dostoevsky book he notes that this openness and dynamism is threatened by two sources of habitualization: on the one hand, the source of habit that is tradition, and on the other hand, by tendencies towards habitualization that are inherent in modernity itself:[20]

> The consolidation of monologism and its permeation into all spheres and ideological life was promoted in modern times by European rationalism, with its cult of a unified and exclusive reason and especially by the Enlightenment, during which the basic generic forms of European artistic prose took shape. [...] Semantic unity of any sort is everywhere represented by a single consciousness and a single point of view. This faith in the self-sufficiency of a single consciousness in all spheres of ideological life is not a theory created by some specific thinker; no, it is a profound structural characteristic of the creative ideological activity of modern times, determining all its external and internal forms.
>
> (*DP* 82)

The novel must combat both the habit that confronts in the epic and also specifically modern habits (some that the novel may acquire in its combat with tradition, for the novel 'is ever questing, ever examining itself and subjecting its established forms to review' (*DI* 39)) that represent a permanent threat of re-monologization. For, if monologism of this sort has come to be a 'structural characteristic' of modern ways of thinking, then it has only come to dominate by processes of habitualization. Bakhtin makes this connection clear at the end of the Dostoevsky book: 'We must renounce our monologic habits so that we might come to feel at home in the new artistic sphere which Dostoevsky discovered, so that we might orient ourselves in that incomparably more complex *artistic model of the world* which he created' (*DP* 272). Bakhtin's ambivalence towards habit persists in so far as the demand that we should come to 'feel at home' (*osvoit'sia*)[21] suggests new and more benign forms of familiarity and habitualization.

Benjamin's attitude to habit is also an indicator of his ambivalent attitude to modernity. By way of example we may take Benjamin's treatment of the concept of ritual. Rituals are patterns of behaviour that have become established over long periods of time until they have become part of habit. In 'On Some Motifs in Baudelaire' (1939), Benjamin describes the traditional amalgam of experience that is preserved by ritual:

> Where there is experience [*Erfahrung*] in the strict sense of the word, certain contents of the individual past combine in the memory with material from the collective past. Rituals with their ceremonies, their festivals [...] kept producing the amalgamation of these two elements of memory over and over again. They triggered recollection at certain times and remained handles of memory for a lifetime.
>
> (*GS I* 611; *SW IV* 316)

Furthermore, as the continuation of the quotation implies, ritual forms part of the world of the storyteller and hence is explicitly linked to the mode of production that is craftsmanship:

> A story does not aim to convey an event *per se*, which is the purpose of information; rather it embeds the event in the life of the storyteller in order to pass it on as experience [*Erfahrung*] to those listening. It thus bears the trace of the storyteller, much as the earthen vessel bears the trace of the potter's hand.
>
> (*GS I* 611; *SW IV* 316)

Here, in the traditional and transmissible world of the storyteller, the cycles of ritual and the rhythm of traditional forms of production, such as the repetitive coiling of a pot by hand or the turning of the potter's wheel, embed the human being into an organic social and physical world. The whole of the person is preserved in all her or his actions. His historical being, his life, is preserved in transmission of the social material that is the story. His physical being, his body, is preserved in the marks that his hands leave in the clay. The story he tells is the same as the story he has heard but also slightly different because of the timbre of his voice and his individual turns of phrase. The repetition of manual production results not in identity but in difference as each earthen vessel will bear slightly different marks, making each pot an authentic and original expression of the whole being of its maker.

In contrast to this image, later in the essay, Benjamin describes the experience of the worker in the modern factory:

> In working with machines, workers learn to co-ordinate 'their own movements with the uniformly constant movements of an auto-maton'. [...] 'All machine work,' says Marx in the same passage cited

above, 'requires prior drilling [*Dresseur*] of the worker.' This drilling must be differentiated from practice [*Übung*]. [...] The unskilled worker is the one most deeply degraded by machine drilling. His work has been sealed off from experience; practice counts for nothing in the factory.

(*GS I* 631–32; *SW IV* 328–29, translation modified)

This is habit of a different form. The regular whirring of the machine is not a human rhythm. *Dresseur* (a term normally used for animals and soldiers) implies that the worker is the passive object of an activity, not its subject as would be the case in *Übung*. The worker's physical experience of his work is also different. Rather than leaving his physical traces on the material world, the material world leaves its traces on him as he is transformed into part of the machine itself.[22] His social being is also annihilated in so far as experience that can be narrated is absent. The repetition of mechanical reproduction produces total identity that relates nothing and tells no stories. Benjamin, then, outlines here two different forms of habit: a traditional form of ritualistic and rhythmic habit in which the full subject-nature of the human being is integrated and preserved, and a modern technological form of habit in which the subject is alienated and reduced to an object. Put simply: traditional habit is a phenomenon which we shape as well as receive, and in which we express our full being; modern habit is something that we fall slave to. This is what Benjamin means when he writes of the bourgeois interior: 'the *intérieur* forces the inhabitant to adopt the greatest number of habits – habits that do more justice to the interior he is living in than to himself' (*GS II* 217; *SW II* 734).[23]

The position that I have just described, however, represents only one part of Benjamin's attitude to modernity. Elsewhere, as in 'The Work of Art', Benjamin thinks in a different vein:

As we know, the earliest artworks originated in the service of rituals – first magical, then religious. And it is significant that the artwork's auratic mode of existence is never entirely severed from its ritual function. In other words: the unique value of the 'authentic' work of art has its basis in ritual, the source of its original use value. This ritualistic basis, however mediated it may be, is still recognizable as secularized ritual even in the most profane forms of the cult of beauty. [...] for the first time in world history, technological reproducibility emancipates the work of art from its parasitic subservience to ritual. [...] But as soon as the criterion of authenticity ceases to be applied to artistic production, the whole social function of art is revolutionized. Instead of being founded on ritual, it is based on a different practice: politics.

(*GS II* 217; *SW IV* 256–57)

Here, Benjamin argues that ritual, in its original cultic forms as well as in its secularized courtly, exhibition and aesthetic forms, is a source of authority. Auratic works of art are embedded in rituals that operate within strict social hierarchies. So, magic rituals are dependent on the power of the magician; religious, on the hierarchy of the priesthood; courtly, on the institution of the Crown; exhibition, on the critic; aesthetic, on the poet. In this ritualistic hierarchy, the work of art wields power over its perceivers. This power is gained from the distance, historical, spatial and hierarchical, that separates it from its perceivers.[24] The distance of ritual ensures that the work of art and the hierarchy within which it is embedded are perceived as untouchable and unchangeable.[25] The result is a perfect tradition of repetition that is authoritarian.[26]

In Benjamin's historical schema, this process of seamless, authoritarian tradition is disrupted by the development of techniques of reproduction (or rather, more correctly, by the orientation of art towards its reproducibility):

It might be stated as a general formula that the technology of reproduction detaches the reproduced object from the domain of tradition. By replicating the work many times over, it substitutes a mass existence for a unique existence. And in permitting the reproduction to reach the recipient in his own situation, it reactivates the object reproduced. These two processes lead to a tremendous shattering of tradition which is the obverse of the present crisis and renewal of humanity. Both processes are intimately linked to the mass movements of our day.

(*GS I* 477–78; *SW IV* 254)

According to Benjamin's argument, it is exactly those mechanical processes of production that he is so critical of in 'On Some Motifs in Baudelaire' and 'The Storyteller' that destroy the authoritarian power of tradition. Furthermore, the exact repetition of sameness that takes place in modern techniques of reproduction such as the rotary press results in the production of difference: replacing a unique existence with a plurality of exact reproductions produces a plurality of possible appropriations by a multitude of receivers. The distance of tradition is broken down by the reproduction which travels across temporal, spatial and hierarchical boundaries to meet the perceiver in her or his specific location. In this process, the authoritarian frameworks of tradition are exploded. The perceiver ceases to be the passive recipient of a closed and unquestionable tradition, but, rather, becomes the active appropriator and reactivator of culture. This is the transformation of the ritualistic basis of art into a new form of democratic politics, for here is the link with the 'mass movements of our day' of which Benjamin speaks. Here, then, is the ambivalence of modernity: modernity's new, authoritarian habits of commodity production, those that result in the 'present crisis of humanity' and whose negative effects we have seen in the essay on Baudelaire, are at the same time liberating forces. These forces enable a new and freer relationship to a once authoritarian tradition that, in the process of the establishment of this relationship, is both shattered and renewed.

Strangely, however, this revolutionary shattering of the habits of tradition is dependent on the creation of new forms of habit. This statement needs some explanation. Among the habit-breaking effects that Benjamin attributes to the impact of film, the phenomenon at the core of 'The Work of Art', is the cinematic opening up of what Benjamin terms the 'optical unconscious'. The montage technique of film with its new perspectives and its ability to slow down and dissect reality reveals to us new, hidden details of what had previously been familiar to us.[27] What was previously unconsciously habitualized becomes conscious.[28] Later in the essay, however, Benjamin, having ascribed such revolutionary power to the optical and habit-breaking possibilities of film, appears to contradict himself. Commenting on the fact that in our perception of architecture it is the tactile and uncon-centrated activity of habit that is equally important in our reception of a building as optical reception, Benjamin states:

For the tasks which face the human apparatus of perception at historical turning points cannot be performed purely by optical means – that is, by way of contemplation. They are mastered gradu-ally – taking their cue from tactile reception – through habit. Even the distracted person can form habits. What is more, the ability to master certain tasks in a state of distraction proves that their perform-ance has become habitual. The sort of distraction that is provided by art represents a covert measure of the extent to which it has become possible to perform new tasks of apperception.

(*GS I* 505; *SW IV* 268)

This new form of habit which will be necessary for resolution of the 'tasks which face the human apparatus of perception' will bear a curious similarity to the old, integrated form of habit that I have described above in relation to the storyteller: its tactility links it to the bodily integrity of the figure of the storyteller. The same is true of distraction: Benjamin has argued earlier in the essay that the viewer of film, the mechanically reproducible medium *par excellence*, develops an attitude of distraction.[29] The element of distraction is also present in the storyteller who distractedly tells his tale whilst working at the wheel or loom.[30] Far from being diametrically opposed, as some critics have claimed, it is now possible to see the common ground between Benjamin's position in 'The Storyteller' and his position in 'The Work of Art'.[31] Orientation towards mechanical reproducibility shatters authoritarian tradition. Its new habits, however, revive certain features of integrated habit that modernity itself seemed to have destroyed.

Automatic and authoritarian habits have to be replaced by new habits in which the old quality of distraction reappears and ensures a critical stance. The opposite of distraction is cultic possession such as when a sacred song 'possesses' its singer, a notion that is analogous to Bakhtin's idea of possession by rhythm in 'Discourse in the Novel'.[32] Distraction (*Zerstreuung*) is a term that bears much of Benjamin's ambivalence about habit. Distraction is a condition of habit formation. We have mastered a process when we can perform it 'without thinking about it'. Distraction is also, however, what happens when habits are disturbed and interrupted by something new or something that momentarily appears unfamiliar.[33] 'Distracted habit' is then the synthetical concept that conjoins Benjamin's sense of positive, integrated habit and his sense of the needs for disruption and newness.

The creation of new habits, furthermore, is a vital and political task. Taussig's comments are useful:

> Habit offers a profound example of tactile knowing and is very much on Benjamin's mind, because only at the depth of habit is radical change effected, where unconscious strata of culture are built into social routines as bodily disposition. The revolutionary task [...] could thus be considered as one in which 'habit' has to catch up with itself. The automatic pilot that functions while asleep has to be awakened to its own automaticity, and thus go traveling in a new way with a new physiognomy – bursting its 'prison-world asunder by the dynamite of a tenth of a second.'[34]

The somaticity of habit means that this new form of critical attitude will carry revolutionary intensity.[35] Benjamin writes in his essay on Surrealism (1929):

> The collective is a body, too. And the *physis* that is being organized for it in technology can, through its political and factual reality, only be produced in that image sphere to which profane illumination initiates us. Only when in technology body and image so interpenetrate that all revolutionary tension becomes bodily collective innervation, and all the bodily innervations of the collective become revolutionary discharge, has reality transcended itself to the extent demanded by the *Communist Manifesto*.
>
> *(GS II* 310; *SW II* 217–18)*

For this to happen, habit must be deployed; there must be complex processes of destruction of the authoritarian habits of certain forms of tradition which also involve the renewal of other forms of integrated habits.[36] 'Distracted habit' takes on political import.

In the position that reveals itself through a consideration of the sum of these essays, we can see that Benjamin's thinking contains a similar structure to that of Bakhtin. Both thinkers have a similar view of the processes of repetition that inhere in life: repetition must produce difference not identity. We have seen above that Benjamin is against those forms of habit in which repetition results in the production of sameness and in favour of those forms of habit in which repetition results in the production of difference. In Bakhtin's conception of language in the Dostoevsky book we find an analogous view:

> 'Life is good.' 'Life is good.' Here are two absolutely identical judgments, or in fact one singular judgment written (or pronounced) by us *twice*; but this 'twice' refers only to its verbal embodiment and not to the judgment itself. We can, to be sure, speak here of the logical relationship of identity between two judgments. But if this judgment is expressed in two utterances by two different subjects then dialogic relationships arise between them (agreement and affirmation).
>
> *(DP* 183–84)*

Bakhtin resists the abstracting and reductionist viewpoint that sees, in apparent regularities of experience, logical relationships of identity rather than plurality and difference. He seeks out the seed of difference within the context of repetition and apparent identity.[37] For both

Bakhtin and Benjamin, a habit that reduces the world to identity is to be rejected in favour of forms whose apparent regularity nevertheless produces difference. Difference-producing repetition may be seen, like Benjamin's distracted habit, as another synthetical unity of habit and its opposite.

There are, however, major differences between the two thinkers. In the essay 'The Problem of the Text in Linguistics, Philology and the Human Sciences' (1959–61), Bakhtin addresses mechanical reproduction:

> Natural uniqueness (for example a fingerprint) and the semantic (signifying) unrepeatability of the text. All that is possible for a finger-print is mechanical reproduction (in any number of copies); it is possible, of course, to reproduce a text in the same mechanical way (i.e. reprinting), but the reproduction of the text by the subject (a return to it, a repeated reading, a new execution, a quotation) is a new unrepeatable event in the life of the text, a new link in the historical chain of speech communication.
>
> (*SG* 106)

Bakhtin's more technical focus on the linguistic nature of the text means that he stops one step short of the conclusion drawn by Benjamin: that the process of mechanical reproduction can, in itself, create new subject positions which represent new executions and new unrepeatable events in the life of the artwork. Benjamin's response seems to emanate more directly from experience of the effect of mechanical reproduction; Bakhtin's more from linguistic theory. Despite this, essential similarities remain between the two thinkers: within modernity there are opposing forces – on the one hand, modernity contains the sources of practices that can liberate subjects from a passive slavery to habit; on the other hand, there are opposing tendencies that lead to new, and yet more authoritarian habits of passivity. And yet, finally there may well be a need to create new forms of habits and to feel at home in a new sort of world. Where the two thinkers seem to differ, however, is in Benjamin's more dialectical insistence that it might be in the debased nature of the modern world (here, commodity production) that one might find sources of resistance to authoritarian practices, whether of the traditional or modern variant. As Benjamin puts it in another context: 'And it is at the scene of the limitless debasement of the word – the news-paper, in short – that its salvation is being prepared' (*GS II* 629; *SW II* 742). In my final chapter, I argue that there is less of a gulf that separates Bakhtin and Benjamin on this point than might appear here.

Tradition and authority

Another way of talking about the set of themes raised under the heading of habit is to examine questions of tradition. After all, tradition might be defined as the historically transmitted habits of a collective. As we have seen, in Benjamin's writings the opposition of habit and the breaking of habit can be mapped onto another (perhaps more fundamental) opposition of tradition and destruction: the tradition of the storyteller versus the destruction of tradition by mechanical reproduction, for example.[38] The aspect of Benjamin's thought that is concerned with tradition has received a fair degree of attention from critics. In Bakhtin scholarship, the theme of tradition does not seem to be common. Nevertheless, it is my contention that at the heart of both writers' thought is a meditation on the relationships between tradition, transmissibility and authority.[39]

Benjamin's conception of tradition is unusual in that he emphasizes the necessary reliance of tradition not on conservation but on destruction. McCole notes: 'What [Benjamin] meant by "tradition" was less a particular canon of texts or values than the very coherence, communicability, and thus the *transmissibility* of experience.'[40] Transmissibility demands that the recipient of tradition is able to integrate the objects of tradition into her or his experience. This is the difference between the tradition of the storyteller and the authoritarian tradition of the aura, described above. In the first case, as I have shown, tradition is integrated into the person of the recipient and continuator of tradition, changing in the process; in the second, the hierarchical distance does not allow the integration of the person, and tradition becomes an authoritarian transmission of identity.[41] Such a form of tradition destroys the very essence of tradition which consists in transmissibility. In the face of this form of tradition, it follows that, in the name of tradition, tradition must be destroyed: hence the dialectic of destruction and tradition that runs through Benjamin's work. Benjamin's search is for a tradition that will not destroy experience; or, put in other terms: a search for cultural forms that do not destroy life.

Bakhtin's view of tradition reveals some similar themes. Bakhtin deals with tradition in his essays of the 1930s and 1940s on the nature of novel. In 'Epic and Novel', he writes.

Let us move on to tradition. The epic past, walled off from all subsequent times by an impenetrable boundary, is preserved and revealed only in the form of national tradition. [...] By its very nature the epic world of the absolute past is inaccessible to personal experience and does not permit an individual, personal point of view or evaluation. One cannot glimpse it, grope for it, touch it; one cannot look at it from just any point of view; it is impossible to experience it, analyze it, take it apart, and penetrate into its core. It is given solely as tradition, sacred and sacrosanct, evaluated in the same way and demanding a pious attitude toward itself.

(*DI* 16)

Immediately it is possible to see features of Bakhtin's conception of tradition that are analogous to Benjamin's view of the authoritarian tradition of the aura in the 'The Work of Art'. Here, like aura, the tradition of epic is characterized by a distance that is established between the objects of tradition and its recipient. First, the distance is hierarchical in so far as it demands our piety. Moreover, this hierarchy is also social in nature since the authoritative word is 'indissolubly fused with its authority – with political power, an institution, a person' (*DI* 343). Second, this hierarchical distance is temporal: the inaccessibility of the epic is the result of its belonging to the walled-off past of the ancestors and in this sense is equivalent to Benjamin's aura that is dependent on the unique historical testimony of the artwork. For Bakhtin, too, the authoritative tradition of the epic is reliant on cultic forms of ritual that elevate the work into a sacrosanct sphere, just as is the case in Benjamin's analysis of auratic works. Furthermore, epic tradition, like the aura, denies a physical integration of the object: 'one cannot grope for it, touch it'. Finally, it denies a plurality of individual perspectives, for, Bakhtin argues, the epic word 'enters our verbal consciousness as a compact and indivisible mass; one must either totally affirm it, or totally reject it' (*DI* 343). The epic word thus reduces the individual to a passive recipient and reduces subjects to objects.[42]

Just as Benjamin contends that the increasing orientation towards mechanical reproducibility is an historical process of the destruction of the authoritarian hierarchies of aura, so Bakhtin argues that the historical development of form contains an antidote to the distance and self-sufficiency of epic forms: 'In the history of literary language, there is a struggle constantly being waged to overcome the official line with its tendency to distance itself from the zone of contact, a struggle against various kinds and degrees of authority. In this process discourse gets drawn into the contact zone' (*DI* 345). His champion in this struggle is the polyphonic novel and the various forms of language consciousness which give rise to it from their birth in the Menippean satire and the Hellenistic romance, through the carnival form of Rabelais, to their full development in the polyphony of Dostoevsky.

Central discrepancies appear between Bakhtin's view of the historical struggle between the authoritative word of the epic and the forces of novelness, and Benjamin's materialist account of the relationship between modes of production and the organization of perception in relation to works of art.[43] The first major discrepancy is to be seen in the two thinkers' understanding of causality. Bakhtin's understanding of the struggle between epic and novel, dialogism and monologism, is an agonistic and almost Manichaean encounter between two forces which, at times, seem to move through history in a decidedly idealist fashion.[44] Benjamin, in contrast, puts his faith in the effects of developments in the mode of production and, more specifically, in technology.[45] As he had already written in 1927 in an article that formed part of a public controversy over Eisenstein's *The Battleship Potemkin*, 'the vital, fundamental advances in art are a matter neither of new content nor of new forms – the technological revolution takes precedence over both' (*GS II* 753; *SW II* 17). The second major discrepancy is between Benjamin's orientation towards visual perception and Bakhtin's towards language. This discrepancy is, perhaps, more serious than the first. Whereas in the first it is possible either to make explicit material and historical determinations which Bakhtin only implies, or to minimize the determinist appearance of Benjamin's account, the distance between perception and language is harder to bridge. As a possible solution one might appeal to the fact that Bakhtin's use of the term 'language' is itself close to the notion of an ideological 'world-view'. Nevertheless, alongside these discrepancies, central similarities also appear in the ways in which the counter-forces of the novel and mechanical reproduction affect tradition.

In a central passage of 'Discourse in the Novel', Bakhtin opposes the 'authoritative discourse' of tradition to the 'internally persuasive word' which is characteristic of the novel. Authoritative discourse, as we have seen, is defined by its closedness within a hierarchical context of distance. The internally persuasive word, on the other hand, is defined by:

> semantic openness to us, its capacity for further creative life in the context of our ideological consciousness, its unfinishedness and the inexhaustibility of our further dialogic interaction with it. We have not learned from it all it might tell us; we can take it into new

contexts, attach it to new material, put it in a new situation in order to wrest new answers from it, new insights into its meanings, and even wrest from it new words of its own.

(*DI* 346)

The internally persuasive word, then, opens up the closedness of traditional language, just as the sensibility of mechanical reproducibility, a sensibility marked by a 'sense of the universal equality of things', wishes to 'pry an object from its shell, to destroy its aura' (*GS I* 479; *SW IV* 255–56, translation modified). Like mechanical reproduction, the internally persuasive word draws the object into the 'familiar zone of contact'; in the phrase the 'zone of familiar contact', with the physical connotations of the term 'contact' (as opposed to the untouchability of the authoritarian word), we see Bakhtin's concern with the somatic aspect of the breaking of tradition. This zone of contact is also the site of an opening up of the singularity of tradition into the democratic plurality of new meanings. Bakhtin's new contexts, new answers and new insights in the quotation above are the counterpart to the effect of Benjamin's mechanical reproduction which 'substitutes a mass existence for a unique existence' and which permits the object of tradition to 'reach the recipient in his own situation', hence reactivating the object. Finally, just as I have argued that, for Benjamin, mechanical reproduction reactivates the subject nature of the perceiver, so, for Bakhtin, the internally persuasive word does not treat its recipient as an object but rather as a co-equal subject with the capacity to answer back. It is 'half ours and half someone else's' (*DI* 345). The internally persuasive word of the novel allows its recipient to enter into dialogue with it as an equally affirmed subject.

For Bakhtin the constitutive feature of authoritative discourse is its historical distance; for Benjamin, the aura is reliant on its historical testimony. Both mechanical reproduction and the internally persuasive word of the novel bring the object of tradition into the zone of contemporaneity. Bakhtin writes:

The internally persuasive word is either a contemporary word, born in a zone of contact with unresolved contemporaneity, or else it is a word that has been reclaimed for contemporaneity; such a word relates to its descendents as well as to its contemporaries; what is constitutive for it is a special conception of listeners, readers, perceivers.

(*DI* 346)

In the case of mechanical reproduction this is effected by the ability of the perceiver to take the mechanically reproduced work into his or her historical context. The creation of an expanded present is also a constitutive feature of cinema, just as the present of a dialogized inter-action of voices is a constitutive feature of the novel. Benjamin notes the extent to which the montage of film presents things that in fact occur at different times as simultaneous events: 'a leap from a window, for example, can be shot in the studio as a leap from a scaffold, while the ensuing fall may be filmed weeks later at an outdoor location' (*GS I* 491; *SW IV* 261). The simultaneity towards which Benjamin's theory of montage strives is a spatialized zone in which everything is possible and nothing has been decided in advance.[46] The creation of spatialized simultaneity is also the goal of the polyphonic novel of Dostoevsky. This is Bakhtin's conception of the novelistic present which is conceived of not as the minimal passing point between past and future, but rather as a moment of decision which expands to fill space and hence can contain a plurality of perspectives:

> Dostoevsky attempted to perceive the very stages themselves in their simultaneity, to juxtapose and counterpose them dramatically, and not to stretch them out into an evolving sequence. For him, to get one's bearings on the world meant to conceive of all its contents as simultaneous, and to guess at their interrelationships in the cross-section of a single moment.
>
> (*DP* 28)

Here we begin to see the kinship between Bakhtin's theory of polyphony and Benjamin's theory of montage which I discuss in more detail in Chapter 3.[47] Interrelationships in the cross section of a single moment are exactly what montage technique creates by ripping fragments out of temporally and spatially diverse contexts and reassembling them in a juxtaposition of equality. For the time being, however, I will only state that the simultaneity of Bakhtin's novel and Benjamin's montage serves the same purpose: they both disrupt the stately temporal progress of a tradition where everything has been determined in advance, and replace it with a spatialized present, pregnant with multiple possibilities.

The novel's and film's cutting up of the seamlessness of tradition can be viewed in another way. In 'The Work of Art', Benjamin draws an analogy between the activity of the cameraman and the surgeon, on the one hand, and the activity of the painter and the magician, on the other:

The surgeon represents the polar opposite of the magician. The attitude of the magician, who heals a sick person by a laying on of
hands, differs from that of the surgeon who makes an intervention
in the patient. The magician maintains the natural distance between
himself and the person treated; more precisely, he reduces it slightly
by laying on his hands, but increases it greatly by his authority. The
surgeon does exactly the reverse; he greatly diminishes the distance
from the patient by penetrating the patient's body, and increases it
only slightly by the caution with which his hand moves among the
organs. Magician is to surgeon as painter is to cinematographer. The
painter maintains in his work a natural distance from reality, whereas
the cinematographer penetrates deeply into its tissue. The images
obtained by each differ enormously. The painter's is a total image,
whereas that of the cinematographer consists of multiple fragments,
its manifold parts being assembled according to a new law.

(*GS I* 495–96; *SW IV* 263–64)

Once again, we see the breaking down of hierarchical (and, here, specifically, cultic) distance. The surgeon delves into the patient's body. To the
magician, the body is a whole that cannot be penetrated. The surgeon
shows it to be an assemblage that is constituted of organs. His clinical
intervention in the body reveals that the seemingly closed unity of the
body is the result of a coming-together of many different things: heart,
brain, spleen and muscles.

The effect of an orientation towards mechanical reproducibility, then,
is to penetrate the surface of things and to reveal their essentially plural
constitution. This is also the effect of novelistic discourse. The opposite
of novelistic discourse, for Bakhtin, is poetry which entails a negation
of the plural nature of language: 'the poet strips the word of other's
intentions' (*DI* 297). The language in a poetic work is a 'unitary and
singular Ptolemaic world outside of which nothing exists and nothing
else is needed. The concept of many worlds of language, all equal in their
ability to conceptualize and to be expressive, is organically denied to
poetic style' (*DI* 286). The novel, by contrast, reveals the fundamentally
plural nature of language as the interrelation and intersection of many
individual and social languages and voices:

The novel orchestrates all its themes, the totality of the world of
objects and ideas depicted and expressed in it, by means of the
social diversity of speech types [*raznorečie*] and by the differing individual voices that flourish under such conditions. Authorial speech,

the speech of narrators, inserted genres, the speech of characters are merely those fundamental compositional unities with whose help heteroglossia can enter the novel; each of them permits a multiplicity of social voices and a wide variety of their links and interrelationships.

(*DI* 263)

Like the surgeon/cameraman penetrating the body/the visual world, the novel penetrates into the complexity of the interrelated and inter-penetrated world and represents it as a plurality rather than the false, abstracted, closed unity that is the object of poetry. Its constitutive languages are utterances in which languages interpenetrate: double-voiced discourse, irony, stylization, the internally persuasive word and so forth.

The explosion of the apparent unity of tradition with the revelation that the world consists in plural interpenetration, however, is more than the mere shattering of tradition. In Bakhtin's view, poetry's sloughing of the traces of all languages other than its own is a mortification of living language. It produces the word as an inert thing: 'Discourse lives, as it were, beyond itself, in a living impulse toward the object; if we detach ourselves from this impulse all we have left is the naked corpse of the word [...]' (*DI* 292). This is exactly what poetry does, according to Bakhtin. Removing the word from the complex interaction of many languages in social life, it kills the word itself. It follows, then, that whilst the novel may be a bitter enemy of tradition, the effect of novelization is the revitalization of the word, that is to say of the essence of tradition: transmissibility. This, then, is Bakhtin's version of the notion of the destruction of tradition that ends up renewing it.

Counter-traditions and the task of the critic

By way of a conclusion to this chapter, one might ask what alternative to authoritarian tradition Bakhtin and Benjamin propose. It is certainly not newness for newness's sake. I have made clear enough the degree of ambivalence of Bakhtin and Benjamin towards the disrupting forces of modernity. Moreover, their central concern for the transmissibility of culture would prevent such a conclusion. The tendency of total newness (total difference, as one might term it) results only in the white noise of absolute intransmissibility. Furthermore, Bakhtin and Benjamin can both be characterized as cultural historians.[48] Their interests do not lie in a wholesale jettisoning of the past. Rather, Bakhtin and

Benjamin both have as one of their underlying aims the establishment of counter-traditions.

We see Bakhtin's construction of a counter-tradition in, *inter alia*, the chapter on 'Characteristics of Genre' in the 1963 version of the Dostoevsky book, in the essays on the novel of the 1930s and 1940s, in particular 'From the Prehistory of Novelistic Discourse' (1940), and in the Rabelais book. Here, a wide variety of cultural phenomena – Menippean satire, the Hellenistic romance, folk culture and Rabelais, and, of course, Dostoevsky himself – are presented as an alternative, vibrant counter-tradition to the authoritarian forms of official culture. This is a counter-tradition in which all the qualities of somaticity, intersubjectivity, familiar contact, dialogue and so forth, that I have discussed above, are preserved and transmitted. This is a form of anti-tradition which, in opposition to official tradition, preserves the essence of transmissibility.

In Benjamin's work one can find something analogous to Bakhtin's construction of a counter-tradition. In 'Discourse in the Novel', Bakhtin describes two lines of the novel's development, one of which, often overlooked and neglected, leads to Dostoevsky. In the second version of 'What is Epic Theatre?' (1939), Benjamin similarly describes two traditions of drama, one of which leads to Brecht:

Plato long ago recognized the undramatic quality of that most excellent man, the sage. In his dialogues, he took this figure to the threshold of the drama; in his *Phaedo*, to the threshold of the Passion play. The medieval Christ who also represented the wise man [...] is the untragic hero *par excellence*. But in Western secular drama, too, the search for the untragic hero has been unceasing. In ways that are ever new, and frequently in conflict with its theoreticians, this drama has differed from the authentic – that is ancient Greek – form of tragedy. This important but poorly marked road, which may serve here as the image of a tradition, wound its way through the Middle Ages in the works of Roswitha and the mystery plays, and through the Baroque period in the works of Gryphius and Calderón; later it can be traced in Lenz and Grabbe, and finally in Strindberg. Scenes in Shakespeare are its roadside monuments, and Goethe crosses it in the second part of *Faust*. It is a European road, but a German one as well – if indeed we can say that the legacy of medieval and Baroque drama has reached us by a road, and not by some obscure smugglers' path. It is this mule track, neglected and overgrown, which in our day comes to light in the dramas of Brecht.

(*GS II* 534; *SW IV* 303–04)

Benjamin's attempts to construct a counter-tradition are not, however, confined to a legitimization of Brecht. His life's work can be construed as an attempt to rescue a whole range of historical and cultural phenomena from obscurity, oblivion and false readings. We see this in his reading of the neglected body of *Trauerspiel* against the grain of the hegemony of standard post-Romantic readings; in his attempt, in his work on the German Romantics, to bring Schelling and Novalis out from under the shadow of Kant and Hegel; in his loving lament for the disappearing and overlooked figure of the storyteller; and in his location of the revolutionary potential of the cinema. This approach to tradition and counter-tradition is summed up in 'On the Concept of History':

> Articulating the past historically does not mean recognizing it 'the way it really was'. It means appropriating a memory as it flashes up at a moment of danger. Historical materialism wishes to hold fast that image of the past which unexpectedly appears to the historical subject in a moment of danger. For both, it is one and the same thing: the danger of becoming a tool of the ruling classes. Every age must strive anew to wrest tradition away from the conformism that is working to overpower it.
>
> (*GS I* 695; *SW IV* 391)

Benjamin's imperative that one wrest tradition from conformism lest its content and its heirs become tools of the ruling class is an approach that Bakhtin's work also adopts.

This reference to Benjamin's writing on the task of the historian might help us understand the ontological status of the counter-traditions that he and Bakhtin construct. In the case of Bakhtin, the question might be put bluntly: are we really to believe in the existence of a counter-tradition that bubbles beneath the mainstream of monologic, official culture, surfacing occasionally in Menippean satire, Rabelais and Dosto-evsky? The answer is, surely, no.[49] To believe in such a thing would be as crazy as to believe in the narrator of Eco's *Foucault's Pendulum*, Casaubon, and his construction of an occult tradition of 'telluric currents' in Europe running from Ancient Egypt, through the Templars, Rosicrucians and Masons, right up to the dimensions of the modern Paris telephone kiosk.[50] Such counter-traditions are constructed by critics like Bakhtin.

To say this, however, is not to devalue the act of construction. The act of construction is the intervention of the historian who has the gift of 'fanning the spark of hope in the past' (*GS I* 695; *SW IV* 391).

To make sense of this it is necessary to examine Bakhtin's and Benjamin's conceptions of criticism. In the case of Benjamin, one finds a highly developed notion of the role of criticism. Much of this is to be found in *The Concept of Criticism in German Romanticism*. Here, Benjamin elaborates a literary theory on the basis of the German Romantics, Novalis, Schlegel and Schelling, in which criticism is the guarantor of the continued life of the artwork:

> Criticism [*Kritik*] when confronting the work of art is like observation when confronting the natural object [...] Thus, criticism is, as it were, an experiment on the artwork, one through which the latter's own reflection is awakened, through which it is brought to consciousness and to knowledge of itself.
>
> (*GS I* 65; *SW I* 151)

It follows from this that, far from being a secondary and parasitic phenomenon in relation to the work of creation, criticism is a necessary 'completion' of the work and, paradoxically, stands prior to it.[51] This 'completion', however, does not mean putting an end to the work, dotting its i's and crossing its t's, but rather drawing it into a continuing after-life of ever-repeated and self-renewing interpretation. In this elevated role, criticism is productive not reactive, and this applies as much to the whole tradition of literature as it does to the individual work. Given this notion of criticism, it is possible to understand how the conscious construction of counter-traditions becomes the foremost task of the critic; the critic must be able to discern the overgrown smugglers' paths which run alongside the broad highway of official tradition.[52]

Bakhtin has a much less developed conception of criticism. Nevertheless, in 1970 in his 'Response to a Question from the *Novyi Mir* Editorial Staff', he sketches a conception of criticism that bears similarities to Benjamin's. Bakhtin shares with Benjamin a rejection of historicism:

> Trying to understand and explain a work solely in terms of the conditions of its epoch alone, solely in terms of the conditions of the most immediate time, will never enable us to penetrate into its semantic depths. Enclosure within the epoch also makes it impossible to understand the work's future life.
>
> (*SG* 4)

Rejection of the explanation of the work 'solely in terms of the conditions of its epoch' parallels Benjamin's rejection of historicism's 'the way it really was'. Historicism 'completes' the work in the bad sense of restricting it to its own historical epoch and of cutting it off from its future life. What Bakhtin has in mind is rather a criticism that supplies the work with a constantly renewed source of life, much as in Benjamin's and Schlegel's sense of 'completion':

> Great works continue to live in the distant future. In the process of their posthumous life they are enriched with new meanings, new significance: it is as though these works outgrow what they were in the epoch of their creation. [...] [Shakespeare] has grown because of that which has actually been and continues to be in found in his works, but which neither he himself nor his contemporaries could consciously perceive and evaluate in the context of the culture of their epoch.
>
> (*SG* 4)

It is the role, then, of the critic to be attentive to the ever-growing semantic richness of the great work, giving it life in his or her own time, rather than consigning it to oblivion:

> Semantic phenomena can exist in concealed form, potentially, and be revealed only in semantic cultural contexts of subsequent epochs that are favourable for their disclosure. The semantic treasures Shakespeare embedded in his works were created and collected through the centuries and even millennia: they lay hidden in the language [...].
>
> (*SG* 5)[53]

What Bakhtin describes as a feature of the passage of great works through time also implies an imperative for the critic. The critic must uncover what has remained hidden, unleash potential, and carefully wipe off the obscuring dust of time from the treasure, thereby revealing new facets visible only to the critic in the present.[54]

Benjamin makes a similar point in 'The Task of the Translator' (1924):

> For in [the work's] afterlife – which could not be called that if it were not a transformation and renewal of something living – the original undergoes a change. Even words with fixed meaning can undergo a maturing process. The obvious tendentiousness of a writer's literary

style may in time wither away, only to give rise to immanent tendencies in the literary creation. What sounded fresh once may sound
hackneyed later; what was once current may someday sound quaint.
To seek the essence of such changes, as well as the equally constant
changes in meaning, in the subjectivity of posterity rather then in
the very life of the language and its works – even allowing for the
crudest psychologism – is to confuse the root cause of a thing with
its essence.

(*GS IV* 12–13; *SW I* 256)

From his or her later historical position, the task of the translator (or
indeed the task of the critic, for Benjamin's conceptions of translation and criticism are intimately linked[55]) is to release the living tendencies immanent in the work, what Bakhtin describes as concealed
semantic phenomena. In so doing the translator/critic revives the work
and rescues it from oblivion, not by virtue of mere historical changes in
the socio-linguistic context, but by virtue of the living essence that has
been slumbering in the work.[56]

At this point, it is worth juxtaposing an image that Benjamin draws
in the essay 'The Storyteller':

In the fourteenth chapter of the third book of [Herodotus'] *Histories*
there is a story from which much can be learned. It deals with Psam-
menitus. [...] This tale shows what true storytelling is. The value of
information does not survive the moment in which it was new. It
lives only at that moment; it has to surrender to it completely and
explain itself to it without losing any time. A story is different. It
does not expend itself. It preserves and concentrates its strength and
is capable of releasing itself even after a long time. [...] Herodotus
offers no explanations. His report is utterly dry. That is why this
story from ancient Egypt is still capable, after thousands of years, of
provoking astonishment and reflection. It is like seeds of grain which
have lain for centuries in the airtight chambers of the pyramids and
have retained their germinative power to this day.

(*GS II* 445–46; *SW III* 148)

A critic like Bakhtin and Benjamin must not see the stone façade of
the mausoleum, but must penetrate the tomb and find in it the seed of
grain that lies overlooked in the corner. Recognizing it as a seed, not
mistaking it for a stone, he must allow it to germinate and come to life;
it must, under his attentive gaze and in his loving hand, be drawn from

the past into the present so that it can break out of the singular, inert and closed form of its exterior and unfold into plural, living and open meanings. In his 'Franz Kafka: On the Tenth Anniversary of his Death' (1934), Benjamin examines this notion of unfolding:

> The word 'unfolding' has a double meaning. A bud unfolds into a blossom, but the boat which one teaches children to make by folding paper unfolds into a flat sheet of paper. This second kind of 'unfolding' is really appropriate to parable; the reader takes pleasure in smoothing it out so that he has the meaning on the palm of his hand. Kafka's parables, however, unfold in the first sense, the way a bud turns into a blossom. That is why their effect resembles poetry [*Dichtung*].
>
> (*GS* II 420; *SW* II 802–03)

The image of tradition that emerges from a consideration of this quotation in conjunction with the passage about Herodotus might illuminate Bakhtin's and Benjamin's understanding of tradition and the critic's construction of counter-tradition. Authoritarian tradition reduces plurality to unity in the manner of the second example of didactic unfolding, where the complexly constituted turns into the flatness of the sheet of paper. Bakhtin's and Benjamin's critical counter-traditions are designed to unfold the cultural objects of the past in the first sense, the way a bud turns into blossom. In 'Author and Hero', we encounter a similar image; in intersubjective encounters, the other must not be reduced to a closed, dead object but rather must be enabled to blossom into living subjectivity. In this context, Bakhtin writes: 'The excess of my seeing [vis-à-vis the other] is the bud in which slumbers form, and whence form unfolds like a blossom' (*AH* 24).

2
Experience

Diachronic contexts from Hegel to *Lebensphilosophie*

Bakhtin and Benjamin are ambivalent towards habit and cognate phenomena such as ritual, tradition and so forth, and their adequacy to the task of preserving the integrity of experience. In the nineteenth century, the influential figure of Hegel, however, had been positive about the benefit (indeed the indispensability) of such customary cultural and social forms for the free development of the individual's subjectivity. In the second part of *Elements of the Philosophy of Right* (1822), Hegel launches a sustained attack on Kant's resolution of the problem of what Hegel terms 'abstract freedom'. Like Kant, Hegel argues that abstract freedom (the unconstrained freedom to do what we want) is illusory, since in acting according to our individual desires we are in thrall to those desires. Similarly, Hegel also argues that freedom is to be achieved in the acting out of our duty: 'I should do my duty for its own sake, and it is in the true sense my own objectivity that I bring to fulfilment in doing so. In doing my duty, I am with myself [*bei mir selbst*] and free.'[1] Against Kant, however, Hegel argues that the fulfilment of one's duty towards an abstractly conceived categorical imperative is not sufficient for the realization of the individual's freedom. Rather, Hegel contends, such a conception of freedom in duty towards an abstract rational imperative pits reason against desire and hence denies human beings the happiness produced by the satisfaction of their natural desires.

In Hegel's solution to this problem, the habits of cultural and social forms play a crucial role. He argues that unity of individual satisfaction and freedom can only be found in conformity to the social ethos and customs of the organic community. In the organic community individual desires and needs are shaped by social custom and hence the satisfaction of those needs and desires benefits the community in a synthesis of the universal and the particular. Hegel writes:

> Just as nature has its laws, and as animals, trees, and the sun obey their law, so is custom the law appropriate to the spirit of freedom. Custom is what right and morality have not yet reached, namely spirit... Education [*Pädagogik*] is the art of making human beings ethical: it considers them as natural beings and shows them how they can be reborn and how their original nature can be transformed into a second, spiritual nature so that this spirituality becomes habitual to them.[2]

Conformity to custom and education into habit set subjects free. At this point a caveat is necessary. Hegel's position does not imply unthinking allegiance to automatized habit. The modern organic society, unlike the organic communities of the ancient world, must be organized according to rational principles so that individuals can recognize the rationality of those principles and hence freely choose to conform to them. If this is not the case, and subjects cease using their capacity for reason, cease an active search for self-realization and act according to blind, unthinking habit, then custom or social habit (*Sittlichkeit*) can become empty habituality (*Gewöhnlichkeit*) with resultant negative effects for individual and social development:

> In habit [*Gewöhnlichkeit*], the opposition between the natural and the subjective will disappears, and the resistance of the subject is broken [...]. Human beings even die of habit – that is, if they have become totally habituated to life and mentally and physically blunted, and the opposition between subjective consciousness and mental activity has disappeared. For they are active only in so far as they have not yet attained something and wish to assert themselves and show what they can do in pursuit of it. Once this is accomplished, their activity and vitality disappear, and the loss of interest which ensues is mental or physical death.[3]

Despite his awareness of the danger of the slipping of *Sittlichkeit* into *Gewöhnlichkeit*, for Hegel the rationally organized, modern organic community ensures the unity of individual and social interest through active participation in habitual social and cultural forms.[4] Cultural forms and individual lives are adequate to each other and it is through customary cultural forms that individuals actualize themselves and their own freedom.

The latter part of the nineteenth century sees a qualitative shift away from Hegel's benign view of the relationship between custom and the life of the individual. This reaction stems from an increasing inability of thinkers to recognize in a fast modernizing world the hallmarks of the organic community as described by Hegel. *Contra* the phrase of the introduction to *Elements of the Philosophy of Right*, the real no longer seemed to be rational. In his *Community and Society (Gemeinschaft und Gesellschaft)* (1887), Friedrich Tönnies made a clear and influential distinction between traditional, organic communities (*Gemeinschaften*) where individual and communal interests stand in harmony, and modern societies (*Gesellchaften*) marked by qualities of abstraction, alienation and specialization that obscure the possibility of such harmony.[5] Max Weber, in his work on rationalization and bureaucracy in a disenchanted world, served further to underline the sense of a disjuncture between cultural forms and the life of the individual.[6] Scepticism about the discrepancy between subjective experience and objective cultural forms becomes increasingly typical of the late nineteenth and early twentieth centuries. This scepticism finds powerful expression in the work of Georg Simmel, a figure who exercises direct influence on both Bakhtin and Benjamin.

In the winter semester of 1912/13, Benjamin attended Simmel's lectures at the University of Berlin.[7] Simmel's influence was to continue in a quiet but often controversial fashion throughout Benjamin's career.[8] His work on Goethe provided Benjamin with a theory of the symbol that became central to the *Trauerspiel* book and, as Buck-Morss notes, survives on into the *Arcades Project*.[9] It was Simmel, rather than Marx, who can be argued to have provided Benjamin with his fundamental understanding of modernity and commodity form. More than Marx, Simmel's analysis of phenomena such as money and fashion informs Benjamin's notion of the symbolic economy of capitalism and the impact of exchange-form on the structures of experience.[10] This attachment to Simmel was to get Benjamin in trouble with his collaborators in the Institute for Social Research, and Adorno in particular. Adorno's criticisms of Benjamin's tendencies to undialectical and unmaterialist thinking in his work on the Paris of Baudelaire stem, in part, from Adorno's objection to Benjamin's use of Simmel.[11] Finally, Simmel's account of the forms of modern (urban) experience as opposed to traditional (rural) experience, particularly as outlined in the essay 'The Metropolis and Mental Life' (1903), informs the structure of Benjamin's meditation on the same themes.

As more recent critics of Bakhtin have recognized, Simmel was a central figure in Bakhtin's intellectual make-up too.[12] Previously, Bakhtin scholarship, focusing on Bakhtin's neo-Kantian roots, had not paid attention to the connection with Simmel.[13] Certainly, unlike Benjamin, Bakhtin does not quote Simmel. Of the Bakhtin Circle members treated here, only Voloshinov makes a direct and, moreover, guarded reference to him.[14] There is no doubt, however, that Bakhtin was familiar with Simmel's work. Simmel's essays had appeared in the Russian edition of the journal *Logos*, a journal which Bakhtin seems to have read.[15] These included Russian translations of 'Zur Metaphysik des Todes' and 'Der Begriff und die Tragödie der Kultur', traces of both of which can be seen in *Toward a Philosophy of the Act* and 'Author and Hero in Aesthetic Activity'.[16] Nevertheless, in following the connection between Bakhtin and Simmel, it is necessary to follow Bakhtin's translations and appropriations, without acknowledgement, of Simmel's ideas into his own language and idiom.

Simmel contests that modern life is characterized by a preponderance of objective culture over the subjective culture of the individual.[17] As modern culture becomes more complex and developed, to a large degree as a result of specialization, the individual is no longer capable of identifying him or herself with this culture and its 'law, language, methods of production, art, science and household objects'. These are phenomena that were originally the products of individual men and women like him or herself.[18] According to Simmel, the birth of objective cultural value, thus, has as its corollary the 'death of the subjective soul' that invests itself in that process of creation.[19] In the face of the increasingly alien domain of objective culture values, the essence of the individual comes under threat. In the modern metropolis, for example:

> such an overwhelming fullness of impersonal Spirit is on offer in buildings, institutions of learning, in the wonders and conveniences of a technology that can defeat space, in the forms of social life and in the visible institutions of the state that the individual [*Persönlichkeit*] cannot, so to speak, keep his own identity in the face of them.[20]

Culture and the life of the individual have suffered a separation that is no less than tragic, with the result that forms and experience no longer equate to each other.

This insight is central to both Benjamin and Bakhtin. Their world is no longer a world in which custom is seen unproblematically as a facilitator of individual experience. It is a world where form, whether the habits and cultural forms of tradition or the new habits of ration-alizing, industrialized societies and commodity exchange, can increasingly also be viewed as alien and authoritarian. The question posed by Benjamin and Bakhtin, following Simmel, is the extent to which the cultural modes of expression, created by the collective activity of men and women, are adequate to the experience of men and women themselves. *Lebensphilosophie*, as represented by Simmel, casts life and cultural form in terms of an opposition of 'life as something hetero-geneous, unorderly, and almost anarchic, and form as homogeneity and law'.[21] The importance of Bakhtin's and Benjamin's thought lies in what they do with this opposition. *Lebensphilosophie* can, in general, be characterized by a tendency to prioritize life over form.[22] Benjamin and Bakhtin's position is not as simple although their starting point is similar.

Modes of experience: *Erlebnis* and *Erfahrung*

Simmel's thinking on the disjuncture between form and life, that was to be so important for Bakhtin and Benjamin, draws on and is part of a debate in nineteenth-century philosophy on the nature of experience which stems from Kant. Kant had argued that experience comes about through the synthetic process that joins the subject's sense perceptions with *a priori* concepts in objectively and universally valid judgements.[23] At the heart of Kant's epistemology is the conviction that subjective intuition alone does not provide the basis for meaningful experience, indeed, for experience of any sort at all.

> For experience [*Erfahrung*] it is not, as is commonly believed, sufficient to compare perceptions and to connect them in one consciousness by means of judging; from that there arises no universal validity and necessity of judgement, on account of which alone it can be objectively valid and so can be experience.[24]

The idea of experience without synthetic judgement (and it can be no more than an idea since Kant's categories are *a priori* and universal) is an illusion. Such experience, were it possible, would be no more than a contingent, disordered and incomprehensible multiplicity.[25] Whilst intuition and perception of concrete, empirical particulars are necessary components of experience, they are only able to enter the realm of experience if they are combined synthetically with universal, general and abstract categories:[26]

A completely different judgment therefore occurs before experience can arise from perception. The given intuition must be subsumed under a concept, which determines the form of judging in general with respect to the intuition, connects the empirical consciousness of the latter in a consciousness in general, and thereby furnishes empirical judgments with universal validity.[27]

Thus, Kant's theoretical framework prioritizes all that is regular, necessary, homogeneous, universal and objective over all that is irregular, contingent, manifold, particular and subjective, and Kant defines experience (*Erfahrung*) as only that in which the latter categories are subsumed by the former. Kant establishes, then, an opposition between the 'manifold of empirical intuition' of particular experiences (*Erlebnisse*) and the homogeneity and universality of *a priori* categories, through whose offices alone true experience or *Erfahrung* can come into being.[28]

In the course of the nineteenth century, this opposition of *Erfahrung* and *Erlebnis* and the evaluative accent that Kant had put on the former was revisited by a range of thinkers. At the beginning of the century, the main approach of philosophers was an attempt to overcome the range of Kantian dualisms, such as the dualisms between subject and object, *Erfahrung* and *Erlebnis*, by means of the construction of various systems of holistic idealism, culminating in the 'absolute idealism' of Hegel.[29] Towards the end of the century, however, a group of thinkers who can be associated with *Lebensphilosophie* and phenomenology took a different approach, accepting, in essence, Kantian dualisms, but subjecting them to different characterizations and evaluations.[30] Thus, Wilhelm Dilthey contrasts the intensity of *Erlebnis* (inner lived experience) to the shallowness of mere *äussere Erfahrung* (outer sensory experience).[31] Similarly, Husserl objected to the scientific and abstract aspects of Kantian notions of *Erfahrung*, and gave priority, instead, to an investigation of the structures of pre-reflexive, inner experience.[32] As Jay notes, in these cases '*Erlebnis* was an honorific term for subjective, concrete intuitive responses to the world that were prior to the constructed abstractions of science or the intellect.'[33] In this tradition, then, both the evaluation and the content of the concepts, *Erfahrung* and *Erlebnis*, have been substantially modified, whilst retaining their connection back to Kant. Returning to Simmel: it is in this context that it is possible to understand the tragedy of culture. Simmel's split between objective and subjective culture, culture and life, represents a split between two modes of experience, that of *Erfahrung* and that of *Erlebnis*. These two modes of experience become important principles in Bakhtin's and Benjamin's thought: in Bakhtin implicitly, in Benjamin much more explicitly.[34]

Beyond the German tradition, Henri Bergson, also a thinker of the loose movement of *Lebensphilosophie* and a thinker who exerted influence on Bakhtin and Benjamin,[35] makes a similar distinction between different modes of experience that can be seen to correspond to *Erlebnis* and *Erfahrung*. Bergson posits two separate categories: *temps*, time as it is measured by science, divisible and repeatable, subject to analytical categories of space and language; and *durée*, time, continuous and changing, as it is experienced by the subject in the flux of inner life, prior to such analytical categories. For Bergson, reality is a matter of *durée*. In this reality, immediately experienced, exist not 'completed things [*choses faites*] but only things that are in the process of being completed, not states that endure but only states that change'.[36] Nevertheless, subjects need stable fulcra (*points d'appui*) in this flux of becoming; likewise, they cannot obviate the practical need for representations of states and things. Hence they abstract (from the flux of becoming) fixed sensations and ideas by substituting the discontinuous for the continuous, stability for mobility, and *temps* for *durée*.

In consequence, Bergson posits two radically different modes of thought and experience, intuition and intelligence, that refer respectively to the direct experience of *durée* and the abstracted cognition of *temps*. Intuition, on the one hand, captures the fluidity of becoming, 'an uninterrupted continuity of unpredictable novelty'.[37] Intelligence provides access only to reconstructed abstractions of repeatable stability that effaces novelty in presenting the new as 'a new arrangement of pre-existing elements'.[38] For Bergson, true experience is accessible only to intuition and its true nature is subject to misrepresentation by the application of analytical intelligence.

Experience is, shall we say, the indivisible and indestructible continuity of a melody where the past enters the present and forms with it an undivided whole that remains undivided and indivisible despite what is added to it at every moment, or rather, because of what is added to it. We are able to gain an intuition of it, but, as soon as we seek an intellectual representation of it, we immediately put together, one after another, a series of states that have become distinct from each other like the pearls which make up a necklace, and that thus need a thread to hold them together, a thread that is neither one thing or the other, that in no way resembles the pearls, that in no way resembles anything at all, but, rather, is an empty entity, a mere word. Intuition gives us something of which intelligence grasps only a spatial transposition and a metaphorical translation.[39]

The abstracted object of intelligence (the pearls of the necklace and most importantly the imputed string that holds the pearls together[40]) is no more than a transposition: a translation of experience into a set of terms that are alien to the nature of experience itself. The objects of intelligence, the only objects that thought can subject to analysis, are, as a result of this process, no more than illusions, and Kant's giving precedence to *Erfahrung* falls prey to an illusion.[41]

The application of intelligence results in failure: 'Intelligence inhabits completed concepts and attempts to seize thereby, as if with a net, something of the reality that passes by [...] But, as a result, it allows to escape from reality that which in its essence consists.'[42] But its failure is made more serious by the fact that it results in a beautiful illusion, a transfiguration and falsification of the nature of experience that allows the true nature of life to slip by. This idea, that abstracting forms of representations of experience as *Erfahrung* not only fail to capture the fragmented immediacy of *Erlebnis* but may also transfigure and falsely represent it, is central to Bakhtin and Benjamin.[43] The desire to abstract closed units from the flux of experience is, perhaps, necessary for practical purposes as Bergson has it. Bakhtin and Benjamin, however, are always aware of the dangers of transfiguration and falsification inherent in representations of this form: in the aura of the traditional artwork or the seductive lure of the commodity for Benjamin, or in the finality of the monologic utterance for Bakhtin. In this sense, *Erfahrung* may be associated with habitualized form; it is experience that has been ordered, made repeatable, a form created out of the flux of a disordered world of immediate experience (*Erlebnis*). But as we have already seen in the previous chapter, habitualized forms of experience contain their own dangers.

For all Bakhtin's and Benjamin's common ground with certain aspects of *Lebensphilosophie* and their use of parts of its conceptual basis, both thinkers see problems inherent in the split that it establishes between *Erfahrung* and *Erlebnis*. The championing of *Erlebnis*, particularly in those quarters of *Lebensphilosophie* associated with irrationalism, could have a dark side. Bakhtin and Benjamin, who were 19 and 22 respectively at the outbreak of the First World War, must have been aware of this. Italian Futurism with the notorious ninth slogan of its manifesto ('We will glorify war – the world's only hygiene – militarism, patriotism, the destructive gesture of freedom-bringers, beautiful ideas worth dying for, and scorn for woman'[44]) had drawn explicitly on Bergson. They found in his thought inspiration for their own championing of raw and irrational experience over exhausted civilized rationality.[45] In the German context, Ernst Jünger had described a similar position in his tellingly entitled long essay on the First World War, *Der Kampf als inneres Erlebnis* ('Combat as inner experience', 1926):

> There is still much of the animal in man who slumbers on the comfortable, woven carpets of a polished, honed, and silently intricate civilization, wrapped up in habit and pleasant formality; and yet when the pointer on the dial of life swings back to the red line of the primitive, the mask falls; naked as ever, he breaks out, primal man, the cave-dweller, in the full unruliness of his unchained instincts. Whenever life reverts to its primal functions, his blood, which up until then has flowed coolly and regularly through his veins in the mechanistic activity of his stony, urban skeleton, foams up, and the ancient rock which has lain for long ages, cold and rigid, in hidden depths, melts once again into white-hot lava.[46]

Here, Jünger opposes the polished, silent mask of the civilization that one can associate with *Erfahrung*, 'covered up in habit and pleasant forms', with the bestial-blood lust of the primal sphere of *Erlebnis*.

For Benjamin, as I shall show, a mythical hypostatization of *Erlebnis*, such as can be seen in Jünger, is one of the pillars of fascism. Bakhtin, too, as I argue below, discerns the bleak and possibly violent consequences of a one-sided celebration of sheer *Erlebnis*. An underlying argument in favour of a more dialectical understanding of the relationship between *Erfahrung* and *Erlebnis* is common to both thinkers. Both are concerned with combating abstracting and authoritarian forms of *Erfahrung* without falling prey to the dangers of a hypostatization of *Erlebnis* and without surrendering the principle of benign form.

Bakhtin and Benjamin: Culture and experience

Bakhtin's tragedy of culture

Bakhtin wrote his extensive fragment, *Toward a Philosophy of the Act*, in difficult material circumstances in Nevel and Vitebsk between 1920 and 1924. This text echoes the concerns of many of the thinkers discussed above in connection with *Lebensphilosophie*. It describes a situation in which human existence is scarred by a rupture between the experience of life and the systems whereby subjects register and give form to that experience:

> The moment which discursive theoretical thinking (in the natural sciences and philosophy), historical description-exposition, and aesthetic intuition have in common [...] is this: all these activities establish a fundamental split between the content or sense of a given act/activity and the historical actuality of its being, the actual and once-occurrent experiencing of it [...]. And as a result, two worlds confront each other, two worlds that have absolutely no communication with each other and are mutually impervious: the world of culture and the world of life, the only world in which we create, cognize, contemplate, live our lives and die or – the world in which the acts of our activity are objectified and the world in which these acts actually proceed and are actually accomplished once and only once.
>
> (*TPA* 1–2)

The strains of a lament over the tragedy of culture can be heard as Bakhtin establishes an opposition between life, on the one hand, as it is experienced, *Erlebnis*, an open, transient and concrete process of becoming, and on the other hand, life as it is systematized in cultural and intellectual forms, *Erfahrung*, repeatable, abstracted and objectified. Bakhtin, like Simmel, highlights the paradoxical nature of cultural forms that not only make life meaningful but also, in the very movement of transferring meaning, remove themselves from life itself. Like Simmel, Bakhtin captures the sense of self-alienation that men and women experience in becoming meaningful selves.

Bakhtin's portrayal of the tragedy of culture, however, differs from the standard view of *Lebensphilosophie* in some important aspects. Simmel contends that the tragedy of culture results in our alienation from ourselves in culture in so far as we are not able to recognize ourselves as the authors of objective cultural values. Thus, Simmel gives precedence to life as the sphere of the subject's authentic being as opposed to culture which is described in terms of alienation. Bakhtin's description is, however, of a more complex situation:

> Contemporary man feels sure of himself, feels well-off and clear-headed, where he is himself essentially and fundamentally not present in the autonomous world of a domain of culture and its immanent law of creation. But he feels unsure of himself, feels

destitute and deficient in understanding, where he has to do with himself, where he is the center from which answerable acts or deeds issue, in actual and once-occurrent life. That is, we act confidently only when we do so not as ourselves, but as those possessed by the immanent necessity of the meaning of some domain of culture.

(*TPA* 20)

Here, Bakhtin also prioritizes the sphere of life, the place where contemporary man 'has to do with himself', that is 'actual and once-occurrent life'. But, for Bakhtin, the subject does not feel at home in this sphere of authenticity that, paradoxically, becomes a site of the experience of alienation. On the contrary, where the subject feels at home is where he or she is not present: that is, in the sphere of culture. This results in a more problematic sense of tragedy than Simmel's. Simmel's tragedy lies in the fact that the subject as authentic being is alienated from the objective cultural products of his or her spirit. Bakhtin locates the tragic divide within the subject itself, in so far as her or his sense of being-at-home takes place beyond her or himself.

Bakhtin's thought in *Toward a Philosophy of the Act* is more than a regurgitation of the basic tenets of *Lebensphilosophie*, and its underlying structure deserves close attention. Bakhtin establishes a distinction between two modes of activity and being: a distinction between the 'given' (*dannyi*) and 'posited' (*zadannyi*)[47] modes of reality. The 'given' mode is complete (*zavershennyi*) and self-sufficient (*samovol'nyi*), and characterized by causality, autonomy and closure. The posited mode is open, in a state of development, and seeks relations and self-confirmation beyond itself. There are three levels on which this opposition operates. The first two are familiar from theories of the tragedy of culture: the split between the given world of general culture and the posited world of life; and the lower level split between the given product of a subject's activity and the posited activity itself – what Simmel terms the objectification of spirit and the subjective spirit that goes into the making of it. The third level represents something new that Bakhtin brings to this debate. This is the level of intersubjectivity. According to Bakhtin, a subject's mode of being can be classified according to categories of passivity and activity, depending on the relations with other subjects. These categories, too, can be understood in terms of the opposition of 'given' and 'posited'. In Coates's interpretation: 'I perceive myself as incomplete and developing, but other people perceive me as completed and whole. Likewise, in my nature as agent I am active and posited, whereas in my capacity as object I am passive and given.'[48] In addition, one can subsume Bakhtin's distinction of the two modes of truth to this same basic opposition between given and posited. Bakhtin distinguishes between truth (*istina*) that tends towards universality and is constant and repeatable and the truth of an event (*pravda*).

Bakhtin does not view these sets of oppositions in neutral terms. He presents the image of a world in which the openness and dynamism of the posited is threatened by the finality and ossification of the given, in which the particular runs the risk of being excluded by the universal, in which difference and heterogeneity is in danger of being swallowed up by equivalence and homogeneity. *Toward a Philosophy of the Act* is a trenchant critique of what Bakhtin terms the 'fatal theoreticism' (*TPA* 27) that we may associate with (neo-)Kantianism.[49] Theoreticism, in its concentration on the universal and abstract rather than the particular, produces a world which excludes life as a unique and open process of becoming in which particular subjects participate. It produces a world in which

> we would find ourselves to be determined, predetermined, bygone, and finished, that is essentially not living. We would have cast ourselves out of life – as answerable, risk-fraught, and open becoming through performed actions – and into an indifferent and, fundamentally, accomplished and finished theoretical Being.
>
> (*TPA* 9)

In theoreticism, which, with Kant, values only what is universal in a particular act, the existence of a particular subject becomes a matter of indifference.[50] Kant's focus is on 'possible experience', not the actual experience of concrete subjects.[51] As Bakhtin comments: 'The theoretical world is obtained though an essential and fundamental abstraction of the fact of my unique being and from the moral sense of that fact – "as if I did not exist" ' (*TPA* 9). What results is a self-enclosed and repeatable sphere of culture which is characterized by concepts of norm and law that have been emptied of practical meaning.

Nevertheless, Bakhtin does not hypostatize the posited mode of reality. He makes it clear that a resort to *lebensphilosophische* stalwarts such as intuition or immediate experience that prioritize the posited is no solution.[52] Contemporary philosophy is in a 'state of crisis':

> The performed act or deed is split into an objective content/sense and a subjective process of performance. Out of the first fragment one creates

a single systemic unity of culture that is really splendid in its stringent clarity. Out of the second fragment, if it is not discarded as completely useless (it is purely and entirely subjective once the content/sense has been subtracted) one can at best extract and accept a certain aesthetic and theoretical something, like Bergson's *durée* or *élan vital* [12 illegible words]. But neither in the first world nor in the second is there room for the actual and answerable performance of a deed.

(*TPA* 21)

For Bakhtin, Bergson's aestheticization of immediate experience does no more than reproduce the split between content and deed in a covert form. Similarly, in Bakhtin's reading of Nietzsche, a Dionysian surrender to the intoxication of immediate experience is also not an option, since from this gesture of surrender to being 'possessed by Being', it follows that 'the passive moment in participation is moved to the fore, while my to-be-accomplished self-activity is reduced' (*TPA* 49). Thus, Bakhtin's understanding of Nietzsche is that his emphasis on the posited aspect of life in fact results in a production of givenness.[53] Against these proposals, Bakhtin makes it clear that theoretical modes that deal with the given cannot simply be jettisoned:

Theoretical cognition of an object that exists by itself, independent of its actual position in the once-occurrent world from the standpoint of a participant's unique place, is perfectly justified. But it does not constitute ultimate cognition; it constitutes only an auxiliary, technical moment of such ultimate cognition.

(*TPA* 48)

Insufficient in itself, theoretical cognition is, nevertheless, an indispensable part of experience. What is needed, instead, is a plane of higher unity that joins these fragmented aspects of activity.

Bakhtin's method is simpler than it at first seems. He confronts two trends of thought. As we have seen, the first trend is the theoreticism that favours theory over practice, the universal over the particular, the abstract over the specific, the objective over the subjective and certainly the primacy of the former categories in comprehending the latter. The second, *Lebensphilosophie* and what Bakhtin describes, perhaps simplistically, as the irrationalism of Nietzsche and the pessimism of Spengler, is a reaction against the excesses of rationalism and abstraction of the first trend that simply reverses that trend's evaluations. Whilst the brunt of Bakhtin's attack is directed against the first trend, Bakhtin is not content simply to reverse the evaluation and champion life over culture in an unreflexive fashion. Rather, *Toward a Philosophy of the Act* aims at a synthesis of the two trends. It is only a synthesis of these oppositions that will take philosophy beyond what Bakhtin sees as false dichotomies, and hence produce a new way to act. This will be a synthesis that is not transcendental, but rooted in the process of experiencing.

Beyond tragedy: responsible participation

The synthesis that Bakhtin proposes is to be found in responsible participation. By responsible participation Bakhtin means that form of activity in which subjects recognize their participation in life in a particular and concrete temporal and spatial context. Here subjects exist in relation to other subjects towards whom they necessarily adopt emotional and evaluative attitudes.

> What does it mean to assert that historical mankind recognizes in its history or in its culture certain things as values? It is an assertion of an empty *possibility* of content, no more. Of what concern is it to me that there is an *a* in Being for whom a *b* is valuable? Insofar as I affirm my own unique place in the unitary Being of historical mankind, insofar as I am its own non-alibi, i.e., stand in an active emotional-volitional relationship to it, I assume an emotional-volitional position in the values it recognizes.
>
> *(TPA 47)*

Bakhtin's point here is that Being is not a neutral state but an evaluative event of a subject's self-activity. Participation means the action of assuming an evaluative stand towards other subjects.[54] This is what Bakhtin means by the 'non-alibi in Being'. We cannot pretend that we are not there and do not have a view. Bakhtin asks us to take a stand, in the double sense of that phrase: both to accept our position in a real and concrete world, and also to accept that we thereby take an evaluative position towards our environment. When we take a stand the world that seems to be made of abstract, universal, equivalent and repeatable identities becomes one that is filled with concrete, individual, variegated and unique elements that are distinguished by subtle shades of evaluation. The abstract and empty categories of space and time thicken and become heavy, and, in Bakhtin's evocative description, 'blaze up with the light of value' *(TPA 59)*. If we act in this fashion and take a stand, then we also take responsibility for our being. The implications of this can be seen by analysing a metaphor that Bakhtin uses to describe this situation:

> Being that is detached from the unique emotional-volitional center of answerability is a rough draft, an unacknowledged possible variant of once-occurrent Being; only through the answerable participation effected by a unique act or deed can one get out of the realm of endless draft versions and rewrite one's life once and for all in the form of a fair copy.
>
> (*TPA* 44)

Theoretically, a draft could be replaced by a different version of which there might be many. A draft offers its writer an alibi: 'Don't take that statement seriously; that isn't what I mean; I'll say it differently in the next draft.' A fair copy, however, is not hypothetical. It is unique and occurs only once. When we offer a document as a fair copy we have to stand by what we have written; we have to make ourselves publicly responsible for it in a more binding sense than when we present a draft.

If we accept the responsible nature of our situatedness in life, our non-alibi in once-occurrent being, if we produce our life in a fair copy, we take responsibility for it and cannot pretend that it is something provisional and hypothetical. This intersubjective act of responsibility (it is an intersubjective act, since it assumes the presentation of our life to others in the same way as we present a document) subsumes the hypothetical and theoretical to the particular and concrete, thereby reconfiguring the spheres of culture and life in the unity of human activity. Only the responsible act, thus conceived, can reunite the two faces of the totality of experience, 'the objective unity of culture' (characterized by *Erfahrung*) and 'the never-repeatable uniqueness of actually lived and experienced life' (characterized by *Erlebnis*):

> It is only the once-occurrent event of Being in the process of actualization that can constitute this unique unity; all that is theoretical or aesthetic must be determined as a constituent moment in the once-occurrent event of Being, although no longer, of course, in theoretical terms. An act must acquire a single unitary plane to be able to reflect itself in both directions – in its sense or meaning and in its being: it must acquire the unity of two-sided answerability.
>
> (*TPA* 2)

Toward a Philosophy of the Act sets out a thesis according to which the split spheres of culture and life, given and posited, *Erfahrung* and *Erlebnis* might be reunited in responsible human activity. Bakhtin's text, however, fails to raise the important question of the ontological status of the responsible act as he describes it. That is to say: it is not clear whether the responsible act belongs to the category of what is or the category of what ought to be, whether it is a descriptive or a deontological category.[55]

The answer would seem to be that it is both. Responsible participation is an element of our activity. Nevertheless, it is an element that is constantly threatened by erosion in the face of tendencies inherent in modernity. On the one hand, one can concur with Hirschkop, one of the few critics to attempt a serious historicization of Bakhtin's thought, who argues convincingly that the Bakhtin of *Toward a Philosophy of the Act* can be read as a critic of modernity.[56] Despite some infelicities, his general picture rings true:[57]

> It required no special power of analysis to see that, in the wake of the First World War, Europe's traditional sources of obligation and its corresponding subjective attribute, 'responsibility', were drying up [...]. In Bakhtin's account, 'oughtness' and 'responsibility' constitute an original dimension of all culture which disappears from view when modern science and juridical thought force it into their two-dimensional frame.[58]

On the other hand, one can also concur with Tihanov that Bakhtin's early work represents 'phenomenological ahistoricism which seeks to grasp the eternal elements of the human condition'.[59] In order to grasp the full force of Bakhtin's text, it is necessary to see that it is Janus-faced, looking both at the eternal nature of the human condition and at Bakhtin's own modernity.

The face that stares disconsolately at the fragmented modern world is viewed in its most powerful form on the last pages of the first of the two sections of Bakhtin's essay. Here, Bakhtin begins a lament that echoes the nostalgia of the cultural conservatives of his day for a world unafflicted by the fragmentation of modernity:

> The contemporary crisis is, fundamentally, a crisis of contemporary action. An abyss has formed between the motive of the actually performed act or deed and its product. But in consequence of this, the

product of the deed, severed from its ontological roots, has withered as well.

(*TPA* 54)

This lament ascribes a role to economic development in the process in which the forces of responsible activity are eroded, arguing that the money-economy may have become the structuring principle of modern morality:

> In relation to the present moment, economic materialism is in the right, although not because the motives of the actually performed act have penetrated inside the product but rather the reverse: the product in its validity walls itself off from the actually performed act in its actual motivation.
>
> (*TPA* 54–55)

One may put this passage in the context of Marx's analysis of commodity fetishism. Bakhtin's notion that the product comes to enjoy an existence independent of its producers bears similarities to Marx's views. Another likely source, however, for this insight is Simmel's *Philosophy of Money* (1900). Like Lukács,[60] Simmel highlights the way in which the development of the money-economy exacerbates tendencies to calculation and abstraction in human activity; he also argues that it fosters indifference and characterlessness:[61]

> This relationship between the significance for life of the intellect and the significance of money leads one, first of all, to a negative characterization of those epochs and areas of activity in which these two things dominate: they have a certain characterlessness. If character always means that people and things are differentiated from other people and things on the basis of their individual form of existence, the intellect is ignorant of this. For the intellect is the indifferent mirror of reality in which all elements are seen as equivalent [...]. This phenomenon can also be seen in the characterlessness of money. Just as money is the mechanical reflex of the values of things according to which all parties are treated the same, so in money-society all people have the same value – not because every person has worth, but rather because no person has worth since the only thing that has worth is money.[62]

Whether or not Bakhtin draws on Simmel, the terms of Simmel's critique of money-society fit Bakhtin's view of a modernity from which participative thinking has been exiled.[63] Characterlessness can be glossed as a failure to assume one's own responsible individuality, intellectuality, which one might understand as the hallmark of theoreticism, indifference and the tendency to treat other subjects as equivalent; all these are signs of a world in which responsible activity is alien.

Bakhtin takes the notion of the tragedy of culture to its logical and pessimistic conclusion. On the one hand, Bakhtin accepts the *lebensphilosophische* idea that theory and culture have become detached from life and form an autonomous, hermetic realm to which subjects have no authentic access. Earlier in the text, Bakhtin sees in the immanent development of technology the ultimate and terrifyingly destructive expression of this detachment:

> Thus [technological] instruments are perfected according to their own inner law, and, as a result, they develop from what was initially a means of rational defence into a terrifying, deadly, and destructive force. All that which is technological, when divorced from the once-occurrent unity of life and surrendered to the will of the law immanent to its own development, is frightening; it may from time to time irrupt into this once-occurrent unity as an irresponsibly destructive and terrifying force.
>
> (*TPA* 7)

On the other hand, Bakhtin demonstrates none of the *lebensphilosophische* belief in the redeeming potential of pure lived experience. The ultimate consequence of the tragedy of culture is that as culture, by losing touch with life, becomes ossified and loses its human aspect, so lived experience begins to deteriorate, reverting to pure biological, non-human nature. The later passage continues with an image of a thorough-going and brutal degradation of experience:

> All the energy of answerable performing is drawn off into the autonomous domain of culture, and, as a result, the performed act, detached from that energy, sinks to the level of elementary biological and economic motivation, that is, loses all its ideal moments: that is precisely what constitutes the state of civilization. The whole wealth of culture is placed in the service of the biological act.
>
> (*TPA* 55)

The result of this is a world of death and a world that is all but dead; a world reduced to the biological and material minimum; a natural world without subjects; the ravaged landscape of trench warfare.[64]

With his use of the term 'civilization', Bakhtin appears to refer directly to Oswald Spengler, and the distinction that Spengler makes between culture and civilization in *The Decline of the West*.[65] Begun in 1911, but first published in 1918 to enormous acclaim, Spengler's monumental account of the decline of the West was widely seen as having received prophetic vindication in the destruction of European culture on the battlefields of the First World War.[66]

> What is civilization, understood as the organico-logical sequel, fulfil-ment and finale of a culture? For every Culture has *its own* Civiliz-ation. In this work, for the first time the two words, hitherto used to express an indefinite, more or less ethical, distinction, are used in a *periodic* sense, to express a strict and necessary *organic succes-sion*. The Civilization is the inevitable *destiny* of the Culture, and in this principle we obtain the viewpoint from which the deepest and gravest problems of historical morphology become capable of solu-tion. Civilizations are the most external and artificial states of which a species of developed humanity is capable. They are a conclusion, the thing-become [*das Gewordene*] succeeding the thing-becoming [*dem Werden*], death following life, rigidity following expansion, intel-lectual old-age and the stone-built, petrifying world-city following mother-earth and the spiritual childhood of Doric and Gothic. They are an end, irrevocable, yet by inward necessity reached again and again.[67]

In the face of this prospect, Bakhtin does not directly contradict Spen-gler's view of the decline of Western culture. Spengler had conceived of history in terms of cycles of decline and fall. Hence, despite his overwhelming pessimism about the West, he thought that the Faus-tian culture which constituted our Western modernity would, passing through the moribund stage of civilization, eventually give way to a new and vital cultural epoch.[68] Bakhtin's criticism is reserved for this: Spengler's faint glimmer of optimism in the possibility of historical renewal. History, Bakhtin argues, as a force conceived of as outside lived-experience, cannot save the contemporary act. The first section, then, ends with a plea for individual subjects to foster in their active existence the responsible participation that alone will keep life alive.

Life can be consciously comprehended only in concrete answerability. A philosophy of life can only be a moral philosophy. Life can
be consciously comprehended only as an ongoing event, and not
as Being *qua* a given. A life that has fallen away from answerability
cannot have a philosophy; it is, in its very principle, fortuitous and
incapable of being rooted.

(*TPA* 56)

Bakhtin's solution in the face of the degradation of experience in the
wasteland of modern existence is a moral imperative. This imperative,
distinct from Kant's moral imperative, is rooted in the event of being,
and hence it is non-categorical, since it is not interested in universally
applicable laws but in specific situations.[69]

We must not allow our lives to fall away from answerability. Despite
the apparent hopelessness of the situation of contemporary culture, this
seems a simple solution. Furthermore, the situation is not as hopeless as
it may seem at first. Bakhtin argues, as I have shown above, that the unity
of culture and life can only be recreated in the unity of human activity.
It follows from Bakhtin's argument that every subject can participate
(indeed, is obliged to participate) in the recreation of that unity. Where
history, as Spengler conceives of it, is powerless, responsible human
participation holds the key to the renewal of life. This imperative is,
moreover, modest in its demands. A change from an attitude of pride
to an attitude of humble responsibility will reverse the eroding effect of
inauthentic habitualization:

The tacit presupposition of life's ritualism is *not* humility, but pride.
One has to develop humility to the point of participating in person
and being answerable in person. In attempting to understand our
whole life as secret [Coates translates this perhaps more appropriately
as 'masked'] representation and every act we perform – as ritual act,
we turn ourselves into impostors or pretenders.

(*TPA* 52)

Bakhtin's modest imperative does not ask us to do different things from
what we do anyway; it simply asks us to do those things in a certain
fashion. Thus, it is concerned with a way of acting rather than acts, with
the process of positing rather than the finished act of the given. Bakhtin
asks us to act in a manner that recognizes difference. Bakhtin asks us to
act with love.[70]

Bakhtin speaks of love in the following terms:

The valued manifoldness of Being as human (as correlated with the human being) can present itself only to a loving contemplation. Only love is capable of holding and making fast all this multiformity and diversity, without losing and dissipating it, without leaving behind a mere skeleton of basic lines and sense-moments. Only un-self-interested love on the principle of 'I love him not because he is good, but he is good because I love him,' only lovingly interested attention, is capable of generating a sufficiently intent power to encompass and retain the concrete manifoldness of Being, without impoverishing and schematizing it. An indifferent or hostile reaction is always a reaction that impoverishes and decomposes its object; it seeks to pass over the object in all its manifoldness, to ignore it or to overcome it. The very function of indifference biologically consists in freeing us from the manifoldness of Being, diverting us from what is inessential for us practically – a kind of economy or preservation from being dissipated in the manifoldness. And this is the function of forgetting as well.

(*TPA* 64)

The loving attitude does not impoverish or schematize the loved one. 'I love him not because he is good.' If one loves someone because he is good, one asserts the primacy of a general category over the specific particularity of the loved one.[71] The particularity of the loved one is seen through the prism of the general and the result is a flattening of that particularity. The difference that is inherent in that particularity is converted into the equivalence of a general value and hence erased. Love does not do this; it values difference and particularity. Indifference, then, is love's opposite: 'Lovelessness, indifference, will never be able to generate sufficient power to slow down and linger intently over an object, to hold and sculpt every detail and particular in it, however minute' (*TPA* 64). For indifference is the lovelessness, the unwillingness to participate, that erases difference.

Earlier in the essay Bakhtin has a passage in which the themes of love and indifference are bound together in a striking fashion:

That he is mortal, for example, acquires its value-sense only from my unique place, inasmuch as I die, my fellow-being dies, and all historical mankind dies. And, of course, the emotional-volitional, valuative sense of my death, of the death of an other who is dear to me, and the fact of any actual person's death are all profoundly different in each case, for all these are different moments in once-occurrent Being-as-event. For a disembodied, detached (non-participating) *subiectum*, all deaths may be equal. No one, however, lives in a world in which all human beings are – with respect to value – equally mortal.

(TPA 48)

In so far as I accept my participation in the world, I must accept the responsibility that I am not indifferent and that I engage evaluatively with others. I recognize my different evaluative and emotive responses to the imagined and real deaths of those around me. This is an attitude of love since it takes as its criterion of valuation those who are dear to me. Love produces a world that is variegated. Lovelessness, however, erases this difference. It transforms variegated deaths that are distinct in the evaluations attached to them into a series of undifferentiated equivalent units to which I am indifferent. Lovelessness and theoreticism are shown by Bakhtin as part of the same continuum. The link that Bakhtin makes between lovelessness, theoreticism and indifference to the particularity of deaths makes him a modern thinker of a century that, in theoreticism turned to radical evil, put technology in the service of genocide.[72]

The loving attitude does not objectify the loved one. Love is interested, in one sense, as Bakhtin states, but it is also disinterested (or rather, un-self-interested).[73] Indifference objectifies the other; it also instrumentalizes the other, ignoring what is 'inessential practically'. If I love someone because he or she is good then a possible implication is that I approach him or her as good for something, for some purpose that is external to him or her. If I love him or her and then secondarily find that he or she is good, my focus remains on him or her. Love does not instrumentalize in this fashion, nor does it not seek to possess the other as an object.[74] Rather, it respects the other as a subject. I, as a subject, am concrete and manifold. When I love, I do not reduce the loved one to an object; hence I preserve his or her subject-nature, that is, his or her concrete and manifold nature. This gives another dimension to the three architectonic categories that Bakhtin gives earlier in the essay. When, unlovingly, I act as I-for-myself, I encounter other subjects as objects, as others-for-me. When I love, however, I act as I-for-the-other, preserving what is subject within the other. Nor do I lose my own subjectivity since I do not merge with him or her. This is the basis of Bakhtin's intersubjective ethics: the world as a world made up of a multitude of different subjects rather than as a world made up of a mass of equivalent objects.

Loving the other in a humble and responsible fashion, not as an object but in such a fashion that her or his subjectivity is preserved and her or his manifold and concrete nature is recognized, means that I must adopt an attitude towards the other that is as close as possible to the attitude that I adopt towards my own subjectivity. This precept has a simple transcription: love your neighbour as yourself. Bakhtin makes this explicit in the final paragraph of the essay:

> The concrete ought is an architectonic ought: the ought to actualize one's unique place in once-occurrent Being-as-event. And it is determined first and foremost as a contraposition of the I and the other... Whence it does not follow at all, of course, that the contraposition of I and the other has never been expressed and stated – this is, after all, the sense of all Christian morality, and it is the starting point for altruistic morality. But this [3 illegible words] principle of morality has still not found an adequate scientific expression, nor has it been thought through essentially and fully.
>
> (*TPA* 75)

The theological readings of Coates and Mihailovic do not draw this conclusion. Both are concerned to put Bakhtin's ethics in the Christological setting of incarnation.[75] Nevertheless, it seems inescapable that the whole thrust of Bakhtin's essay is a secularized philosophical argument for a Christian ethics in a modern world.[76]

A key for understanding Bakhtin's thinking here may be found in a thinker whose work seems, so far, not to have found resonance in Bakhtin scholarship: Thomas Hobbes. Given Bakhtin's extreme disdain for acknowledgement, the fact that Bakhtin mentions Hobbes is striking. Bakhtin gives a brief but accurate summary of the central thrust of Hobbes's *Leviathan* (1660):

> At one time man actually established all cultural values and now is bound by them. Thus the power of the people, according to Hobbes, is exercised at one time only, in the act of renouncing themselves to the ruler; after that the people become slaves of their own free decision.
>
> (*TPA* 35)

Bakhtin objects to Hobbes's notion of sovereignty. The Leviathan stands as the result of the final objectification of the cultural and theoretical sphere into an authoritarian political realm whose subjects, having relinquished all activity and all responsibility once and for all, are mere slaves. Nevertheless, Bakhtin's and Hobbes's thought display a similar structure, despite radical dissimilarities.[77]

Like Bakhtin, Hobbes's work has as its basis an examination of experience. From his theoretical investigations into the nature of experience, he concludes that man lives in a fragmented and divided world.[78] He argues from this that subjects must find some way of establishing a unity.[79] The means by which Hobbes argues that such a unity can be established is by following an imperative, the central, second law of nature from which all the other laws are derived:

> From this Fundamentall Law of Nature, by which men are commanded to endeavour Peace, is derived this second Law; *That a man be willing, when others are so too, as farre-forth, as for Peace, and defence of himselfe he shall think necessary, to lay down this right to all things; and be contented with so much liberty against other men, as he would allow other men against himselfe*...This is the Law of the Gospell; *Whatsoever you require that other should do to you, that do ye to them.* And that Law of all men, *Quod tibi fieri non vis, alteri ne feceris.*[80]

Hobbes, whose narrative of human nature has nothing to do with a biblical narrative, manages to bring the 'Law of the Gospell' and the 'Law of all men' into a relationship of concordance without inserting a theological element into his secular argument.[81] In a similar fashion, Bakhtin's *Toward a Philosophy of the Act* attempts to give Christ's new commandment an 'adequate scientific expression' and to think it through 'essentially and fully' on a secular basis. There is, however, a profound difference between Hobbes and Bakhtin on this point. Whilst Hobbes's law of nature does not possess force that is binding, it is nevertheless, Hobbes implies, a maxim or imperative that men and women will, in the course of time and with experience, see that it is in their best interest to follow. Thus, Hobbes, despite his initially negative characterization of human nature, can be seen to contain an unexpected optimism. This is not the case for Bakhtin. In Bakhtin's tragedy of culture, as described in the admittedly unfinished work *Toward a Philosophy of the Act*, his imperative for responsible activity remains no more than a plea.

Benjamin's crisis of experience

Many critics have noted Benjamin's use of the terms *Erlebnis* and *Erfahrung*.[82] Few, however, have recognized the extent to which Benjamin develops a theory of different modes of experience that emerges from his early engagement with Simmel and notions of the tragedy of culture. Nevertheless, Jay traces this heritage, commenting that what set Benjamin apart from his immediate predecessors in German thought, people like Dilthey and Husserl, 'was his disdain for both the alleged immediacy and meaningfulness of *Erlebnis* and the overly rational, disinterested version of *Erfahrung* defended by the positivists and the neo-Kantians'.[83] One reason for critics' slowness to point out this connection is that Benjamin's use of these terms can be confusing. Benjamin takes from Simmel and the *lebensphilosophische* tradition a notion of the split between *Erlebnis* and *Erfahrung*. The confusion arises from the fact that the synthetic mode of experience that Benjamin proposes as a solution to this tragedy is itself termed by Benjamin a qualified form of *Erfahrung*. This, however, should not blind the reader to the fact that Benjamin shares with Bakhtin a similar view of the limits of *Erfahrung* in the traditional, Kantian sense. In its place, Benjamin seeks a variety of forms of *Erfahrung* which are qualified in various ways, depending on the context in which he is writing: as 'future', 'higher', 'absolute', 'disappearing' and 'narratable'. Whilst Benjamin rejects much of Kant, he still uses *Erfahrung* as the term for a synthesis of the particularity of *Erlebnis* with some other quality. The difference lies in Benjamin's rejection of the notion that this other quality, necessary for *Erfahrung*, is universality. Benjamin tends to substitute for Kant's 'universality' the term 'narratable' (*mitteilbar*). Narratability lies somewhere between the particular and the universal: it is common to a number of subjects as communication, hence not particular, but restricted historically and culturally, hence not universal. It is the notion of narratability that leads Benjamin to literary and art criticism: an analysis of historically and culturally located artistic works yields a view of the central quality of narratability.

In the academic year 1912–13, Benjamin was, as we have seen, at the University of Berlin. Here, as well as attending the lectures of Simmel and others, he became deeply involved in a wide range of student and youth associations.[84] It was in this context that he contributed to the journal *Der Anfang*. In the opening paragraph of an article in the August 1913 issue, Benjamin writes as follows:

> The present accuses those whose souls are most powerfully inhabited by a feeling of a future task [*Aufgabe*] of being 'lacking in a sense of history'. For this is what they call a sense of the definite, not the indefinite, a sense of the given [*das Gegebene*], not the posited [*das Aufgegebene*]. So strong is its sense of history, this sense of facts,

restraint and caution, that the present is probably most especially poor in actual 'historical ideas'. These it generally calls 'Utopias' and has them fail in the face of the 'eternal laws' of nature. It rejects a task that cannot be contained by a programme of reform, a task that demands a new movement of spirits and a radical new way of seeing.

(*GS II* 57)

This was followed by a piece, more a manifesto of the youth movement than an article, in the October issue. The piece bears the title 'Erfahrung':

In our fight for responsibility, we fight against someone who is masked. The mask of the adult is called experience [*Erfahrung*]. It is expressionless, impenetrable, and ever the same. The adult has already experienced [*erlebt*] everything [...] We have not yet experienced [*erfuhren*] anything. [...] That is what they have experienced, this one thing, never anything different: the meaninglessness of Life. Its brutality. Have they ever yet encouraged us to anything great or new or forward-looking? Oh no, precisely because these are things one cannot experience.

(*GS II* 54; *SW I* 3)

Beneath the youthful, provocative rhetoric of these two statements, which one can take together, lie the germs of Benjamin's life-long meditation on the nature of experience.

As in Bakhtin's critique of theoreticism in the contemporary crisis of the act, Benjamin describes a form of experience (*Erfahrung*) that is characterized by its regularity and repeatability, its habitual nature, its conformity to 'eternal laws' and its sense of the given (*das Gegebene*). This experience erases difference, representing always the one thing (*das Eine*), and never anything different (*das Andere*). This experience is expressionless (*ausdruckslos*) and unchanging like a mask. Thus, like the ritualism of Bakhtin's impostor, the mask of *Erfahrung* is a way of disclaiming responsibility. Similarly, *Erfahrung* is impenetrable (*undurchdringlich*); it neutralizes participation. Benjamin's conception of *Erfahrung* brings to our attention an aspect of Bakhtin's notion of theoreticism that I have not yet commented on. *Erfahrung* is character-ized by restraint (*Gebundenheit*) and caution (*Vorsicht*). Bakhtin argues similarly that if we are governed by theoreticism 'we would have cast ourselves out of life – as answerable, risk-fraught, and open becoming' (*TPA* 9). The theoreticism of *Erfahrung* excludes the risk of life. Finally, Benjamin argues that *Erfahrung* results in the acceptance of brutality (an idea that is close to Bakhtin's idea that theoreticism is indifferent to death). Benjamin also brings new themes to this discussion. Benjamin establishes a parallel between ontogenesis and phylogenesis. *Erfahrung* is the experience of the adult. The process of becoming adult is a process of the ossification of true experience, parallel to the historical ossification of experience.[85]

This early Benjamin differs radically from Bakhtin, however, in his vitalism and, indeed, Decadence:

> Nothing is so hateful to the philistine as the 'dreams of his youth' [...]. And most of the time sentimentality is the protective camouflage of his hatred. For what appeared to him in his dreams was the voice of the spirit [*Geist*], that once called him just as it calls every man. Youth is the eternal, reproachful reminder of this. That is why he combats it. He tells the young of that grim, overwhelming experience [*Erfahrung*] and teaches the young man to laugh at himself [...]. Again: we know of another experience [*Erfahrung*]. It can be hostile to spirit and destructive to many blossoming dreams [*Blütenträume*]. Nevertheless it is the most beautiful, most intangible, most incommunicable, since it can never be without spirit as long as we remain young. As Zarathustra says, the individual can experience [*erlebt*] himself only at the end of his wanderings. The Philistine has his 'experience' [*Erfahrung*]; it is the eternal one of spiritlessness [*Geisteslosigkeit*]. The young man will experience [*erleben*] Spirit [...].
> (*GS II* 56; *SW I* 4–5)

This passage, in its celebration of the possibility of destruction of illusion (the *Blütenträume*), in its hostility to spirit (*Geist*) that paradoxically preserves spirit from the spiritlessness (*Geisteslosigkeit*) of the Philistine, and in its rejection of sentimentality, strongly echoes Nietzsche. It echoes not only Nietzsche's *Thus Spake Zarathustra* (1883–85) but also 'The Genealogy of Morals' (1887) and its noble barbarian, free from social constraints, who constitutes the antithesis to nihilistic, *ressentiment*-bound, mediocre, contemporary humanity.[86] Thus, whilst he speaks of the youth movement's need for 'another form of experience' (*eine andere Erfahrung*), Benjamin here, in Nietzschean and *lebensphilosophische* mode, may be seen to be championing *Erlebnis*.

Benjamin's uncritical enthusiasm for *Erlebnis* will be subjected to thoroughgoing revision.[87] One point remains, however, to be drawn from this essay on experience. In this essay, Benjamin draws out of the term *Erfahrung* a shade of meaning that becomes central to his later thinking on experience. The German word *Erfahrung* carries a sense of the transmissibility of experience. What one has learned (*erfahren*), one can also teach or pass on as tradition.[88] In the example here, the adult generation attempts to pass on its experience in the form of *Erfahrung*. This is the bitter and conservative 'experience' of the adult who, in saying, 'don't attempt to change anything; I thought about trying as a young man and I failed', presents the world as immutable. Here, the form of tradition that is passed from adults to the younger generation is authoritarian. In the face of this authoritarian conservative tradition of *Erfahrung*, the necessary force of destruction is represented by the barbarous revolt of youth and the vitalism of *Erlebnis*.

Benjamin revises this position in his later critique of *Lebensphilosophie*, an expression of which can be found in a review article, 'Theories of German Fascism'. Published in 1930, it deals with a collection of rightist mémoires of the experience of the First World War, edited by Ernst Jünger. As we have seen, Jünger and his comrades had seen in war the expression of a vibrant if brutal *Urerlebnis* and a radical rejection of the ossified and exhausted forms of modern, bourgeois experience. They implicitly identify with the aristocratic barbarian of the Decadent and Nietzschean imagination. Benjamin recognizes this association: 'The most rabidly decadent origins of this new theory of war are emblazoned on their foreheads: it is nothing other than an uninhibited translation of the principles of *l'art pour l'art* to war itself' (*GS III* 240; *SW II* 314).[89] The celebration of the rawness of life, in Benjamin's reading, results, in fact, in a transfiguration of life into the aesthetic. Benjamin makes a similar criticism of *Lebensphilosophie* in 'On Some Motifs in Baudelaire':

> Since the end of the last century, philosophy has made a series of attempts to lay hold of 'true' experience as opposed to the kind that manifests itself in the standardized, denatured life of the civilized masses. These efforts are usually classified under the rubric of *Lebensphilosophie*. Their point of departure, understandably enough, was not the individual's existence in society. Instead, they have evoked poetry [*Dichtung*], or preferably nature, and, most recently, the age of myths. Dilthey's book *Das Erlebnis und die Dichtung* represents one of the earliest of these efforts, which culminate with Klages and Jung, who made common cause with fascism.
>
> (*GS I* 608; *SW IV* 314)

Lebensphilosophie, by ignoring 'the individual's existence in society', ends in a conception of life as a hypostatized mythical nature which, paradoxically, excludes life itself. This constitutes its kinship with fascism. Similarly, the vitalist Jünger believes that he is celebrating the life of man. In reducing his conception of the life of man to the biological and animal, however, the true essence of life escapes him and the experience which he champions is no more than aesthetically produced illusion.

Benjamin argues that these rightist theorists of war have failed to understand the true nature of their subject. In their focus on the archetypal, aristocratic individual warrior who rediscovers in war a lost *Urerlebnis*, they fail to capture the specificity of this war with its massed ranks of modern men. In their emphasis on the eternal nature of war, which they wrap up in archaic, cultic rhetoric, Jünger *et al.* fail to recognize the essentially historical and modern nature of war. The historical and modern nature of war is to be found in its relationship to technology:

> War – the 'eternal war' that they talk about so much here, as well as the most recent one – is said to be the highest manifestation of the German nation. It should be clear that behind their 'eternal' war is concealed the idea of cultic war, just as behind the most recent war hides the idea of technological war; and it should also be clear that these authors have had little success in perceiving these relationships.
>
> (*GS III* 241–42; *SW II* 314–15)

The relationship of technology to modern ('imperialist') war is described by Benjamin as follows:

> Without going too deeply into the significance of the economic causes of war, one might say that the harshest, most disastrous aspects of imperialist war are in part the result of the gaping discrepancy between the gigantic means of technology and the minuscule moral illumination it affords. Indeed, according to its economic nature, bourgeois society cannot help insulating everything technological as much as possible from the so called spiritual, and it cannot help resolutely excluding technology's right of determination in the social order. Any future war will also be a slave revolt [*Sklavenaufstand*] of technology.
>
> (*GS III* 238; *SW II* 313)

Here we see a creative synthesis of Simmel's notion of the tragedy of culture and Marx's theory of the fetish-character of the commodity.[90] Benjamin attributes the particular, modern, brutal power of war to two, mutually reinforcing sources: the crushing weight of an objective culture that has been divorced from the subjective realm, and a commodity society where fetishized products control their creators. As for Bakhtin in *Toward a Philosophy of the Act*, so for Benjamin, technology, the product of objective culture, has become separate from human beings' subjective and volitional activity, with devastating consequences.

The abyss between subjective and objective culture neutralizes subjective activity in such a way that any objections we might have to make, whether about the forms of social organization or the moral justification for war, are irrelevant.[91] Hence, just as Marx argues that in commodity form, which determines the capitalist mode of production, the products of our collective activity come to be animated and exercise control over their creators, so here in war, technology rebels against its owners. The correct relationship between man, technology and nature has been violently inverted. As Benjamin puts it in the 'The Work of Art':

> the destruction caused by war furnished proof that society was not sufficiently developed to master the elemental forces of society. [...] *Imperialistic war is an uprising on the part of technology, which demands repayment in 'human material' for the natural material society has denied it.* Instead of draining rivers, society directs a human stream into a bed of trenches; instead of dropping seeds from airplanes, it drops incendiary bombs over cities.
>
> (*GS I* 507–08; *SW IV* 270)

Jünger's celebration of the subjective sphere gives a mythologizing justification to this total and annihilating victory of objective culture as technology. With technology set free for barbarism, modern war, in the age of technological capitalism, is the final act in the tragedy of culture.

In his essay on theories of fascism, Benjamin does not attack simply the mythologizing forces of Jünger's vitalism. Benjamin also locates what Leslie terms an 'ethical aporia' in the Idealist philosophy that Benjamin treats as capitalism's philosophical counterpart and that we might associate with Bakhtin's theoreticism.[92] The generalizing and abstracting forces of Idealism are held responsible for their complete inability to account for the material aspect of existence, a material aspect that comes shockingly to the fore in the ripped-open bodies of the battlefield:

It should be said as bitterly as possible: in the face of this 'landscape of total mobilization', the German feeling for nature has had an undreamed-of upsurge. The pioneers of peace, who settle nature in so sensuous a manner, were evacuated from these landscapes, and as far as anyone could see over the edge of the trench, the surrounding had become the terrain of German Idealism; every shell crater had become a problem, every wire entanglement an antinomy, every barb a definition, every explosion a thesis.

(GS III 247; *SW II* 318–19)*

Kantian idealism cannot account for the brutally material nature of this world. It transforms it into an abstract language of ethical justification which bypasses its intense materiality. The categorical imperative with its emphasis on universal laws does not deal with a concrete war; it can, hence, be complicit in allowing war to happen and even in justifying it on abstract ethical grounds. The ravaged landscape of the trenches is a transformed but familiar version of Kant's ethical landscape. Benjamin stresses the compatibility of Kantian ethics and totally mobilized war in the continuation of the words quoted above: 'by day the sky was the cosmic interior of the steel helmet, and at night the moral law above' *(GS III* 247; *SW II* 319). This is Benjamin's bitter travesty of Kant.[93]

This image of the desolate landscape of the trenches where Kant's starry firmament has become the inside of a helmet and the moral law is suspended in the fearful night of the battlefield is a prelude to a passage in 'The Storyteller':

Experience [*Erfahrung*] has fallen in value. [...] Was it not noticeable at the end of the war that men who returned from the battlefield had grown silent – not richer but poorer in communicable experience? What poured out in the flood of war books ten years later was anything but experience that can be shared orally. And there was nothing remarkable about that. For never has experience been more thoroughly belied than strategic experience by tactical warfare, economic experience by inflation, bodily experience by mechanical warfare, moral experience by those in power. A generation that had gone to school on horse-drawn streetcars now stood under the open sky in a landscape where nothing remained unchanged but the clouds, and, beneath those clouds, in a force-field of destructive torrents and explosions, the tiny, fragile human body.

(GS II 439; *SW III* 143–44)*

Modern war, with its bombardment of shock and its flood of fragmented bodily experience (*Erlebnis*), displaces the subject and brings about an absolute break with tradition and the possibility of communicable experience (*mitteilbare Erfahrung*). The mechanism whereby the psyche transforms that which has been lived through (*erlebt*) into experience that can be communicated (*Erfahrung*) has ceased to function as a result of an overload of the sensory apparatus. In 'On Some Motifs in Baudelaire', Benjamin expands this notion to account for the role of shock experience in urban life. Drawing on Freud's theory from *Beyond the Pleasure Principle* on the psychical mechanism for dealing with trauma, he suggests:

> the greater the share of the shock factor in particular impressions, the more constantly consciousness has to be alert as a screen against stimuli; the more efficiently it does so, the less do these impressions enter experience [*Erfahrung*], tending to remain in the sphere of a certain hour of one's life [*Erlebnis*]. Perhaps the special achievement of shock defence may be seen in its function of assigning to an incident a precise point in time in consciousness at the cost of the integrity of its contents.
>
> (*GS I* 615; *SW IV* 319)[94]

Nevertheless, it is not only the change in the nature of *Erlebnis*, the material and random shocks of life, that makes communicable experience impossible.[95] The objective structures of the modern world themselves have been transformed by technology in the broadest sense. Technology transforms strategy into tactics and economic experience into inflation. Processes of urbanization and the development of increasingly complex structures of social organization create the environment of urban shock. Thus, it is also the changed, organized structures of objective culture that displace the subject.

The contrast between the human, whose frail physicality in a world of violent flux is highlighted in 'The Storyteller', and the unchanging heavens is an absolute contrast between the particular and the general. That is to say: a participative relationship between man and nature has been recast in terms of fixed antinomies between the given realm of nature and the posited fragility of being. Hence, Benjamin's statement on the uselessness of modern *Erlebnis* for communicable experience is also a statement on the powerlessness of Kantian *Erfahrung*: whilst the tripartite structure of Kantian experience (*Erfahrung*) persists (sense experience, universal law and the embodied subject), the communication between these three coordinates no longer functions. Sense experience and abstract cognition have been forced apart and a synthesis of the two in the *mitteilbare Erfahrung* of narrative is impossible.

This is a crisis of experience, a division between two modes of experience which cannot be brought together. In the modern world, sources of an experience that would make sense of the world in a universal and communicable fashion (*Erfahrung*), whether these be the communal, narratable experience of storytelling or the theoretical, moral experience of the Kantian tradition, are no longer accessible and no longer relevant. The structure of experience of this sort has dissolved in the incomprehensible workings of technological capitalism. On the contrary, *Erlebnis* (now transformed by those same workings of technological capitalism into the mere shock of isolated and apparently unrelated events that act directly on the body) has become the norm. This is, in Benjamin's various descriptions, the experience of the trenches, the syncopated, dislocating rhythm of the factory, the jostle of the crowd and the rush of traffic in the big city, the swift intercutting of images in the montage technique of cinema, the click of the camera that isolates a moment, the flare of a match, or the juxtapositions of articles on the page of a newspaper. The increase in the power and frequency of *Erlebnisse qua* shock and the subsequent development of mechanisms to combat shock bring about what Benjamin diagnoses as the modern atrophy of experience (*Erfahrung*).

In their treatment of Benjamin's conception of experience, critics do not focus on the fact that the atrophy of *Erfahrung* is paralleled by a degradation of *Erlebnis*. Nevertheless, both facets of experience have been flung apart and both have suffered in the process. If we look back to *Lebensphilosophie*, we shall remember that *Erlebnis* constituted for thinkers such as Simmel, Dilthey and Bergson a form of intense subjectivity. Bergson's intuition, for example, might be loosely paraphrased as what one 'knows in one's bones', one's 'gut feelings', before one subjects it to the faculty of reason. If we compare this notion of intense subjectivity with Benjamin's notion of *Erlebnis*, it will be clear that, in Benjamin's analysis, an immense historical shift has occurred. Intense subjectivity has been replaced by intense objectivity; the body, far from 'knowing things in its bones' or having 'gut feelings' as a pre-rational form of subjectivity, has become an object, buffeted about by the shocks prepared for it by the modern world. The new forms of *Erfahrung* that are the object of Benjamin's search can never be *Erfahrung* in the Kantian sense of the term.[96] They will have to be capable of avoiding the pitfalls of Kant as well as capable of assimilating this new and degraded form of *Erlebnis*.

Beyond crisis: a new and higher form of experience

Benjamin's most systematic treatment of the limitations of Kantian experience is to be found in his early text 'On the Programme of the Coming Philosophy' (1918). This essay bears many similarities to Bakhtin's *Toward a Philosophy of the Act*, being both an attempt to go beyond the dominant Kantian tradition and searching for a philosophy yet to come.[97] Unlike Bakhtin, Benjamin does not rework Kant by countering Kant's analysis of experience and cognition with a phenomenological account of the experience of the subject; rather, Benjamin works from within and attempts to expand Kant's framework. This essay is more, however, than a critique of Kant. McCole comments:

> [Benjamin's] interest in systematically extending Kant's theory of experience aimed not only at overcoming Kant's exclusive orientation of epistemology toward the mathematical natural sciences but also – perhaps more so – at recapturing the full range of experience from the monopoly being surrendered by default to the vitalist right.[98]

The 'coming philosophy' that Benjamin calls for here is a philosophy that will go beyond the tragedy of culture as represented by the split between Kantianism and vitalist irrationalism.

In Benjamin's view, Kant's fundamental mistake is to be traced to the unconscious historical parochialism that undermines his claim to construct a theory of knowledge that would be universally valid. Kant's epistemology is defined in relation to a distinct form of experience, which Benjamin describes in the following terms as:

> the conception of the naked, self-evident experience, which for Kant, as a man who somehow shared the horizon of his times, seemed to be the only experience given, indeed, the only experience possible. This experience, however, [...] was unique and temporally limited.
> (*GS II* 158; *SW I* 101)

Kant defines knowledge in relation to his own epoch's narrow notion of Newtonian mathematical and scientific empirical experience. Hence, he limits himself to an equally narrow conception of the world accessible to knowledge. The notion of experience that results is, in Benjamin's view, impoverished.[99] 'The very fact that Kant was able to commence his immense work under the constellation of the Enlightenment indicates that his work was on the basis of an experience virtually reduced to a nadir, to a minimum of significance.' This Newtonian conception of experience in which the world is law-bound and calculable is, in Benjamin's view, 'one of lowest forms of experience or views of the world' (*GS II* 159; *SW I* 101). Kant had excluded knowledge of the noumenal from his epistemology, since, in so far as the noumenal transcends the bounds of Newtonian experience, claims to knowledge of this sphere must remain hollow and ungrounded. Yet, for Benjamin, any theory of knowledge that relinquishes its claim to metaphysics and knowledge of the noumenal is not worth its name. A theory of knowledge based on the prosaic regularities of the phenomenal world promotes a conception of existence that Benjamin dubs inferior.

Benjamin's criticisms of Kant's theory of experience, then, are, in part, similar to Bakhtin's critique of theoreticism. Benjamin also criticizes the abstracted and repeatable nature of Kant's image of experience. Similarly, Benjamin criticizes the inability of Kantian philosophy to account for the intersubjective nature of being. Benjamin argues that Kant's desire to move epistemology away from the slippery ground of metaphysical speculation is itself prey to what he terms a 'metaphysical blindness'. This metaphysical blindness of Kant stems, in Benjamin's view, from his assumption that knowledge can only be conceived of in terms of the relation between subject and object. This assumption, Benjamin argues, is a result of Kant's bias towards a human empirical consciousness that encounters the world as a knowing subject confronted with the objects of its knowledge: 'The subject nature of this cognizing consciousness stems from the fact that it is formed in analogy to the empirical consciousness, which of course has objects confronting it' (*GS II* 161; *SW I* 103).

In Benjamin's view, for philosophy to do justice to the fullness of being, what is necessary is a 'new and higher form of experience that is yet to come [*einer noch kommenden neuen und höhern Art der Erfahrung*]' (*GS II* 161; *SW I* 103). By way of anticipation of such a form of experience, Benjamin describes modes of experience in which subjects encounter the world in a fashion in which the boundary between subject and object is not rigidly patrolled:

We know of primitive peoples of the so-called pre-animistic stage who identify themselves with sacred animals and plants and name themselves after them; we know of insane people who likewise identify themselves in part with objects of their perception, which are thus no longer objects placed before them; we know of sick people who do not relate the sensations of their bodies to themselves, but rather to other beings, and of clairvoyants who at least claim to be able to feel the sensations of others as their own.

(*GS II* 161–62; *SW I* 103)

These modes of experience are modes which do not comply with the precepts of modern reason, least of all modern empirical science. Modern (Kantian) reason would classify these ways of viewing the world as myth-ologies. And yet, Benjamin argues, in so far as a modern, rational world-view is blind to its own limitations, it is as much a mythology.[100] These non-rational modes of experience, however, imply a possible approach with which to challenge narrowly instrumental reason that conceives of a strict boundary between the knowing subject and the objects of that knowledge. Benjamin's new and higher form of experience shares the same aim as Bakhtin's responsible activity: it resists the reduction of the world to a series of passive and repeatable objects; rather, it seeks to preserve the subject-nature of both knowing subject and the subjects which that subject confronts.

This early essay does not define precisely what this new and higher form of experience might be; it is, after all, only 'coming' and Benjamin is clearer on what it is not and what it should be able to encom-pass than on positive definitions. Similarly, Bakhtin's early essay is less than full in his description of the practical sources which human beings may draw on to engage in responsible participation. Benjamin gives us an indication, however, towards the end of the essay: 'the great transformation and correction which must be performed upon the concept of experience [*Erfahrung*], oriented so one-sidedly along mathematical-mechanical lines, can be attained only by relating know-ledge to language [...]' (*GS II* 168; *SW I* 107–08). Benjamin's argu-ment is that Kant's mathematical bias and his desire for the abstract universality and certainty of the mathematical formula means that he ignores the fact that human experience is always articulated in language:

For Kant, the consciousness that philosophical knowledge was absolutely certain and *a priori*, the consciousness of that aspect of philosophy in which it is fully the peer of mathematics, ensured that he devoted almost no attention to the fact that all philosophical knowledge has its unique expression in language and not in formulas or numbers.

(GS II 168; *SW I* 108)*

Bakhtin has a similar insight into the importance of language to responsible participation. 'Historically language grew up in the service of participative thinking and performed acts, and it begins to serve abstract thinking only in the present day of its history' *(TPA* 31). Bakhtin argues, similarly to Benjamin, that there is an aspect of language that resists abstraction and might be the source of responsible participation. In the next chapter, I shall show how both Bakhtin and Benjamin come to seek in language the model for what they have termed respectively 'responsible participation' and a 'higher form of experience'. First, however, I shall consider the extent to which Benjamin's responses to the crisis of experience may be compatible with Bakhtin's ethics of a non-categorical imperative, discussed above.

Politics and ethics

Unlike the early Bakhtin, Benjamin is not obviously a philosopher of ethics.[101] Benjamin's thought seems to contain so little moral theory because of the perspective of actuality that he assumes.[102] The demand of actuality is that we must not forget our relationship to our present. From the standpoint of actuality, overtly ethical thinking may tend towards unsituated abstraction. Hence, in Benjamin's work ethical ideas tend to dissolve into political activity. Furthermore, Benjamin's work seems to claim that his particular situation does not allow the luxury of expressly ethical behaviour; rather, it demands political commitment. In 'The Storyteller', he speaks of the righteous man who has disappeared from the world along with the narrative community of storytelling: 'The hierarchy of the creaturely world, which has its apex in the righteous man, reaches down into the abyss of the inanimate by many gradations' *(GS II* 460; *SW III* 159). In a modern world whose landscape has been transformed by the forces of modernity, the righteous man has no place. Benjamin makes a similar point at the end of 'Theories of German Fascism':

Until Germany has exploded the entanglement of such Medusa-like beliefs that confront it in these essays, it cannot hope for a future. Perhaps the word 'loosened' would be better than 'exploded,' but this is not to say it should be done with kindly encourage-ment or with love, both of which are out of place here; nor should the way be smoothed for argumentation, for that wantonly persuasive rhetoric of debate. Instead, all the light that language and reason still afford should be focused upon that 'primal exper-ience' [*Urerlebnis*] from whose barren gloom this mysticism of the death of the world crawls forth on its thousand unsightly conceptual feet.

(*GS III* 249; *SW II* 320–21)

The emptiness of love and wise words are not sufficient here to the actual threat of fascism. It seems that we are a long way from Bakhtin and his imperative to love.

A closer examination, however, exhibits a different situation. Bakhtin's form of ethics is also against a conception of love that is general. For Bakhtin, love must be specific and located. Any other form of love would similarly be empty and powerless. Bakhtin's ethics, then, are concerned with actuality. Furthermore, Benjamin's 'On the Concept of History' contains an implicit ethical dimension that may usefully be compared with Bakhtin. Here, Benjamin argues that the task of the historical materialist is to fight on behalf of the vanquished of the past in a form of historiography that seeks to rescue the tradition of the oppressed. The historical materialist must not be indifferent to the past: 'for it is an irretrievable image of the past which threatens to disappear in any present that does not recog-nize itself as intended in that image' (*GS I* 695; *SW IV* 391). Rather the historical materialist participates with the past, not as something that is given, but as something that is still posited. Here, Benjamin contrasts the approach of the historical materialist with that of the historicist:

Universal history has no theoretical armature. Its procedure is additive; it musters a mass of data to fill the homogeneous, empty time. Materialistic historiography, on the other hand, is based on a constructive principle. Thinking involves not only the flow of thoughts, but their arrest as well. When thinking suddenly stops in a configuration pregnant with tensions, it gives that configuration a shock, by which it crystallizes into a monad. The historical mater-ialist approaches a historical subject only where he encounters it as a monad. In this structure he recognizes the sign of a messianic cessation of happening, or (to put it differently) a revolutionary chance in the fight for the oppressed past.

(*GS I* 702–03; *SW IV* 396)

The indifference of the historicist reproduces history as a sequence of equivalent and abstract units all of which add up to a closed conception of history as an inevitable progression towards a given present. The historical materialist who is not indifferent but stops to linger over the past preserves the specific nature of past moments and hence produces an open history of difference that preserves the posited nature of temporal experience. Time is no longer homogeneous and empty, but filled with the bodily presence of subjects.

Similarly Bakhtin's love is able to 'slow down and linger intently over an object, to hold and sculpt every detail and particular in it, however minute' (*TPA* 64). In this way, Bakhtin's loving attention transforms the nature of time:

Only the value of mortal man provides the standards for measuring the spatial and the temporal orders: space gains body as the possible horizon of mortal man and as his possible environment, and time possesses valuative weight and heaviness as the progression of mortal man's life, where, moreover, the content of the temporal determination as well as its formal heaviness possess the validity of rhythmic progression. If man were not mortal, then the emotional-volitional tone of this progression of life – of this 'earlier', 'later', 'as yet', 'when', 'never' and the tone of the formal moments of rhythm would be quite different. If we annihilate the moment constituted by mortal man, the value of what is actually experienced will be extinguished: both the value of rhythm and the value of content.

(*TPA* 65)

Without love, time is mathematically identical, homogeneous and empty. With loving attention to the value of mortal man, time gains weight and space gains body. Bakhtin's loving attention is also an activity that is directed towards history. Indifference 'is the function of forgetting as well' (*TPA* 64). The paradigm of love, for Bakhtin, seems to be loving remembrance of the dead. Benjamin demands the same ethics of memory. In *The Arcades Project* Benjamin comments:

The corrective to this line of thought lies in the reflection that history is not simply a science but also and not least a form of remembrance [*eine Form des Eingedenkens*]. What science [*Wissenschaft*] has 'determined', remembrance can modify. Remembrance can make the incomplete (happiness) into something complete, and the complete (suffering) into something incomplete.

(*GS V* 589; *AP* 471)

(Loving) remembrance, for both Bakhtin and Benjamin, is a weapon against a forgetful science that presents past suffering as given, necessary and hence repeatable. Remembrance attempts to complete happiness whilst not taking suffering for granted. In its emphasis on the necessity of remembrance, Benjamin's notion of critical attentiveness and commitment (a term that is common to the vocabulary of both love and political struggle) comes to be the political corollary to Bakhtin's ethical notion of love.[103] Both point beyond the tragedy of culture.

3
Language

Language, the tragedy of culture and intersubjectivity

In *Toward a Philosophy of the Act*, Bakhtin writes:

> I think that language is much more adapted to giving utterance precisely to that truth [the *pravda* of responsible activity], and not to the abstract moment of the logical in its purity. That which is abstract, in its purity, is indeed unutterable: any expression is much too concrete for pure meaning – it distorts and dulls the purity and validity-in-itself of meaning. That is why in abstract thinking we never understand an expression in its full sense.
>
> (*TPA* 34)

Bakhtin's point here is that language cannot be reduced to abstract, logical or mathematical expression alone. The utterance always bears some of the traces of its genesis in a particular, historically and socially located context. The corollary of this is that the attempts at stating only the logical purity of the given, utterances such as mathematical equations, are unutterable in language.[1] In 'On the Programme of the Coming Philosophy', Benjamin similarly argues that Kant's inability to account for the fullness of possible experience is the result of his tendency to seek the model of knowledge not in language but in mathematical formulae. For both thinkers, language contains a fuller form of experience than the minimal experience that is grasped by abstract thinking.

Language contains a double orientation: on the one hand, as a medium of communication between different subjects in different situations, language must contain an orientation towards abstraction, generality and repeatability. On the other hand, as the medium of expression for specifically located subjects and their evaluative positions and itself emerging from such positions and evaluations, it must contain an orientation towards the concrete and must be able to express the unrepeatability of actual being. Hence, language might be the site of participative action by virtue of this double orientation towards both the sphere of the given and the sphere of the posited. It might bear the marks of a higher experience that the abstraction of mathematical formulae fails to grasp. This seems to be the insight that is common to both Bakhtin in *Toward a Philosophy of the Act* and Benjamin in 'On the Programme of the Coming Philosophy'. Nevertheless, at this early point, neither thinker has developed a conceptual vocabulary that articulates such an idea with any degree of clarity. During the course of the 1920s, however, Bakhtin, in association with other members of his circle, turns his attention increasingly towards linguistics and the philosophy of language and puts language at the heart of his search for paths beyond the tragedy of culture.[2] As a result, we can turn to another member of the Bakhtin Circle, Valentin Voloshinov, and his text of 1929, *Marxism and the Philosophy of Language*, where this conception of language is expressed in a more detailed and explicit fashion.

Voloshinov's *Marxism and the Philosophy of Language* represents a reformulation of Bakhtin's concerns in *Toward the Philosophy of the Act*. Furthermore, it is characterized by the same structure. Where Bakhtin seeks a synthesis between Kantian theoreticism and *Lebensphilosophie*, Voloshinov, likewise, seeks a synthesis between opposing trends.[3] In the first part of his study, Voloshinov describes the split between what he terms psychologists and anti-psychologists over the relationship between the psyche and ideology. Psychologists are individualistic subjectivists, who maintain that ideology is the product of individual psychical activity. Psychologists, then, give precedence to the posited sphere of life. Anti-psychologists are abstract objectivists, who maintain that the psyche is derived from ideology. They, then, give precedence to the given sphere of culture.

Voloshinov argues that the inability of thinkers to bring these two positions together represents Simmel's tragedy of culture in which the product of psychical activity (ideology, as Voloshinov terms it, or, in Simmel's original term, objective culture) has become divorced from the psyche (or in Simmel's terms, life). Voloshinov, who observes admiringly that Simmel's analysis of the tragedy of culture 'contains no small number of acute and interesting observations', describes the basic deficiency of Simmel's conception:

> For Simmel, an irreconcilable discrepancy exists between the psyche and ideology: *he does not know the sign of a form of reality common to both psyche and ideology* [...]. Moreover, though a sociologist, he utterly *fails to appreciate the thoroughgoing social nature of the reality of ideology, as well as the reality of the psyche* [...]. As a result the vital dialectical contradiction between the psyche and existence assumes for Simmel the shape of an inert, fixed antinomy by resorting to a metaphysically colored dynamics of the life process.
>
> (*MPL* 40)

For Voloshinov, the underlying unity of meaningful existence is the social realm of ideological signification. Conceptions of the individual and the social are secondary abstractions from this fundamental unity and result in a fixed and tragic antinomy.[4] As Voloshinov concludes on Simmel:

> Only on the grounds of a materialistic monism can a dialectical resolution of all such contradictions be achieved. Any other grounds would necessarily entail either closing one's eyes to these contradictions or transforming them into a hopeless antinomy, a tragic dead end.
>
> (*MPL* 40)

One must not be put off by the rather dourly Marxist-sounding term 'materialistic monism'. This monism is the plural and concrete sphere of intersubjective interaction to be found in social communication. Simmel's anxiety at the tragedy of culture, according to Voloshinov, is no more than the anxiety that results from the bourgeois attitude that is unable to see the social significance of all phenomena, including the individual psyche, and that instead wishes to see the individual as the fundamental building block.

Like Bakhtin, Voloshinov's answer to Simmel and the tragedy of culture is to be found in the intersubjective aspect of experience. Unlike Bakhtin, however, Voloshinov's linguistic approach gives him a set of terms with which to describe this form of intersubjectivity, the essence of which he finds in language. *Marxism and the Philosophy of Language* describes two trends in linguistic thought that correspond to the psychologists and the anti-psychologists: the individualistic subjectivism of the Vossler school and others and the abstract objectivism of Saussure and the Geneva school. These two trends can likewise be mapped onto the opposition between the posited and the given respectively.[5] Drawing on Wilhelm von Humboldt and the distinction that Humboldt draws between *ergon* and *energeia*, Voloshinov notes that individualistic subjectivism, on the one hand, conceives of language as the expression of the subject (*energeia*), that is to say, language as concrete, posited activity. Abstract objectivism, on the other hand, conceives of language as an inert objective system (*ergon*), that is to say, language as abstract, given product.[6]

Voloshinov characterizes these trends by means of an analysis of their differing preferences for what he terms 'meaning' and 'theme'. Meaning, on the one hand, the focus of abstract objectivism, consists in 'signification without regard to the concrete situation of utterance in life. It is those aspects of the signification of an utterance that are most abstract and general, reproducible and self-identical in all instances of repetition' (*MPL* 100). This is the word of dictionaries and grammar that, abstracting from lived speech, aims at the inert stability and repeatability of signification. Theme, the focus of individualistic subjectivism, on the other hand, is the expression of the concrete temporal situatedness of the utterance in the mouth of a speaking subject in the midst of life: 'The theme of an utterance is concrete – as concrete as the historical instant to which the theme belongs' (*MPL* 100). Theme is the subject's expression of concrete relations to and evaluations of the temporal, spatial and social environment. This split between a focus on theme and a focus on meaning constitutes an articulation of the tragedy of culture.

Voloshinov's insight is that both theme and meaning are contained in the primary unity of language as social and intersubjective activity. The bifurcation of language into the individual aspect of theme and the objective aspect of meaning results from a failure to recognize this fundamental unity. Voloshinov, and subsequently Bakhtin, view language as, in essence, intersubjective:

Any true understanding is dialogic in nature. Understanding strives to match the speaker's word with a counter word [...]. There is no reason for saying that meaning belongs to a word as such. In essence, meaning belongs to a word in its position between speakers; that is, meaning is realized only in the process of active, responsive understanding. Meaning does not reside in the word or in the soul of the speaker or in the soul of the listener. Meaning is the effect of interaction between the speaker and listener produced via the material of a particular sound complex.

(*MPL* 103)

The primary focus of the Bakhtin Circle's philosophy of language is neither the individual utterance nor the system of language but rather the interaction of utterances, the utterance in reaction to, with reference to, or in pre-emption of another's utterance: (free) indirect discourse (Voloshinov), the word with a sideways glance, the internally dialogized word (Bakhtin).

In a sense that seems at first glance paradoxical, the word of the other must always precede the word of the self. Deleuze and Guattari, drawing on Voloshinov, make explicit something of the strange nature of this situation:

> Language in its entirety is indirect discourse. Indirect discourse in no way supposes direct discourse; rather, the latter is extracted from the former, to the extent that the operations of significance and proceedings of subjectification in an assemblage are distributed, attributed, and assigned, or that the variables of the assemblage enter into constant relations, however temporarily. Direct discourse is a detached fragment of a mass and is born of the dismemberment of the collective assemblage; but the collective assemblage is always like the murmur from which I take my proper name, the constellation of voices, concordant or not, from which I draw my voice [...]. My direct discourse is still the free indirect discourse running through me, coming from other worlds or other planets.[7]

Just as we have seen that, for Voloshinov, the individual psyche is constituted secondarily out of the ideological material of social life, so it follows that the individual word, conceived of in isolation is a secondary abstraction from the essence of language which is to be found in the other's word. This theory allows Voloshinov and Bakhtin to replace a primary division between subject and object with a primary unity of intersubjectivity in language, from which subject and object are falsely abstracted. We now see, then, the reason for the significance that Bakhtin and, I shall argue, Benjamin ascribe to language. Language becomes the medium in which the fundamental schism that opened up in Western philosophy since Descartes, the schism between cognizing subject and cognized object-world, is revealed as already healed. As Williams comments of Voloshinov's conception of language: 'It is of and to this experience – the lost middle term between the abstract entities, "subject" and "object", on which the propositions of idealism and orthodox materialism are erected – that language speaks.'[8]

For Voloshinov, indirect discourse is the phenomenon in which the true nature of language is to be observed:

> As we know now, the real unit of language that is implemented in speech (*Sprache als Rede*) is not the individual, isolated monologic utterance, but the interaction of at least two utterances – in a word dialogue. The productive study of dialogue presupposes, however, a more profound investigation of the forms used in reported speech, since these forms reflect basic and constant tendencies in the active reception of other speakers' speech [...]. What we have in the forms of reported speech is precisely an objective documentation of this reception.
>
> (*MPL* 117)

Bakhtin, in his study of the novel, in particular, seeks to isolate the artistic use of linguistic forms in which the essentially intersubjective, dialogic nature of all language is preserved and allowed to flourish. Dialogic prose is in opposition to the monologic word which renders mute the word of the other that resides in the word of the self and hence reproduces the fixed antinomies of subject and object. In his notes of 1970–71, however, Bakhtin makes an intriguing comment that suggests that an understanding of language as the lost middle term between the antinomies of subject and object can be gained in other ways as well:

> Quests for my own word are in fact quests for a word that is not my own, a word that is more than myself; this is a striving to depart from one's own words, with which nothing essential can be said. [...] This is now the most critical problem of contemporary literature, which leads many to reject the genre of the novel altogether, to replace it with a montage of documents, to bookishness [*lettrism*], and, to a certain degree, also to the literature of the absurd. In some sense [...] these [quests] can be defined as various forms of silence. These quests led Dostoevsky to the creation of the polyphonic novel. He could not find the word for the monologic novel. A parallel path led Leo Tolstoy to folk stories (primitivism), to the introduction of biblical quotations (in the final parts of his novels). Another route would be

to cause the world to begin speaking and to listen to the word of the world itself (Heidegger).

(SG 149)

Dostoevsky's quest for his own word in the word that was not his own, his desire to reproduce and honour the intersubjective nature of language and, indeed, existence *per se*, led him to the complex forms of the polyphonic novel. Benjamin, as we shall see, is largely concerned with the other possible paths that Bakhtin identifies. In what follows, I shall examine the ways in which Benjamin's theory of language may be seen to approximate Bakhtin's philosophy of language in these other paths: the word of the world, quotation, montage and silence.

Jay, in his article 'Experience without a Subject', suggests that Benjamin's search for higher experience 'without a subject' in language might have, but did not, led him to a theory of indirect discourse such as that of Voloshinov and Bakhtin. Jay traces the development of the concept of indirect discourse and its variants from Lorck's *erlebte Rede* through Voloshinov to Benveniste's similar concept of the 'middle voice'.[9] In both indirect discourse and the middle voice, Benjamin's longed-for sphere of neutrality towards both subject and object can be achieved. As Derrida argues, 'the middle voice, a certain nontransitivity, may be what philosophy, at its outset, distributed into an active and a passive voice, thereby constituting itself out of this repression'.[10] Furthermore, Jay notes the importance of Voloshinov's dialogical and intersubjective understanding of this sphere of 'experience without a subject'. The notion of the middle voice in which subject and object are subsumed in undifferentiated unity carries a certain threat and 'may even prove an unwitting hand-maiden of an authoritarian politics, as Heidegger's philosophy itself based on a search for experience without a subject, unfortunately did'.[11] Instead, Jay sees the more open space of Bakhtin and Voloshinov's indirect discourse as 'a less settled notion of a unity prior to a split into direct and indirect discourse, active and passive voice' where 'experience without the subject turns out to be experience with more than one subject inhabiting the same space'.[12]

According to Jay, the question of indirect discourse is something that Benjamin happens not to notice. Benjamin 'failed to appreciate' the confirmation of his conception of absolute experience by the linguistic evidence of indirect discourse in the novel.[13] The contention of what follows is first, that Benjamin does have an approach to the notion of intersubjective, indirect discourse (even if he never calls it this by name); and second, moreover, that Benjamin goes as far as to display this in his reading of the modern novel. As well as looking at the extent to which Bakhtinian ideas of indirect discourse can shed light on Benjamin, this chapter will also try and show how Benjaminian ideas such as quotation, montage and mutism can shed light on Bakhtin.

'The Word of the World' and translation

In order to understand Benjamin's philosophy of language and its affinities with Bakhtin, we have to move a long way from Voloshinov and his Marxist and semiotic vocabulary. This is because the primary engagement of the young Benjamin's theory of language is with the very different world of German Romanticism. Nevertheless, Benjamin shares the same concerns as Voloshinov: the desire to transcend the fixed antinomies of subject and object by coming to an understanding of the nature of language. As we have seen, Benjamin's criticism of Kant's theory of experience is, to a large extent, directed at Kant's inability to conceive of the world other than in terms of the division between cognizing subject and cognized object. In this, Benjamin echoes the concerns of the German thinkers following Kant (Schiller, Fichte, Schlegel, Schelling, Novalis, Hölderlin, Hegel) who likewise realized that the world as represented by Kant is split by a set of dualisms (reason and nature, duty and inclination, freedom and necessity, and so forth) that stem from the fundamental dualism of subject and object. In particular, Benjamin has great affinities with Hölderlin.

In a fragmentary text of 1795, Hölderlin addresses the question of subject and object. His text is a dialogue not so much with Kant directly, but rather with Fichte, who, in the *Wissenschaftslehre* (1794), had proposed that Kantian dualism can be overcome by positing an absolute ego in which, through reflection, both subject and object are contained. Hölderlin maintains, *contra* Fichte, that no sort of 'I', absolute or not, can precede a division between subject and object, since, in so far as it is capable of judging, it must always be defined in relation to an object that is distinct from it. He makes this point with a piece of word-play:

> Judgement – is in the highest and most strict sense the original separation, that separation which makes object and subject first possible, the judgement [*Ur – theilung*, original – separation]. The concept of judgement already contains the concept of the reciprocal relation of object and subject to each other, as well as the necessary precondition of a whole of which object and subject are the parts.[14]

On the verso of the scrap of paper on which this fragment appears, Hölderlin addresses the question of Being. Being is the standpoint of unity of subject and object that precedes the judging I:

> Where subject and object simply are, and not just partially, united, such that no separation can take place without injuring the nature of that which is to be divided, only there and nowhere else can there be talk of being as such, the same is the case in intellectual intuition.[15]

Subjectivity, for Hölderlin, is a breaking up of this underlying unity of 'absolute Being' as opposed to the 'absolute I'. Absolute being, however, is necessarily unknowable. As Hölderlin writes to Schiller a few months later: 'the unity of subject and object is possible aesthetically, but, in the intellectual way of seeing things [*in der intellectualen Anschauung*] of theory, possible only through infinite approximation [*unendliche Annäherung*]'.[16] Aesthetically, however, such a unity may be more approachable.

Increasingly, Hölderlin abandons philosophy for poetry and, by giving voice to nature, attempts in his verse to reconstitute the broken ground of being. For here, in poetic inspiration, when the subject is 'alone and less conscious of himself [...] what is speechless gains speech by him and through him, and what is general and unconscious achieves the form of particularity and consciousness'.[17] When he is 'less conscious of himself', the subject nature of the poet begins to recede. Accordingly, the object nature of the natural world also falls away. Nature finds voice as a subject. We approach a mode of neutrality vis-à-vis subject and object, exactly the situation that Benjamin describes as necessary for higher experience in 'On the Programme of the Coming Philosophy'. This must be an 'absolute', non-subjective experience:

> All genuine experience rests upon the pure 'epistemological (transcendental) consciousness', if this term is still usable under the condition that it be stripped of everything subjective. [...] The task of future epistemology is to find for knowledge the sphere of total neutrality in regard to the concepts of subject and object; in other words, it is to discover the autonomous, innate sphere of knowledge in which this concept in no way continues to designate the relation between two metaphysical entities.
>
> (*GS II* 163; *SW I* 104)

This sphere of neutrality is what is achieved by the poet who, as Bakhtin puts it above (with reference to Heidegger), causes 'the world to begin speaking' and listens 'to the word of the world itself'.[18]

In Hölderlin's conception, the poet must receive and transmit the speech of nature. Thus, subject and object are reunited in language.[19] We can now see how Hölderlin can be brought alongside Bakhtin. Despite the vast difference in approach, despite his resolute emphasis on the 'holy' sphere of poetry not the 'profane' sphere of prose, Hölderlin's aesthetics are, at base, comparable with Bakhtin's insistence on the importance of indirect discourse in the novel: at the heart of both there is a search for the other's word as the ground of a wholeness of being that does not know of the antinomies of subject and object. Moreover, whilst Hölderlin's thinking on being and language bears certain broad similarities to Bakhtin's approach, in Benjamin's adaptation of it greater affinities become apparent.

We see the outlines of Benjamin's theory of language in his essay of 1916, 'On Language as Such and on the Language of Man'. This essay is dauntingly theological, if not straightforwardly mystical. As well as drawing on his 1914 essay, 'Two Poems of Friedrich Hölderlin', this essay represents a creative synthesis of the long tradition of language mysticism and ontologies of linguistic being that stretches from Boehme to Hamann and Schlegel.[20] It seems curious that a few years after Saussure has given his ground-breaking lectures in general linguistics in Geneva, establishing a radically modern linguistics, and at the same time as the Vienna Circle is developing its mathematically orientated philosophy of language, Benjamin is delving back into what seems to be pre-modern obscurantism in order to construct a mystical theory of language.[21]

How does this affect our reading of the essay? One does not have to accept or reject the essay *in toto* on the basis of an acceptance or a rejection of mysticism. The essay contains fundamental insights into the relationship between Man, nature and language that can be understood in secular terms.[22] Benjamin's language-mysticism can, in part, be explained by his inability to present his underlying intuition of the nature of language in any other way.[23] For all the importance that he accords to language in his thinking, Benjamin does not engage thoroughly with theoretical linguistics. Benjamin's 1935 review article, 'Problems in the Sociology of Language: An Overview', which deals with, amongst others, Bühler, Bally, Vygotsky, Piaget and Marr and hence provides a point of contact with the world of the Bakhtin Circle, reveals his inability to deal with what was then the cutting edge of linguistics. His own philosophical purposes intrude to the detriment of the coherence of the subject that he discusses.[24] The position of Bakhtin and Voloshinov is different.[25] They live in an environment in which linguistics is, arguably, the model discipline for the humanities. Here, a strong domestic linguistic tradition fuses with the new linguistics from Geneva;[26] Soviet thinkers are well informed about the most recent developments in linguistics in the French- and German-speaking world. As a result, Bakhtin and Voloshinov possess a set of linguistic terms and concepts that Benjamin does not.[27] A reader with an awareness of the linguistic concepts and terminology found in Bakhtin and Voloshinov can reassess Benjamin's theory of language.

A central matter in this context lies in the fact that Benjamin repeatedly speaks of Man's relation to nature, whereas Bakhtin repeatedly speaks of the relation of one subject to another.[28] This appears to constitute a fundamental difference between the two thinkers. Rochlitz argues that 'Benjamin discovers intersubjectivity, which has very little place in his thinking, only through the detour of the mystical or poetic relation to nature'.[29] In this chapter I argue against this that Benjamin's thinking has a form of intersubjectivity at its very heart. Nevertheless, Benjamin's immersion in the German Romantic tradition, on the one hand, and his lack of linguistic expertise, on the other hand, result in his being able to come close to a theory of intersubjectivity only through the detour of Man's relation to nature. It is precisely at this limit of Benjamin's approach that a comparison with the thought of Bakhtin is valuable.

In 'On Language as Such and on the Language of Man', Benjamin argues that since God created the world through the word, so he necessarily implanted language within things. Nature is possessed of its own linguistic being which is the residue of the Word of God. Man, however, was created differently. Benjamin points out that God created man out of earth: 'God did not create man from the word, and he did not name him. He did not wish to subject man to language, but in man God set language which had served *Him* as medium of creation, free' (*GS II* 149; *SW I* 68). Language, originating in God, is present first in nature and not, as such, in Man. God gives Man the capacity of language, but he does not give Man language itself which is to be found instead in nature. Man finds language already inhabited. As Bakhtin comments in the Dostoevsky book:

> When a member of a collective comes upon a word, it is not as a
> neutral word of language, not as a word free from the aspirations

and evaluations of others, uninhabited by others. No, he receives the word from another's voice and filled with that other's voice. [...] His own thought finds the word already inhabited.

(*DP* 202)

In Bakhtin's theory, the word is already inhabited by the subjectivity of the other. So it is with Benjamin. Nature has its own share of subjectivity in so far as it is possessed of language.[30] Man, too, however, possesses a share of subjectivity, albeit a different form of subjectivity granted by the freedom of the faculty for language.

For Benjamin, unlike Rousseau, Eden is not characterized by an unmediated relationship between Man and nature; Man is not nature, but is already, by virtue of his language-faculty, separate from it. Nor does Benjamin's image, despite an outward similarity, tally with the medieval philosophy of the 'book of the world', as described by Foucault:

In its original form, as it was given to men by God, language was a sign of things that was absolutely certain and transparent because it resembled them. Names were imprinted on the things that they designated, just as strength is inscribed on the body of the lion and royalty is inscribed in the gaze of the eagle.[31]

Man does not possess the absolute lordship of subject over object that would be contained in a ready-made, God-given language. His lordship resides merely in the capacity to respond to the language that already inheres in nature. Man's relation to the sphere of nature is, as a result, the relation of one sort of subject to a subject of another sort. As Bröcker comments: 'The language of man is bound to the object-world but man does not stand in a subject-relation to it [the world]. [...] In the paradisiac state of creation, subject and object do not face each other as alien.'[32] The relation between Man and nature is, then, analogous to a relation of intersubjectivity. This notion of intersubjectivity is a departure from Hölderlin's poetic absolute. In Hölderlin's theory, the boundaries of subject and object are abolished in a moment of undifferentiated unity of being, whereas, in Benjamin's image, relations persist as relations between subjects without objects.[33]

Benjamin makes clear his objections to a philosophy of language based on the relation between a subject and an object-world, in his criticisms of what he terms the 'bourgeois conception of language':

Anyone who believes that man communicates his mental being *by* names cannot also assume that it is his mental being that he communicates, for this does not happen through the names of things, that is, through the words by which he denotes a thing. And, equally, the advocate of such a view can only assume that man is communicating factual subject matter to other men, for that does happen through the word by which he denotes a thing. This view is the bourgeois conception of language, the invalidity and emptiness of which will become increasingly clear in what follows. It holds that the means of communication is the word, its object factual, its addressee a human being.

(*GS II* 143–44; *SW I* 64–65)

Language is not an instrument. In essence, for Benjamin, 'all language communicates itself' and only secondarily any particular content. Benjamin's resistance to the instrumentalization of language shows his affinities with the Symbolist thinking of Stefan George, Hugo von Hofmannsthal or Stéphane Mallarmé.[34] Yet, in so far as a non-instrumental conception of language does not reduce the world to an object, it is clear that the effect of Benjamin's conception of language also relates to his criticism of Kant's concept of experience. Language provides the basis of Benjamin's 'higher experience'. Language is the intersubjective unity (understood as a plural rather than an undifferentiated phenomenon) that precedes the tragic antinomies of the division into subject and object. Here is a space of experience, like the space of indirect discourse, that is inhabited by more than one subject.

Benjamin's theory of the internally differentiated unity of Man and nature is grounded in a theory of translation.[35] Man is not given language, merely the capacity of language. Hence, in expressing his own essence as the one with the capacity for language, he must orientate himself outside himself towards the language that is immanent in nature as the residue of God's creative word. He does this by translating the mute language of things into his own language in the process of naming:

In name the word of God has not remained creative; it has become in one part receptive, even if receptive to language. Thus fertilized, it aims to give birth to the language of things themselves, from which in turn, soundlessly, in the mute magic of nature, the word of God shines forth.

(*GS II* 150; *SW I* 69)

Man's search for his own word is a search for the word of the other, albeit in a rather different sense from that of Bakhtin. Nevertheless, this form of translation is analogous to indirect discourse. It must be double-voiced, fulfilling the same role as indirect discourse in Bakhtin and Voloshinov: it must preserve the subject nature of the other, giving birth to the language of nature rather than reducing it to an object. Benjamin, like Bakhtin and Voloshinov, raises a secondary activity, translation, to the status of a primary activity.[36] Translation becomes the foundation for all language: 'Translation attains its full meaning in the realization that every evolved language [...] can be considered as a translation of all the others' (*GS II* 151; *SW I* 69–70). At first sight paradoxically, translation, which is 'much too far-reaching and powerful to be treated in any way as an afterthought, as has happened occasionally' (*GS II* 151; *SW I* 69), becomes the primary means whereby the subject finds his own words, and hence comes to a subjectivity that does not sacrifice the subjectivity of the other.

Benjamin develops his theory of translation in his 1924 essay, 'The Task of the Translator'. This essay opposes a number of commonly received ideas about translation. It opens by stating that no artwork is intended for the recipient and no translation is intended for a reader who does not understand the language of the original.[37] This contradicts Benjamin's position elsewhere, particularly in the 'The Work of Art', on the role of the recipient of the artwork. But Benjamin's intention here is different: the idea that translation does not serve a reader reinforces Benjamin's insistence on the non-instrumental nature of language: 'Any translation which intends to perform a transmitting function cannot transmit anything but information – here, something inessential. This is the hallmark of a bad translation' (*GS IV* 9; *SW I* 253). A translation is not a tool by means of which the reader gains mastery over the object that is contained in the original.

Benjamin counters two standard views of translation: the first, the theory of the translator's licence, holds that a translation should be as free as possible in order to preserve the meaning of the idea that the original expresses; the second, the theory of the translator's fidelity, holds that the translation should be as literal as possible in order to preserve the original itself. The problem of the first is that it assumes that the meaning of the original is not present in its language and hence reduces meaning to information. The problem of the second is that it treats the original text as an object that can be reproduced in another language by literal imitation of its structures, words and idioms. In both instances, translation attempts mere reproduction of a fixed and inert object, whether this be some absolute meaning conceived of as lying beyond the text, or the corporeal matter of the original language itself. Again, we see Benjamin's objection to processes of reproduction that result in, or aim at, the repetition of inert identity. Instead, translation is, as I have already argued, a form of indirect or double-voiced discourse:

> The task of the translator consists in finding the particular intention toward the target language which produces in that language the echo of the original. This is a feature of translation that basically differentiates it from the poet's work, because the intention of the latter is never toward the language as such, at its totality, but is aimed solely at specific linguistic contextual aspects. Unlike a work of literature, translation finds itself not in the center of the language forest but on the outside facing the wooded ridge; it calls into it without entering, aiming at that single spot where the echo is able to give, in its own language, the reverberation of the work in the alien one.
>
> (*GS IV* 16; *SW I* 258–59)

Translation aims to allow the original language to reverberate and echo in its own language. Unlike the language of original poetry which is focused on specific contexts, translation is focused on another's language. It is a word that looks at a referential context, but by means of a 'sideways glance' at the language of another, a search for the other's word. In notes for a broadcast that Benjamin planned in the mid-1930s, 'Translation – For and Against' (1935 or 1936), Benjamin makes this point again: 'Stresemann's dictum (intended as a *bon mot*) that "French is spoken in every language" is more serious than he thought, for the ultimate purpose of translation is to represent [*repräsentieren*] the foreign language in one's own' (*GS VI* 159–60; *SW III* 251).

In the image of the language forest above, it is possible to see affinities with Bakhtin's distinction between poetry and dialogized discourse in 'Discourse in the Novel':

> The trajectory of the poetic word toward its object and toward the unity of language is a path along which the poetic word is continually encountering someone else's word, and each takes new bearing from the other; the records of the passage remain in the slag of the creative process (as scaffolding is cleared away once construction is finished) so that the finished work may rise as unitary speech, one co-extensive with its object, as if it were speech about an 'Edenic' world.
>
> (*DI* 331)

The poet, according to Bakhtin, must studiously ignore and clear away the traces of the social complexity of intersecting voices in his language in order to find his own voice which is stripped of all intentions but his own. This is possible, in the terms of Benjamin's image, from within the depths of the language forest. In these depths, poetry, according to Bakhtin, cultivates wilful ignorance of a language other than its own:

> Poetry behaves as if it lived in the heartland of its language territory and does not approach too closely the borders of this language, where it would inevitably be brought into dialogic contact with hetero-glossia; poetry chooses not to look beyond the boundaries of its own language.
>
> *(DI* 399)

Poetic language attempts to ignore the existence of other languages. Ignoring the existence of other languages is not possible for the trans-lator who stands outside the language of the text that he translates. His 'outsidedness' – to use a term of Bakhtin – means that he must direct his own language at the language of the other, at the language forest itself.

Translation is, for Benjamin, an interaction between two languages which revives both the language into which the text is translated and the language from which it is translated:

> While a poet's words endure in his own language, even the greatest translation is destined to become part of the growth of its own language and eventually be absorbed by its renewal. Translation is so far removed from being the sterile equation of two dead languages that of all literary forms it is the one charged with the special mission of watching over the maturing process of the original language and the birth pangs of its own.
>
> *(GS IV* 13; *SW I* 256)

In translation, historical sterility, deadness, and even the monument-ality of 'endurance' are rejected in favour of a sense of language as historical, growing, alive and new. Translation is also (returning to the themes of the first chapter) a means of keeping tradition alive as the production of difference rather than the tradition of inert objects that remain the same. Like the critic whose task it is to release the meaning of the cultural object for the present that is concealed within it, the task of the translator is a task of liberation: 'It is the task of the translator to release in his own language that pure language which is exiled among foreign tongues, to liberate the language imprisoned in a work in his re-creation of the work' (*GS IV* 19; *SW I* 261).

We see here the extent to which Benjamin's notion of the effect and role of translation is not so far removed from Bakhtin's notion of the power and effect of heteroglossia. There are clearly substantial differences between Bakhtin's heteroglossia and Benjamin's translation. In his essay, Benjamin is describing what he thinks good translation is and how translations should be. In his work on heteroglossia, Bakhtin purports to describe an historical and social phenomenon that manifests itself in language. Nevertheless, both ideas express Bakhtin's and Benjamin's views on what language is, in its essence, as well as what it should be.[38] In heteroglossia:

> The new cultural and creative consciousness lives in an actively polyglot world. [...] Languages throw light on each other: one language can, after all, see itself only in the light of other languages. [...] All this set into motion a process of active, mutual cause-and-effect and inter-illumination. Words and language began to have a different feel to them; objectively they ceased to be what they had once been. Under these conditions of external and internal inter-illumination, each given language – even if its linguistic composition (phonetics, vocabulary, morphology, etc.) were to remain absolutely unchanged – is, as it were, reborn, becoming qualitatively a different thing for the consciousness that creates it.
>
> (*DI* 12)

Similarly, the interaction of language in translation is the guarantee of newness and creativity as opposed to the sterility of the language that stands alone and does not look out of the darkness of its solitary language forest.

Towards the end of the essay on translation, Benjamin produces a quotation from Pannwitz:

> Our translations, even the best ones, proceed from a wrong premise. They want to turn Hindi, Greek, English into German instead of turning German into Hindi, Greek, English. Our translators have a far greater reverence for the usage of their own language than for the spirit of the foreign works [...]. The basic error of the translator is that he preserves the state in which his own language happens to be instead of allowing his language to be powerfully affected by the foreign tongue. [...] He must expand and deepen his own language

by means of the foreign language. It is not generally realized to what extent language can be transformed, almost the way dialect differs from dialect.

(GS IV 20; SW I 261–62)

A good translation would be the double-voiced discourse implied in the transformation of German into Hindi. This is the interaction of the other in the word of the subject. It is also heteroglossia in action, one language being deeply affected by another. Pannwitz's reference to dialect at the end of the quotation also points to an awareness of the existence not only of 'national' languages but also of the internal stratification of languages into dialects, idiolects, *argots* and so forth, which also may be the subject of 'translation'. Additionally, however, Pannwitz notes that most translation is bad translation.

Whilst Benjamin's essay is, in one part, a blueprint for what the translator should do, in another significant part, it is a polemic against bad translation. The epitome of bad translation is the paradox that is aimed at by the majority of translators: that the free translation should read as if it were originally written in the language into which the text has been translated. This would be an appearance of originality and would hence represent a falsification. In such a translation, the language of the original has been obliterated. The word of the other has been reduced to silence. In 'Translation – For or Against', Benjamin describes a confrontation with such a translation:

As I was passing an open-air bookstall a few days ago, I came across a French translation of a German philosophical book. Looking through it, as one does with books on the *quais*, I looked for the passages which had often engrossed me. What a surprise – the passages were not there. You mean, you didn't find them? Oh yes, I found them alright. But when I looked them in the face, I had the awkward feeling that they no more recognized me than I did them.

(GS VI 157–58; SW III 249)

Here the language of the original no longer speaks through the translation. There is no friendly greeting. Translation has become, what Bakhtin terms in his early works, transcription, a process in which concrete subjectivity is erased through a process of abstraction, the form of translation of which Bakhtin speaks in his notes towards a reworking of the Dostoevsky book: 'I translate into the language of an abstract worldview that which was the object of concrete and living artistic visualization and which then became a principle of form. Such a translation is inadequate' (*DP* 288).

There is, however, more in Benjamin's radio dialogue. In the 'awkward feeling' the translation 'no more recognizes' Benjamin than he, it, one can discern an echo of Benjamin's statements on the nature of the aura in 'On Some Motifs in Baudelaire'. The first incarnation of this theory is to be found in Benjamin's essay 'A Short History of Photography' (1931). In early photography, Benjamin notes, the long exposure times meant that the person being photographed had to concentrate in a way which the more modern snapshot does not require: 'The procedure itself caused the subject to focus his life in the moment rather than hurrying on past it; during the considerable period of the exposure the subject as it were grew into the picture' (*GS II* 373; *SW II* 514). This concentration of the subject's gaze is one of the reasons for the aura which we experience when looking at early photographs. Speaking of an early portrait of Kafka, dressed up in a 'humiliatingly tight child's suit' in the bizarre artificial environment of the photographer's studio, Benjamin comments:

> This picture in its infinite sadness forms a pendant to the early photographs in which people did not look out at the world in so excluded and god-forsaken a manner as this boy. There was an aura about them, an atmospheric medium, that lent fullness and security to their gaze.
> (*GS II* 375–76; *SW II* 515)

Aura here is the ability of the subject's gaze to survive the process of objectification that is inherent in having one's photograph taken. Auratic experience is a form of, or intimation of, intersubjectivity.[39] As Habermas comments: 'the auratic appearance can occur only in the intersubjective relationship of the I with its counterpart, the alter ego'.[40] Put simply: auratic experience is a form of dialogue. What we see in the image of the translation encountered on the *quai* is a translation in which the subjectivity of the original has been erased and from which the original subject can no longer look out. A further definition of the aura, this time from 'On Some Motifs in Baudelaire', serves to put Benjamin's thinking into perspective:

> Experience of the aura thus arises from the fact that a response characteristic of human relationships is transposed to the relationship between humans and inanimate or natural objects. The person we

look at, or who feels he is being looked at, looks at us in turn. To experience the aura of an object we look at means to invest it with the ability to look back at us.

(GS I 646–47; SW IV 338)

If the aura is experiencing the object as subject, in bad translation the subject of the original text is experienced as an object that cannot look back at the reader of the translation and cannot recognize him or her.

Bad translation is the practice of the majority of translators.[41] Benjamin comments in the notes for the radio broadcast: 'The fact that a book is translated already created a certain misunderstanding of it. Jean Christophe: what is selected is usually what could also be written in the translator's own language' (*GS VI* 159; *SW III* 250–51).[42] Translation usually focuses only on those texts which do not require the complex interaction of languages. Benjamin's theory of good and bad translation implies that there are two different ways of translating, two different forms of linguistic practice that are opposed to each other, but both equally possible. Caygill remarks of Benjamin:

> Human language is equivocal: it can either reduce all other linguistic surfaces to its own level, confining them within its limits at the price of exclusion and distortion, or it can transform the character and limits of its own surface in the translation of other languages.[43]

These two tendencies can be rephrased, in the terms of Bakhtin's Dostoevsky book, as the tendencies towards monologization and dialogization:

> Whatever discourse types are introduced by the author-monologist, whatever their compositional distribution, the author's intentions and evaluations must dominate all the others and must form a compact and unambiguous whole. Any intensification of others' intentions in a certain discourse is only a game, which the author permits so that his own direct or refracted word might ring out all the more energetically. [...] The artistic task Dostoevsky takes on is completely different. He does not fear the most extreme activization of vari-directional accents in double-voiced discourse; on the contrary, such activization is precisely what he needs to achieve his purpose.

(DP 203–04)

Where monologic language excludes, distorts and confines the other within its own limits, dialogic language is itself transformed by the language of the other. Monologue is German making Hindi German. Dialogue is German being powerfully affected by Hindi. There is a great difference between Bakhtin and Benjamin, however: Benjamin expresses his idea of translation with the powerful but vague image of the good translation that is German being affected by Hindi. Bakhtin, in the chapter on 'Discourse in Dostoevsky', by contrast, provides sophisticated linguistic analysis of the different ways in which dialogic discourse can function in the novel.[44]

Quotation and montage

Benjamin's use of quotation is at the core of all his writing. It finds its fullest expression in *The Arcades Project*, much of which is no more than lists of quotations. Here, Benjamin indicates that quotation is a form of montage: 'This work has to develop the highest degree of citing without quotation marks. Its theory is intimately related to that of montage' (*GS* V 572; *AP* 458). In the same section, he elaborates:

> Method of this project: literary montage. I needn't *say* anything. Merely show. I shall purloin no valuables, appropriate no ingenious formulations. But the rags, the refuse – these I will not inventory but allow, in the only way possible, to come into their own: by making use of them.
>
> (*GS* V 574; *AP* 460)

The montage of quotations is a means of seeking the other's word: Benjamin need not speak but is able to allow the other's voice to be heard.

In the case of Bakhtin, quotation often occurs without acknowledgement; in his work more generally, quotation frequently takes the form of the use of many different variations and reformulations of similar arguments, a phenomenon which constitutes a form of hidden self-quotation, a technique also employed by Benjamin.[45] His work, then, is also akin to a montage of quotations.[46] He remarks in his notes from 1970–71:

> The unity of the becoming (developing) idea. There is also a certain internal unfinishedness in many of my thoughts. But I do not wish to make a vice into a virtue: in my works there is good deal of external

unfinishedness, an unfinishedness not of thought itself, but of its expression and exposition. Sometimes it is difficult to separate one kind of unfinishedness from the other [...]. My love for variations and for a multiplicity of terms for a single phenomenon. A multiplicity of perspectives. A bringing close of the distant without an indication of mediating links.

(*SG* 155)

Bakhtin's 'bringing close of the distant without an indication of mediating links' is analogous to Benjamin's 'citing without quotation marks'.[47] Variations are, as already argued, forms of quotation; multiple perspectives and unfinishedness are all hallmarks of montage. (One need only think of montage in cinema to see the link with Bakhtin's 'multiple perspectives'.) The same holds for 'unfinishedness': the piece of montage is cut (once again, one can hear the association with cinema) from a larger whole to which it still points; it is, then, necessarily unfinished, just as a quotation is a fragment of a larger context and is hence also, in this sense, unfinished. Finally, Bakhtin's 'bringing close' is also a function of montage that takes material from different and distant contexts and brings them together on one plane. One thinks of the montage of Dada or Surrealist collage which takes cuttings and scraps from different sources and juxtaposes or overlays them in proximity on the canvas.[48]

Bakhtin's thought demonstrates a concern with forms of language that are comparable to the montage of quotations. In his theory of the polyphonic novel, Bakhtin champions the fragmentation of perspective and voice which the novel effects on what he terms 'unitary languages'. In the face of the unities which come into being through the centripetal forces of monologic discourse, Bakhtin is concerned with the plurality of polyphony: 'alongside verbal-ideological centralization and unification, the uninterrupted processes of decentralization and disunification go forward' (*DI* 272). The plurality of the novel – 'the dispersion into the rivulets and droplets of social heteroglossia' (*DI* 263) – is a plurality of fragments. The world of the polyphonic novel of Dostoevsky, then, is a montage of perspectives and voices, quoted directly and indirectly. Nevertheless, just as Benjamin insists that the montage of quotations in the *Arcades Project* retains a relation to the totality of nineteenth-century Paris, so Bakhtin insists that the fragmented voices of polyphony retain a complex relation to 'social totality'.

I have argued in Chapter 1 that montage and dialogized discourse are both ways of opening up the closedness of authoritarianism, whether this be the authority of the aura and tradition or the authority of the monologic utterance. Both forms, then, have an ideological import. Both thinkers, however, insist on the historical specificity of their particular forms. These are not forms of which they merely approve because of their innovative or ideological effects; both grow necessarily out of their social and historical circumstances. Buck-Morss points out the extent to which montage in the *Arcades Project* was more than just a formal principle:

> Crucial is Benjamin's understanding of 'montage' as a form which, if already visible in the early arcades, in the kaleidoscopic, fortuitous juxtaposition of shop sign and window displays, was raised by technology during the course of the century to the level of a conscious principle of the nineteenth century.[49]

Montage is both the form of construction of nineteenth-century Paris and the only way of representing it without distorting it. Something similar holds for Bakhtin's treatment of Dostoevsky in a passage that I have quoted above:

> By relativizing all that was eternally stable, set and ready made, carnivalization with its pathos of change and renewal permitted Dostoevsky to penetrate into the deepest layers of man and human relationships. It proved remarkably productive as a means for capturing in art the developing relationships under capitalism, at a time when previous forms of life, moral principles and beliefs were being turned into 'rotten cords' and the previously concealed and unfinalized nature of man and human *thought* was being nakedly exposed. [...] Capitalism, similar to that 'pander' of Socrates on the market square in Athens, brings together people and ideas.
>
> (*DP* 166–67)

In this passage, Bakhtin asserts both the emergence of dialogue from the spirit of capitalism and its status as the only faithful means of its representation.[50]

There are, however, marked central differences between Bakhtin and Benjamin. Benjamin's employment of montage is linked to a much more explicitly political task than Bakhtin's theory of polyphony. Jennings comments: 'Benjamin's practice [of montage] stems from the Dadaist conviction that it is only that which lies unused or already discarded that is free of the ideological contamination of the ruling formation.'[51]

Thus it is not merely the form of montage that is political but also its content. Benjamin's montage, as practised in *One-Way Street* and the *Arcades Project*, elevates to the level of attention all that is unsuccessful, marginal, misused, obsolescent, forgotten or overlooked.[52] Bakhtin does not explicitly address this aspect of polyphony in his theory of the novel. Such an attitude, it might be argued, is more strongly present less in Bakhtin himself than in his model Dostoevsky, whose fiction gives voice to the unsuccessful, the obsolescent, the misused and the overlooked.

Some of the general connections between Benjamin's notions of quotation and montage and Bakhtin's theory of the polyphonic novel should now be clear. To examine this in more detail, I turn to a review of Alfred Döblin's novel of 1930, *Berlin Alexanderplatz*, which Benjamin published under the title 'The Crisis of the Novel'. This review also reveals the extent to which Benjamin comes close to the formulation of a theory of the polyphonic novel. Benjamin writes:

> The stylistic principle governing this book is that of montage. Petty-bourgeois printed matter, scandal-mongering, stories of accidents, the sensational incidents of 1928, folk songs and advertisements rain down in this text. The montage explodes the framework of the novel, bursts its limits both stylistically and structurally, and clears the way for new epic possibilities.
>
> (*GS III* 232; *SW II* 301)

The technique of montage, as, for example, pioneered in Dadaism, is the taking of fragments of the real world and incorporating them in the work of art. These are the ticket-stubs and scraps of newspaper stuck onto Dadaist paintings that Benjamin refers to in 'The Work of Art'. In literary form, montage consists of the direct quotation of fragments of reality such as the songs and advertisements referred to in Benjamin's review. Just as Benjamin argues in 'The Work of Art' that montage destroys the artwork's aura of authenticity and originality, so here he argues that the montage of quotations 'explodes the framework of the novel' that consists of authorial authority.

Montage of quotation subverts the authority of the author and pushes him to the edge of his own work:

> The texture of [Döblin's] montage is so dense that we have difficulty hearing the author's voice. He has reserved for himself the street-ballad-like epigraphs to each character; otherwise, he is in no great hurry

to make his voice heard. (Even though he is determined to have his say in the end.) It is astounding how long he trails behind his characters before risking any challenge to them.

(*GS III* 233; *SW II* 301)

The characters gain independence from the authorial context to the extent that the author 'trails behind them' not daring to challenge them. This is an explosion of the framework of the novel and a clearing of the way for new narrative possibilities that is analogous to the Copernican revolution that Bakhtin claims Dostoevsky effects in the creation of the polyphonic novel: as the world takes on a whole 'new look', 'not only the reality of the hero himself, but even the external world and the everyday life surrounding him are drawn into the process of self-awareness, are transferred from the author's to the hero's field of vision' (*DP* 49). According to Bakhtin, Dostoevsky renounces his position of authority above his characters and descends to a plane on which he is, in certain respects, their equal. In Benjamin's analysis of Döblin, the author is also reduced to a peripheral figure who 'trails behind his characters'.

Benjamin's characterization of Döblin's novel as montage derives from a saying of Döblin himself that Brecht was fond of quoting. Brecht's formulation of this bears examination:

[Actually, there is a] dramatic element in epic works, and an epic element in the dramatic. The bourgeois novel in the [nineteenth] century developed much that was dramatic, by which one means the strong centralization of the story, a momentum that drew the separate parts into a common relationship. [...] The epic writer Döblin came up with an excellent characterization when he said that with an epic, as opposed to a dramatic, work you can as it were take a pair of scissors and cut it into individual pieces which remain fully capable of life.[53]

Brecht recognizes the aspect of the dramatic, traditional novel that centralizes and draws separate parts into a common relationship. This common relationship is analogous to what Bakhtin describes as the single consciousness of the monologic author. The epic writer, however, according to Brecht, produces a form of montage that consists of parts that can be cut up. This sort of cutting-up into fragments is one in which, perhaps paradoxically, the individual pieces 'remain fully capable of life'. Hence, just as Döblin's characters are able to walk in front of their author, so, in Brecht's and Benjamin's theory, montage does not kill the 'life' in the material. It is the closedness of authoritarian forms that does that.[54] Similarly, Bakhtin writes of the polyphonic novel: 'In Dostoevsky's larger design, the character is a carrier of a fully valid word, and not the mute, voiceless object of the author's discourse' (*DP* 63). The monologic approach that stems from a sense of a false wholeness kills life, reducing it to a series of mute objects. It is precisely because Bakhtin insists that the world be conceived of as a unity of living subjects who are carriers of meaning that it must be represented in the form of a montage of multiple perspectives and voices.

Benjamin goes on to characterize Döblin's mode of narration:

> He approaches things in a relaxed way as befits an epic writer. Whatever happens – even when it happens suddenly – seems to have been prepared for well in advance. In this attitude, he has been inspired by the spirit of Berlin dialect – a dialect that moves at a relaxed pace. For the Berliner speaks as a connoisseur, in love with the way things are said. [...] The book is a monument to the Berlin dialect because the narrator makes no attempt to enlist our sympathies for the city based on any regional loyalty. He speaks from within Berlin. It is his megaphone. His dialect is one of the forces that turn against the reserved nature of the old novel.
>
> (*GS III* 233; *SW II* 301)

We may first note the theme of habit that re-emerges in the notion of Döblin's relaxed attitude. This is the relaxation that comes from a sense of familiarity. More important in this context, however, is Benjamin's discussion of the role of dialect. When Benjamin says that Döblin 'speaks from within Berlin', he means that Berlin speaks from within Döblin. Döblin's text is interpenetrated with different forms of language: thieves' cant, the biblical, prostitutes' slang, the Yiddish-influenced German of newly arrived *Ostjuden*, and, above all, the heterogeneous, linguistic monster that is *berlinerisch*. This is akin to Bakhtin's description of heteroglossia in 'Discourse in the Novel':

> Languages do not exclude each other, but rather intersect with each other in many different ways: the Ukrainian language, the language of the epic poem, or early Symbolism, of the student, of a particular generation of children....[...] as such these languages live a real life, they struggle and evolve in an environment of social heteroglossia.
>
> (*DI* 292–93)

Specifically, Döblin achieves this not merely by dialogue and by the montage of direct quotation but also by indirect quotation, that is, a variety of different forms of double-voiced discourse. This can be seen in the following passage:

> Dann wird mit einemmal die Unterhaltung am Nebentisch laut, der eine Neue führt das grosse Wort. Der will singen, dem ist es hier zu ruhig[...] Franz kaut denkt: die meinen mir. [...] Daß der alter Georg Dreske sich mit solchem Grünzeug zusammensetzt und nicht mal zu ihm rüberkommt, hätt er auch nicht für möglich gehalten. Son oller Stiebel, ist verheiratet, n ehrlicher Stiebel, und sitzt bei det junge Gemüse und hört sich die ihr Geschnatter an.[55]

The standard German of the first clause represents authorial direct discourse which is lightly inflected by the discourse of Franz in the second half's colloquialisms ('der eine Neue', 'das grosse Wort'). The next sentence is double-voiced, free indirect discourse of Franz's thoughts which gradually becomes more and more inflected by Franz's speech patterns (although these are already present in the dialect use of the dative for the accusative in the sentence, 'die meinen mir'). Finally, authorial discourse is almost forced out entirely in the strong dialect forms ('oller', 'det') and slang expressions ('det junge Gemüse', 'Stiebel') of the last sentence which is heavily stylized discourse.

It is in the range of forms of double-voiced discourse that Döblin speaks from within Berlin and Berlin speaks from within him. Benjamin neither performs such analysis of Döblin's prose nor does he possess the technical vocabulary to do so. Nevertheless, Döblin's narrator finds the other's word and achieves the sphere of neutrality vis-à-vis subject and object that has been the goal of Benjamin's philosophy since his early writings. Here, in his analysis of Döblin, Benjamin seems to have intuited that the indirect discourse of the polyphonic novel transcends the antinomies of subject and object.[56]

Silence

In May 1916, Martin Buber wrote to the young Benjamin asking him to contribute an article to the first issue of a new journal, *Der Jude*. In effect, Buber was asking Benjamin to take a political position within the current debates on Zionism and the position of the Jews in Germany. Benjamin refused, arguing that to assume that writing is 'capable of influencing the ethical world and human actions' would be to present 'language and writing as powerless, and diminished to the role of a pure medium' (*Briefe* 125–26). Benjamin goes on to oppose this debased form of instrumentalized language to what he calls the 'essential being' of language and writing:

> I can understand writing in general, whether poetic, prophetic, or objective in its effect, only magically, that is, only immediately. Every sound and healthy effect of language – indeed every effect that does not represent a self-demolition of language, touches upon mystery (of the word, of language). Whatever the form in which language is capable of proving itself effective, this cannot be through communication of its contents, but rather through the purest revelation of its own worth, and its own essence. [...] My conception of straightforward and at the same time highly political style and writing is to indicate that which fails words; only there, only where the sphere of wordlessness reveals itself in its pure power can the magic spark between word and deed arise.
>
> (*Briefe* 126)

If language is to go beyond its 'self-demolition', it must not limit itself to an auxiliary role as the instrument of communication. Effective language must reveal that aspect of itself that is incommunicable and express the unsayable (*Das Unsagbare*) which cannot be assimilated to the mere communication of content. Here, language finds the expression of its 'essential being'. Many of the concerns of this chapter are recognizable here. The rejection of an instrumental conception of language may be political in so far as it resists the reduction of the world to manipulating subjects and manipulated objects. Nevertheless, its claim of absolute political significance does not prevent it from falling into the apolitical abyss of silence.

Benjamin abandons this theory of silence in favour of a study of literary and artistic forms in which language is not reduced to mere instrumentality. Nevertheless, the search for the other's word through silence is something that reappears sporadically. It is there in the statement on montage that I have given above, where Benjamin claims that he need not speak but merely allow the rags and refuse of montaged quotations to come into their own. It is there in Benjamin's approving comment on Kraus: 'Kraus has written articles in which not a single word is his own' (*GS II* 1093). The sacrifice of one's own voice may sometimes be necessary if one is to find the voice of the other.

Bakhtin's theory of silence is to be found in his essays on the novel. Over the course of Bakhtin's work it is possible to observe a gradual shift in his formulation of the ideal position of the author in relation to his work. In the early work, the author is a benign but over-arching, all-encompassing figure whose creative word shapes his hero. In Bakhtin's writing on Dostoevsky this position has changed; here, the author has relinquished the position of absolute authority and has descended to the level of his characters, and the author's word is to be no more authoritative than those of his characters. By the time of the essays on the novel, this position has changed yet again. Here, 'it is as if the author has no language of his own':

> The author is not to be found in the language of the narrator, not in the normal literary language to which the story opposes itself [. . .] but rather the author utilizes now one language, now another, in order to avoid giving himself up wholly to either of them.
>
> (*DI* 311)

The author's unwillingness to speak in his own voice is another way of allowing the other to come to voice. His silence is an act of self-renunciation and a quest for the other's word.[57]

The history of language: Fall, monologism and mutism

Bakhtin and Benjamin see language as a practice that is rooted in history and the nature of which changes historically. Furthermore, we have seen that they both conceive of language as the site of opposing tendencies and phenomena (instrumental and non-instrumental language; bad and good translation; the authoritative and the internally persuasive word; monologue and dialogue) in which one side of the opposition is generally preferred. These tendencies and the relationships between them also develop historically.

In *Toward a Philosophy of the Act*, Bakhtin writes: 'Historically language grew up in the service of participative thinking and performed acts, and it begins to serve abstract thinking only in the present day of its history' (*TPA* 31). In this early text, Bakhtin is perhaps thinking ahead of himself to the theory of language discussed above, according to which language is the site of an intersubjective unity that precedes the antinomies of subject and object. Language, Bakhtin argues, emerges from responsible participation but, in the face of modern forces of theoreticism, becomes degraded and instrumentalized. In his work taken as a whole, however, Bakhtin has a contradictory account of the historical fate of language: on the one hand, modern theoreticism and monologism, sometimes explicitly associated with the Enlightenment and the modern era, threaten to obliterate the participative nature of language as dialogue. On the other hand, dialogue itself seems to grow out of the very social and historical forces of modernization. A contradiction is to be found between the narrative of the liberation of the dialogized word from authoritarian contexts in Bakhtin's theory of the development of the novel, and the narrative of the decline of the participative word and the threat of monologization.[58]

Benjamin's work also contains a history of the fate of language. To discuss this, I return to 'On Language as Such and on the Language of Man', whose theological narrative of the Fall nevertheless contains the essence of Benjamin's ideas about the historical existence of language in the secular world. The Fall is brought about by Adam and Eve's seduction by the serpent into eating of the fruit of the tree of knowledge of good and evil. Benjamin points out that since God created the world and saw that it was good, the knowledge of good and evil is worthless and vain (*nichtig*). Such knowledge's vanity has two sources: first, knowledge of good and evil stands beyond the created world, which is of itself good, and is hence meaningless (Benjamin uses Kierkegaard's term, prattle [*Geschwätz*]); second, in attempting to replace God's judgement of the world as good, it becomes a parody of God's creative word.

By establishing himself as subjective judge, Man brings evil into the world. Subjectivity, then, is the origin of evil and the source of the meaninglessness of 'prattle'. As the knower of good and evil, Man abandons the language of name in which he knew an intersubjective unity with God and nature and enters the sphere of judgement: 'this judging word expels human beings from paradise; [...] In the Fall, since the eternal purity of names was violated, the sterner purity of the judging word arose' (*GS II* 153; *SW I* 71). Here is Hölderlin's *Ur-theilung*. In setting himself up as autonomous judge of the external world, Man is separated from it and is condemned, by his own actions, to the mediated existence of a subject in an alien world of objects.[59] This is how Benjamin understands the expulsion from Paradise. Benjamin draws further consequences from the introduction of the prattle of judgement. First, 'man makes language a means (that is knowledge inappropriate to him), and therefore also, in one part, a *mere* sign' (*GS II* 153; *SW I* 71).[60] Language comes to be dominated by its instrumentality, which is linked to its acquiring an arbitrary nature. Second, the Fall is the origin of abstraction in so far as its knowledge is unnameable, whereas name is rooted in the concrete.[61] Benjamin's narrative of the Fall brings us, once again, to Bakhtin. As Coates has pointed out, there is a theme of the Fall that runs through Bakhtin's work. In her reading of 'Author and Hero', the Fall is the result of Man's attempt to claim self-sufficiency from God.[62] This is analogous to Benjamin's understanding of the Fall as the imposition of human terms of judgement. In both cases, Man attempts to speak his own definitive word without listening to the voice of God. The fallen word, for both Bakhtin and Benjamin, is the self-sufficient word that is deaf to the word of the other.

The theme of judgement as a consequence of the Fall forms a further bridge between Benjamin and Bakhtin. Brandist has argued forcefully for the influence of the Marburg School's theory of law and the juridical person on Bakhtin.[63] Whilst it is difficult to accept many of his arguments for the extent of this influence, his observation that Bakhtin's thinking often carries a framework of judgement seems correct.[64] We might explain this by noting that in Dostoevsky's novels, characters are always on trial. Bakhtin does not share with Benjamin an aversion to the notion of judgement on the philosophical grounds that I have discussed above; indeed, right from his early work, he insists that every act has an evaluative, that is to say, a judging function. Nevertheless, Bakhtin is always keen to stress that the act of judgement must be just. If, in the dialogic utterance, the position of the other being judged is taken into account (his specific circumstances, his possible excuses), the monologic utterance is an unjust judgement that imposes the judgement without regard for the position of the judged and judges an inert object. The former may be approximated to the act of Benjamin's namer who listens to the language of God in nature and knows it. The latter may be approximated to the arbitrary judgement that fallen Man imposes on the object world.

Benjamin contends that the original language is not utterly destroyed. Language itself has been fractured in the same way that Man's relationship with God and nature has been fractured. In the damaged and distorted state of fallen language, traces of the language of names survive. Benjamin notes such a trace in the act of naming children. In a fallen world, instrumental and non-instrumental aspects, signs and names, concrete and abstract, judgement and knowledge coexist. Benjamin's essay here deals with the mythical time of Genesis. His account of the fate of language, however, holds relevance for a modernity that is increasingly characterized by abstraction and instrumentality. It is here that the realm of the aesthetic is of importance – for, Benjamin implies, the fracturing of language can be seen in the division of linguistic practice into the mimetic language of art and the discursive language of communication.[65] Benjamin writes: 'The language of poetry is partly, if not solely, founded on the language of names' (*GS II* 156; *SW I* 73). The language of poetry strives, despite the fallen state of language, to draw closer to the original language. In this way, poetry seeks to be a profane echo of the primordial language of names, and ultimately it seeks to restore by human means the unity of Man, God and nature destroyed by the Fall. This view of the language of poetry is not a mere repetition of the view of Hölderlin, for Benjamin concedes that 'it is certain that the language of art can be understood only in the deepest relationship to the doctrine of signs' (*GS II* 156; *SW I* 73). Poetry, then, contains both name and sign. More generally, language, as what Benjamin calls elsewhere an 'archive of non-sensuous similarities', even in its corrupt form, bears the traces of the relation of name.[66]

Before I move on to a discussion of the special language of art in the next chapter, I wish to consider a final effect of the Fall of language, namely the muteness and melancholy of nature:

> After the Fall, however, when God's word curses the ground, the appearance of nature is changed. Now begins its other muteness, which we mean by the deep sadness of nature. It is a metaphysical truth that all nature would begin to lament if it were endowed with language. [...] This proposition has a double meaning. It means, first: she would lament language itself. Speechlessness: that is the great sorrow of nature (and for the sake of her redemption the life and language of man – not only, as is supposed, of the poet – are in nature). This proposition means secondly: she would lament. Lament, however, is the most undifferentiated, impotent expression of language; it contains scarcely more than the sensuous breath; and even where there is only a rustling of plants, in it there is always a lament.
>
> (*GS II* 155; *SW I* 72–73)

Once again, the problem arises of how this powerful and eloquent image is to be read outside its theological framework. At the simplest level, this passage is driven by a pathetic fallacy: in his separation from nature, Man laments the essential alienness to him of the natural world. This is the melancholy of alienation.

Another way of looking at this is provided by Bernstein in the context of a discussion of German Romantic aesthetics. Bernstein describes the changed relations between Man and the natural world that arise with Descartes's establishment of the *cogito* as the fundamental principle of knowledge, relations that are underscored by Kant's Critiques. With the establishment of the enquiring and analytical *cogito*, nature loses its self-evidence. Sensuous nature is replaced by the immaterial and mechanical forms of physics. Bernstein gives as a paradigmatic example of this Descartes's image of the dissolution of the sensuously resplendent piece of wax into its physical properties (malleability, extension) that are comprehensible only to abstract thought.[67] He continues:

> This dematerialization denies that there might be a unique, irreducible language of nature, and this is equivalent to the delegitimation of the authority of nature in favour of the authority of scientific reason. Thus the disenchantment of nature, which included the human body, its pains and pleasures, leaves it dispossessed of voice or meaning, since all meaning is given to nature by (mathematical) reason. To say that reason delegitimates the authority of nature means at least that the promptings of the body come to lack *normative* authority, that is they no longer operate as reasons, and so cannot be thought of as raising claims and demands that should (or should not) be heeded. Such items become causal facts no different in kind than those of dead nature.[68]

This is a useful approach. First, it makes clear the extent to which thinking about nature, particularly in the German Romantic tradition, is necessarily a meditation on human beings understood as part of nature, a meditation on human nature (*menschliche Natur*). The alienation from nature that the Romantics and Benjamin often describe in terms that today sound mystical might be as much about the relationship of the subject with the body as they are about mountains and trees. Second, this passage brings us back to the concerns of Benjamin's 'On the Programme of the Coming Philosophy'. The rationalist and mathematical standards of the Enlightenment do, indeed, deny normative authority to the promptings of the body. They impoverish a conception of experience – not only for 'primitive people' who identify with sacred animals or the mentally ill who feel that the objects of their perception are parts of their body, but also for the average person who no longer thinks that it is legitimate to feel things in her or his 'bones' or who has to ascribe the melancholy of November to 'Seasonally Affected Disorder'. Third, Bernstein's use of the terms 'promptings', 'reasons', 'demands' leads us to understand how this is a problem of language: modern rationalism no longer allows nature to speak to us.

The melancholy of nature is the result of the imposition of Man's arbitrary subjectivity on a world that is thereby reduced to an object, and hence is denied a voice. Bakhtin's thought contains a similar insight on the muteness that the monologic utterance imposes on its object. In the totally instrumental and monologic form of the language of the natural sciences, the world is mastered and deprived of voice:

> The entire methodological apparatus of the mathematical and natural sciences is directed toward mastery over *mute objects, brute things*, that do not reveal themselves in words, that do not comment on themselves. Acquiring knowledge here is not connected with receiving and interpreting words or signs from the object itself under consideration.
>
> (*DI* 351)

So too, in the monologic novel, characters are denied a voice, they are objectified, and fall silent. As I noted in the Introduction, Bakhtin, however, often seems to be lacking the dimension of melancholy that Benjamin is so painfully aware of.

The image of mournful nature that Benjamin describes at the end of 'On Language as Such and on the Language as Man' is a landscape emptied of people and frozen in melancholy. This image of the muteness of alienation makes clear the absolute need for the construction of a new relationship towards the object world and the absolute need for the invigoration of intersubjectivity. If Bakhtin's life-affirming world of the novel is a modern, crowded world of dynamic possibilities, Benjamin's image of a depopulated, mute nature is also a modern landscape. Bakhtin and Benjamin present conflicting yet coexistent aspects of modernity: landscapes of desolation as well as of possibility.

4
Totalities

Bakhtin's and Benjamin's modernity is a world of human experience that is marked by fragmentation and division. In the face of this situation, Bakhtin and Benjamin are concerned with the overcoming of these divisions in order to bring about a restoration of a wholeness of experience.[1] Despite the emphasis on the provisional, unfinished and contested nature of dialogue in his writings, Bakhtin's work marks out a necessary space for a finalizing and totalizing perspective. This is what he describes in a text of 1959–60 as the perspective of the third-person superaddressee. Dialogue consists of the first-person subject of utterance and the second person to whom that utterance is addressed:

> In addition to this addressee (the second party), the author of the utterance, with a greater or lesser awareness, presupposes a higher *superaddressee* (third) whose absolutely just responsive understanding is assumed, either in some metaphysical distance or in distant historical time (the loophole addressee). In various ages and with various understandings of the world, this superaddressee and his ideally true responsive understanding assume various ideological expressions (God, absolute truth, the court of dispassionate human conscience, the people, the court of history, science and so forth).
>
> (SG 126)

The superaddressee, the judge in a final court of appeal, is the embodiment of the hope for just resolution that underlies all human utterances. The orientation towards the superaddressee is an orientation towards a totality by the standards of which the partial and unfinished fragments of dialogue are always implicitly judged. Benjamin's conception of fragmentation contains a similar relation to the notion of totality. It may be axiomatic that, for Benjamin, as one critic puts it, the world is 'splintered into fragments, is legible only in fragments, and is representable solely through fragments'.[2] Nevertheless, as a whole, his work is structured by a longing for wholeness in the face of historical forces of fragmentation. This longing is best captured in the image of the angel in Benjamin's 'On the Concept of History':

> His face is turned toward the past. Where a chain of events appears before *us*, *he* sees one single catastrophe, which keeps piling wreckage upon wreckage and hurls it at his feet. The angel would like to stay, awaken the dead, and make whole what is smashed. But a storm is blowing from Paradise and has got caught in his wings; it is so strong that the angel can no longer close them. This storm drives him irresistibly into the future, to which his back is turned, while the pile of debris before him grows toward the sky. What we call progress is *this* storm.
>
> (*GS I* 697–98; *SW IV* 392)

On the one hand, Benjamin's image presents history as an experience of catastrophic fragmentation that can only truthfully be represented by fragments (rather than by the falsely complete narrative of human progress). On the other hand, this image resounds to the painful yearning of the angel, in the face of the storm, to stay and make whole what is broken.

One sphere in which an intimation of totality may be discovered is the sphere of art. Art, for Bakhtin and Benjamin, may be, at its best, a space for benign form-giving, in which the unruly activity of life is gathered up without sacrificing the integrity and specificity of its contents. Artistic form strives to be form that does not violate life, that does not attempt to achieve mastery over life as an object but rather preserves and promotes the complexity of life as the experience of interconnected subjectivity. For both thinkers, artistic form goes some way to being the totalizing solution to the problems that emanate from the fractured nature of existence.[3]

The negative totalities of art

There are three main reasons for art's special status in Bakhtin's and Benjamin's thought. First, returning to the topic of the first chapter: artistic forms may, on the one hand, provide benign models of habitualization and tradition, and on the other hand, provide the tools for challenging authoritarian forms of habit and tradition. Second, returning to the conclusion of the second chapter: art provides a model of the loving attention and remembrance that may be a possible way out of the tragedy of culture. By virtue of its orientation towards the specific, art expresses and preserves plural participative activity in the face of abstraction and indifference. This notion is at the heart of Bakhtin's theory of polyphonic prose that 'recreates not a world of objects, but precisely these other consciousnesses with their worlds' (DP 68). A similar notion forms the core of Benjamin's analysis of the synthetic production of new forms of *Erfahrung* out of fragments of *Erlebnis* in writers such as Proust and Baudelaire. Bakhtin's and Benjamin's thinking centres on the ways in which art might preserve and promote 'responsible activity' and 'higher forms of experience' in a situation where these phenomena are under permanent threat. Third, returning to the topic of the previous chapter: we have seen that Bakhtin and Benjamin share a view of language as the original and/or potential, if endangered, site of unity where the poles of the given and the posited, the general and the particular, object and subject, are held together. Bakhtin's and Benjamin's focus on the forms of art, and on verbal art in particular, stems from an understanding that art is the testing ground on which language strives to capture and recapture its own essence as the site of this unity. In artistic forms, such as dialogic prose for Bakhtin and montage for Benjamin, language claims and reclaims its power.

The importance that the two thinkers accord to the aesthetic is neither surprising nor original. Since Kant's *Critique of Judgement* and the revisions of Kant in the aesthetics of the Romantic movement, the German philosophical tradition had seen aesthetic experience as the realm in which the antinomies of subject and object, general and particular, might be overcome. In *Toward a Philosophy of the Act*, Bakhtin makes such special claims for aesthetic activity:

> The world of aesthetic seeing – the world of art. In its concreteness and its permeatedness with an emotional-volitional tone, this world is closer than any of the abstract cultural worlds (taken in isolation) to the unitary and unique world of the performed act. An analysis of this world should help us to come closer to an understanding of the architectonic structure of the actual world-as-event.
>
> (*TPA* 61)

This position seems to be a mere reformulation of a standard position of German Idealist aesthetics.[4] As in Kant, aesthetic activity provides a ground on which we may develop responsible and participatory activity that, in turn, may serve indirectly to heal the rifts encountered in the contemporary non-aesthetic sphere. Similarly, Benjamin's career-long search for the higher experience of the 'Programme on the Coming Philosophy' in literary and artistic forms may seem to do little more than refine and give new emphasis to familiar themes in the main strand in German aesthetics from Kant onwards. Thus, Benjamin's statement, in 'On Language as Such and on the Language of Man', that the language of poetry is partly founded on name seems to imply that the original relationship of wholeness between God, man and nature may survive in the aesthetic realm, and hence that this realm may provide a resource for the reinstitution of totality. In this way, Benjamin is close to thinkers such as Schiller for whom art is a means 'to restore by means of a higher Art the totality of our nature which the arts themselves have destroyed'.[5] Both thinkers, then, stand in the tradition that thinks of art as a sphere for education understood as *Bildung*: the cultivation of the aesthetic will help to educate ourselves into a more harmonious relationship with ourselves and our world.[6]

Nevertheless, whilst there is no doubt that Bakhtin and Benjamin work within this tradition, their conclusions on the role of aesthetic experience and on those artistic forms that best promote it go beyond and significantly alter that same tradition. Most notably, their contribution to this tradition lies in their parallel recognition that art, in the cause of permanent and transcendent wholeness and completion, must adopt a provisional aesthetics of fragmentation and openness –[7] for both thinkers, in the end, celebrate not artistic forms that produce images of totality, forms such as the traditional organic artwork whose parts combine into a harmonious whole, but rather forms such as the polyphonic novel and montage which present the world in terms of open fragmentation.[8] Totality, for Bakhtin and Benjamin, is best represented indirectly by means of and against the backdrop of its negation.

Allegory and dialogue

Benjamin's *Habilitationsschrift*, written in 1924–25, *On the Origin of the German Play of Lamentation*[9] is not just a contribution to the literary history of the German Baroque. Benjamin's *Trauerspiel* book keeps an eye on its own present and is, in significant measure, a justification of the aesthetics of the Avant-garde.[10] In the first section of the work '*Trauerspiel* and Tragedy', Benjamin sets out to establish the autonomy of the Baroque tragic drama from classical models of tragedy. According to Benjamin, Ancient Greek tragedy must not be seen as a universal, transhistorical genre; on the contrary, tragedy arises from a specific historical moment: humanity's struggle against myth, as exemplified by the tragic hero who battles the forces of Fate in order to assert his or her ethical autonomy. *Trauerspiel* had traditionally been viewed by scholars as a degenerate form of tragedy. Benjamin insists, however, that *Trauerspiel* also corresponds to its own, completely distinct historical moment and must not be judged by the terms of tragedy. What organizes *Trauerspiel* is not the conflict of the tragic hero, but history, understood by the Baroque sensibility in terms of the inescapable transience and fragmentation of worldly things that finds its expression in lamentation. Far from seeing it as a degenerate and fragmented form of tragedy, Benjamin reads an internal, formal coherence into *Trauerspiel* that is provided by its cultivation of fragmentation.[11]

Benjamin's choice and definition of *Trauerspiel* as subject matter bears comparison with Bakhtin's approach to the polyphonic novel and to Dostoevsky's work in particular. In the opening chapter of the Dostoevsky book, Bakhtin reviews the work of Dostoevsky's critics who stress the contradictory, heterogeneous, plural, fragmentary and unresolved nature of Dostoevsky's world:

> Snatching [...] chunks of reality, extending empiricism to its utmost extreme, Dostoevsky does not for a single moment permit us to lose ourselves in joyous recognition of that reality (as Flaubert does, or Leo Tolstoy); instead he frightens us, and this is precisely because he snatches and rips everything out of the normal and predictable chain of the real; in transferring these chunks to himself, Dostoevsky does not transfer along with them the predictable links familiar to us from our experience: the Dostoevskian novel is bound up in an organic unity that has nothing to do with plot.
>
> *(DP* 20)

One notes here the attributes of montage, shock and renewal of the familiar (integral aspects of Benjamin's aesthetics) that appear in this characterization of Dostoevsky's art. Bakhtin's comments reinforce a sense of these characteristics:

> Indeed, the monologic unity of the world is destroyed in a Dosto-evskian novel, but those ripped-off pieces of reality are in no sense directly combined in the unity of the novel: each of these pieces gravitates toward the integral field of vision of a specific character; each makes sense only at the level of a specific consciousness. If these

chunks of reality, deprived of any pragmatic links, were combined directly as things emotionally, lyrically or symbolically harmonious in the unity of a single and monologic field of vision, then before us would be the world of the Romantic, the world of Hoffmann, for example, but in no way could it be the world of Dostoevsky.

(*DP* 20–21)

Bakhtin asserts here the impossibility of judging Dostoevsky's polyphonic novel by the standards of the totalizing forms of the realist novel or Romanticism. Dostoevsky's novel of chunks and ripped-off pieces of reality must be judged in its own terms. As in Benjamin's approach to *Trauerspiel*, Bakhtin sets himself the task of seeing an internal coherence to Dostoevsky's work that emerges from its very lack of coherence.

The second section of Benjamin's *Trauerspiel* book is devoted to allegory. Benjamin approaches this through an immanent critique of the Romantics' characterization of the relationship between symbol and allegory. For the Romantics, the orthodox conception of the symbol was 'the appearance of the Idea in the artwork' (*im Kunstwerk die Erscheinung einer Idee*) (*GS I* 336; *OGTD* 160). The term 'Idea' here carries the full Idealist sense of a transcendent, absolute and timeless value. Appearance implies that the idea does not merely occur in a work of art, which serves as an incidental vehicle, but shines forth in and through the work, lending it beauty and totality. Through the symbol, works of art entail a claim to totality and to an unmediated communion with the absolute in and of themselves: 'as a symbolic construct, the beautiful is supposed to merge with the divine in an unbroken whole' (*GS I* 336; *OGTD* 160).

Benjamin objects to the notion of the aesthetic symbol because of the way that the symbol may falsify human, historical experience. For Benjamin, the philosophy of art since Romanticism has suffered under 'the tyranny of a usurper' in the form of the Romantic symbol (*GS I* 336; *OGTD* 159). In a deconstructive play on the terms that ground the Romantic doctrine of the symbol, Benjamin's critique reveals the semantic richness and resultant ambiguity of Romantic theory. The appearance (*Schein*) of totality in the symbol, Benjamin argues, transfigures (*verklären*) its object.[12] At the heart of this is the double meaning of the word *Schein*. *Schein*, like the English 'appearance', carries two meanings: on the one hand, it means appearance in the sense of actual manifestation; on the other hand, it means appearance in the sense of illusion. The symbol's insistence on the *Schein* of the transcendent transfixes men and women with its seductive glow and blinds them to the transient reality of their profane existence. Benjamin's objection is to the seductive and false projection of totality.

For the Romantics, the arbitrary and conventional nature of allegorical expression was a testament to its degeneracy. These critics denigrated allegory in their keenness to exalt the aesthetic symbol. Schopenhauer, for instance, contends that allegory was, like script, a mere conventional relationship between a signifying image and its meaning. Reading the Romantic critics against themselves, however, Benjamin contends that allegory is indeed like script and bears the marks of its origin in convention; yet this, he argues, is its distinctive strength.[13] Allegory, like script, 'immerses itself in the abyss between pictorial being and meaning' (*GS I* 342; *OGTD* 165). In so doing, it probes the inevitable discrepancy between arbitrary signs and absolute, stabilized significance. Allegorical expression bears witness to the failure of human language and signification to capture and stabilize that which is intended. It flaunts its own fragmentation and asserts the fundamentally unsuccessful and fragmented nature of human existence. As opposed to the symbol's image of harmonious totality, allegorical expression transforms all it touches into fragments and ruins:

> Whereas romanticism inspired by its belief in the infinite, intensified the perfected creation of form and idea in critical terms, at one stroke the profound vision of allegory transforms things and works into stirring writing. [...] In the field of allegorical intuition the image is a fragment, a rune. Its beauty as a symbol evaporates when the light of divine learning falls upon it. The false appearance of totality is extinguished.
>
> (*GS I* 352; *OGTD* 176)

An allegorical mode of thinking, then, acts as a critical and deconstructive weapon against the false totalizing of the symbolic mode.

In the symbol, sign and meaning are unmediated. There is, in the symbol, an indivisible unity of form and content, even if this unity represents a falsified image of the world. In contrast, allegory is characterized by a conventional and arbitrary relationship between sign and meaning which is semiotic in character.[14] It is this semiotic character of allegory that allows for a reconstituted, open-ended relationship between the sacred and the profane. Allegory recognizes the unbridgeable gap between these two realms, yet calls all the more pain-fully for the abolition of that gap. Benjamin writes:

> Any person, any object, any relationship can mean absolutely anything else. With this possibility a destructive, but just verdict is passed on the world in which the detail is of no great importance. But it will be unmistakably apparent, especially to anyone who is familiar with allegorical textual exegesis, that all of the things which are used to signify derive, from the very fact of pointing to something else, a power which makes them appear no longer commensurable with profane things, which raises them onto a higher plane, and which can, indeed, sanctify them. Considered in allegorical terms, then, the profane world is both elevated and devalued.
>
> (*GS I* 351; *OGTD* 175)

The arbitrary nature of allegory means that it continually fails to capture its object. In this failure lies a truthful but negative relation between the transient and historical world of the profane and the eternal realm of the sacred. If allegory rips the totality of the symbol out of the illusory site of transparent meaning, and thereby destroys the false experience of the world which the symbol contains, it goes on to create a new relation to the object, preserving something of the relation to a world beyond that the symbol claimed to represent.

By refusing to present the false reconciliation of the symbol, allegory projects a transgredient perspective from which this world can be judged and justified. In so doing, it contains within its world of mournful fragments of history a negated image of a higher ahistorical totality.[15] An analogous notion can be observed many years later in Benjamin's analysis of Baudelaire:

> If Baudelaire, in the 'Spleen' and in 'Vie antérieure' holds in his hands the scattered fragments [*auseinandergesprengten Bestandsstücke*] of genuine historical experience, Bergson has alienated himself from history much more with his notion of the durée [...]. It [the durée] is the quintessence of an *Erlebnis* that parades in the borrowed robe of *Erfahrung*. The spleen in contrast, exhibits the *Erlebnis* in all its nakedness [*stellt das Erlebnis in seiner Blösse aus*].
>
> (*GS I* 643; *SW* 336)

Unlike Bergson's vitalism, Baudelaire's poetry of the fragments of urban experience (*Erlebnis*) refuses false totalizing.[16] The result is that his poetry creates a negative relation to the experience (*Erfahrung*), the disintegration of which his verse demonstrates so clearly:

> Of all the experiences which made his life what it was, Baudelaire singled out his having been jostled by the crowd as the decisive, unmistakable experience. [...] Baudelaire battled the crowd – with the impotent rage of someone fighting the rain or the wind. This is the nature of the immediate experience (*Erlebnis*) to which Baudelaire has given the weight of long experience (*Erfahrung*).
>
> (*GS I* 652–53; *SW IV* 343)

It is in the most debased and fragmented of phenomena (the shock-experience of urban life) that a negative image of totality (bearing the weight of *Erfahrung*) may come into being.

Bakhtin shares with Benjamin a fear of false totalization. Just as Benjamin contends that the symbol lays claim to an untimely confidence in the totality of transcendence, so Bakhtin finds and condemns in monologue a pretence to its own finality and self-sufficiency:

> Monologism denies that there exists outside of it another consciousness, with the same rights, and capable of responding on an equal footing, another and equal I (thou). For a monologic outlook (in its extreme form) the other remains entirely and only an object of consciousness, and cannot constitute another consciousness. No response capable of altering everything in the world of my consciousness is expected of this other. The monologue is accomplished and deaf to the other's response; it does not await it and does not grant it any decisive force. Monologue makes do without the other; that is why to some extent it objectivizes all reality. Monologue pretends to be the last word.
>
> (*DP* 292–93)

Monologue shares, then, a number of characteristics with the symbol: its imperviousness corresponds to the imperviousness of the untouchable symbol; its claim to finality and direct signification corresponds to the symbol's claim to eternal value. Monologue, like the symbol, presents itself as being outside the course of history, hence it represents a falsification of human experience. As Hirschkop comments of monologue:

> In fact poetic discourse and all the variants that it spawns in the course of 'Discourse in the Novel' (different species of monologism,

'serious' discourse, authoritarian discourse, myth) are worth polem-
icizing with precisely because they represent a kind of false, official
transcendence of the individual, a transcendence which offers power
as a substitute for fulfilment and redemption.[17]

Hirschkop is right to emphasize the connection between monologue's
false transcendence and power. Like the Romantic symbol that Benjamin
accused of exercising the 'tyranny of a usurper', Bakhtin identifies in
monologue the twin threats of violence and self-appointed authority of
the monologic utterance.[18] Monologue in its claim to the final word,
like the symbol in its claim to transcendence, pretends to a position of
power. In so doing, both phenomena pretend to a throne that is not
theirs.

Just as Benjamin favours the failed and permanently deferred mode
of allegorical representation, so Bakhtin favours the ever-provisional
and open form of dialogic discourse. Once again, dialogue shares many
of the characteristics of allegory. Dialogue, like allegory, bears the
imprint of its own failure. In its expectation of an answer back, dialogue
recognizes its inherent instability and incapacity for absolute signification. Dialogue is thoroughgoingly historical, immersed in the concrete
language of social reality. (In Bakhtin's words: with the development
of dialogic discourse, 'for the first time in artistic-ideological consciousness, time and the world become historical' (*DI* 30).) The essence of
dialogue is indirect discourse, a word directed at the other's word.
Allegory, too, whose signifier must always refer to other signifiers and
not to the being of the signified, is a word with a sideways glance.
The dialogic word is polyvalent since its meaning is contested and
it is subject to competing evaluations, like allegory whose conventional and arbitrary nature opens it up to plural meanings and plural
accents.

Like allegory, moreover, dialogue possesses a double orientation. First,
it possesses a critical function in relation to the pretence of totalizing
monologue; second, by virtue of this function, it retains a negative relation to the totality to which monologue lays claim. Both these aspects
are present in the following observations on dialogic discourse in the
Dostoevsky book:

> We might add that Rabelais taunts the deceptive human word by
> a parodic destruction of syntactic structures, thereby reducing to
> absurdity some of the logical and expressively accented aspects of
> words. [...] Turning away from language (by means of language of

course), discrediting any direct or unmediated intentionality and expressive excess (any 'weighty' seriousness) that might adhere in ideological discourse, presuming that all language is conventional and false, maliciously inadequate to reality – all this achieves in Rabelais the maximum purity possible in prose. But the truth that might oppose such falsity receives almost no direct intentional and verbal expression in Rabelais, it does not receive its own word – it reverberates only in the parodic unmasking accents in which the lie is present. Truth is restored by reducing the lie to an absurdity, but truth itself does not seek words; she is afraid to entangle herself in the word, to soil herself in verbal pathos.

(*DI* 307)

On the one hand, the dialogic discourse of Rabelais acts deconstructively on monologic claims to an unmediated form of signification: in Bakhtin's view, parodic laughter exposes the conventional and arbitrary nature of monologic seriousness for what it is, and, hence, such laughter is able to dethrone the pretender. On the other hand, this movement of deconstruction restores, albeit negatively, a relation to truth. Truth here does not speak her name (once again, we see Bakhtin's recourse to silence) but is nevertheless restored to her throne.

Theology and politics

Benjamin's allegorical mode of thinking structures his work. It is at the heart of his conception of theology rooted in Jewish conceptions of the incommensurability of the realm of the sacred and the profane, the unutterability of God's name, and the prohibition on graven images.[19] In the apocalyptic strand of this tradition, the more catastrophic and the more negative the nature of historical life, the more forceful the testament to the need for and imminence of the abolition of historical life which will be brought about by the Messiah.[20] Benjamin displays a strong affinity with this tradition. In Benjamin's allegorical mode of thought, the very debased nature of the profane in all its transience carries an index to the Messianic. In the 'Theological-Political Fragment' (written either 1920–21 or 1937–38), he writes:

The profane, therefore, though not itself a category of [the Messianic Kingdom], is a decisive category of its most unobtrusive approach. For in happiness all that is earthly seeks its downfall [*Untergang*], and only in happiness is its downfall destined to find it. [...] For nature is messianic by reason of its eternal and total passing away [*Vergängnis*].

To strive for such a passing away – even the passing away of those stages of man that are nature – is the task of world politics, whose method must be called nihilism.

(*GS II* 203–04; *SW III* 305, translation modified)

It follows from this that the task of the writer and the critic is not to attempt to construct visions of a better world of transcendence, for this is impossible and ultimately mythic. Rather, he is to reveal the broken nature of the world of history and transience in anticipation of the word of God that will come as abolition or, as we shall see, in anticipation of the voice of revolution that will come as destruction.

A view of the correct and the incorrect way to represent the relationship between the sacred and the profane can be found in Benjamin's essay on Karl Kraus (1931). Here, Benjamin quotes approvingly from one of Kraus's poems from 1929, a polemical attack directed at the poet Stefan George. In the poem, Kraus confronts George, the self-styled priest-poet and 'object of worship':

Who in the temple dwells from which
He never had to drive the traders and the lenders,
Nor yet the Pharisees and scribes
Who, therefore, camped about the place, describe it.

(*GS II* 359; *SW II* 451)

In Kraus's poem and in Benjamin's reading of it, George's error is two-fold: first, George's hieratic 'cult of language' lays claim to the language that can describe the temple. His poetic mystifications are, as Britt puts it, 'a kind of linguistic idolatry'.[21] Second, George occupies the space of the temple. In opposition to the Messiah who comes and clears the holy place of the moneylenders and traders, George's blasphemous claim to occupy the holy space presents an obstacle to Messianic happening.

It is possible to interpret Benjamin's interpretation of Kraus's poem as follows: the words that prepare the way of the Messiah must not be prematurely full of the mere appearance of the divine, but empty and emptying. Such are the words of allegorical form. The arbitrary emptiness of allegory makes space for the authentic, full word of the Messiah. This is the significance of Kraus and his liberation of language through destruction. Kraus is one of the incarnations of Benjamin's destructive character. In the wilderness of fallen language, Kraus cries 'make way for the Lord!' – for, Benjamin seems to argue, it is in the space that has been cleared away that the Messiah can come and speak. Breithaupt comments:

> [The destructive character] makes space [...] only because it was thought to be occupied by some phenomenon or fiction. When this fiction is emptied out, the space remains. In this space, the future is not blocked. Someone or something could arrive. Benjamin says: 'There will be someone who might need this place without occupying it.' The empty space is the podium for possible speakers. For Benjamin, this empty space is the only sphere for politics, a politics of advent. Benjamin does not make an image of this person who might come and need this space. Every image or phenomenon would only occupy the space and thereby block the future. Some-times, Benjamin calls this coming and space-needing person the Messiah.[22]

As at the Passover Seder a cup of wine is poured for the prophet Elijah (and indeed, as in certain extreme forms of Protestantism, a space is left at the table for an always-expected Christ), so the forms of language that carry an index to redemption and authentic totality are those that make space and those that, in their brokenness, are empty and emptying. This negative, allegorical mode of thinking need not operate on the theo-logical plane alone. Such a mode of thinking is at work in Benjamin's adherence to the dictum of Brecht (another of Benjamin's destructive characters) that the cause of political change is best served by starting with the bad new things, rather than with the good old ones. It is to be found in his argument that mechanical reproduction that, on the one hand, destroys benignly auratic modes of experience (such as those, for example, inherent in storytelling) also fashions, on the other hand, a new and liberated organization of collective subjects. It follows that such a mode of thinking is also at the heart of Benjamin's appropriation of revolutionary Marxism.

Benjamin's Marxism is a rejection both of the vulgar form of Marxism that sees the revolution as the natural and inevitable result of economic and technical progress, and of the view of so-called progressivists in the Social Democratic parties who conceive of the cause of social justice proceeding by step-by-step reform. Both positions project a political situation (revolution, a just position for the working classes) as the goal and fulfilment of historical tendencies. Rather, Benjamin conceives the revolution as the interruption of a historical evolution which otherwise leads to catastrophe.[23] As Benjamin puts it in a striking reworking of Marx: 'Marx says that revolutions are the locomotive of world history. But perhaps it is quite otherwise. Perhaps revolutions are an attempt by the passengers on this train – namely, the human race – to activate the emergency brake' (*GS I* 1232; *SW IV* 402). It is the sight of the catastrophe ahead on the railway line of history – the boulders that block the track – that forces the proletariat to pull the revolutionary emergency brake and bring history to an end. It is this form of Marxism that leads Benjamin to put his faith not in Stalinist optimism but in what he terms, in the essay on Surrealism, the 'organization of pessimism':

> Surrealism has come ever closer to the Communist answer. And that means pessimism all along the line. Absolutely. Mistrust in the fate of literature, mistrust in the fate of freedom, mistrust in the fate of European humanity, but three times mistrust in all reconciliation: between classes, between individuals, between nations. And unlimited trust only in I. G. Farben and the peaceful perfection of the air force.
>
> (*GS II* 308; *SW II* 216–17)

Benjamin's argument is that precisely in the most debased phenomena of capitalist society are to be found both an unmasking of false freedoms and a negative relation to true freedom. This view is an alternative form of Marxism that nevertheless stays close to Marx – for Marx argues that, for example, the very nature of the commodity, the separation of buying and selling, which makes capitalism possible, contains the seed of the economic crises which are to bring about capitalism's downfall.[24] Likewise, he asserts that the progressive immiseration of the proletariat, the most brutal and negative effect of advanced capitalism, is the process by which capitalism produces and increases its own gravediggers, the revolutionary proletariat. For Marx, as for Benjamin, hope is to be found in the most negative of phenomena.

In this optimistic pessimism, Benjamin moves sharply away from any tendencies in his work towards cultural conservatism. Benjamin's silence in response to Buber had been a resignation in the face of the impossibility of saying anything meaningful in a fallen, instrumentalized and alienated language. Benjamin's theological-political convictions, however, lead him beyond this position. Far from rejecting modernity in a nostalgic lamentation of all that has disappeared, Benjamin's embrace of modernity in all its degeneracy constitutes an act of theological and political responsibility. So too in the sphere of art,

Benjamin, on the one hand, turns to champion those artistic forms that reveal the nature of fallen experience, and, on the other hand, directs his destructive critical powers at those forms that seek to falsify the transience and brokenness of historical life. Revolutionary forms are those such as montage or Brecht's political theatre that interrupt and create space for political action.

In the case of Bakhtin, it is, perhaps, less clear that his celebration of open form is, in a measure equal to that of Benjamin, a provisional gesture which is predicated on the projection of some future totality. Many critics insist on Bakhtin's absolute resistance to the form of finalization that this would imply:

> Dostoevsky's text is presented as a confrontation of discursive instances: an opposition of utterances, a contrapuntal, polyphonic ensemble. It does not form a totalizable structure: without unity of subject or meaning, anti-totalitarian and anti-theological, the Dostoevskian model has nothing in common with Hegelian dialectic.[25]

Despite the undoubted attraction of such a view with its utopian projection of a world of possibility, this conception of Bakhtin's thought gravely impoverishes it, reducing it to a mere openness for its own sake. An emphasis on eternal openness in Bakhtin would constitute a denial that one is responsible for one's utterances and hence a form of what he terms an alibi-in-non-being. As Hirschkop comments: 'Discourse is historical; it lacks theological certainty. But this does not mean that its essence is to lack any form of certainty and therefore every statement is equally, and hence absolutely, provisional.'[26] To claim otherwise is, in a curious fashion, to erase difference from Bakhtin's thought. If all statements, though contradictory, retain equal rights, then their difference evaporates and the result is an eternal continuum of undecidability.

One way of approaching this problem is to turn to Bakhtin's collaborator, Voloshinov. In *Marxism and the Philosophy of Language*, Voloshinov argues that utterances gain their signification in a dialogic interaction that is social and open-ended. The vision of signification is one that appears to be explicitly anti-authoritarian and democratic. No utterance is immune to a potential answer back. The dialogic nature of language itself means that evaluative meaning cannot be permanently fixed within the flux that is language. Voloshinov contrasts the closed forms of monologic utterance that seek to have the final word, with the open forms of indirect discourse which remain true to the nature of language.

Behind this view lies an historical narrative of the development of language. This story is the story of language's liberation. It begins in pre-history with the enslavement of the native word at the hands of the conquering foreigner and his ideology-transmitting counterpart, the priest.

> [One's native word] contains no mystery; it can become a mystery only in the mouths of others, provided they are hierarchically alien to us – in the mouth of the chief, in the mouth of priests. But in that case, it has already become a word of a different kind, externally changed and removed from the routine of life (taboo for usage in ordinary life, or an archaism of speech); that is, if it had not already been from the start a foreign word in the mouth of a conqueror chief. [...] This grandiose organizing role of the alien word [...] led to its coalescence in the depths of historical consciousness of nations with the idea of authority, the idea of power, the idea of holiness, the idea of truth, and dictated that notions about the word be pre-eminently oriented toward the alien word.
>
> (*MPL* 75)

The word described here is closed: closed off by the hierarchical distance that I have discussed in Chapter 1. It is wrapped up in an impenetrable aura of holiness, power and unfamiliarity. It is the word of a tradition that strives to stay forever the same and seeks to organize and subordinate its community in fixed relations of power. Voloshinov charts the unravelling of this form of monologic discourse through dialogization in the development of genres of indirect speech. This development opens up the closed word of the philologist and priest into the plural world of modernity. The closed word of authority is relativized by the intrusion of varied, individual points of view. This is a process of secularization and demystification in which the hieratic speech of the priest becomes the demotic speech of the people, a process of democratization in which the authoritarian word of the single chief is wrested from his mouth for the many mouths of competing classes, and a process of the opening up and dissolution of a single, immutable truth into the plural sphere of many claims to truth. It is, then, once again, the 'profaning of all that is holy', the 'disturbance of social relations', the melting of the solid into air that we have already seen in the Communist Manifesto.

Just as in Marx, however, Voloshinov's narrative of the liberation of the word does not end here. The dialogization of monologic discourse is not to be celebrated *per se* but only in so far as it is a necessary precondition for a higher form of freedom:

> The victory of extreme forms of the picturesque style in reported speech is not, of course, to be explained in terms either of psychological factors or the artist's own individual stylistic purposes, but is explainable in terms of the general, far-reaching subjectivization of the ideological word-utterance. No longer is it a monument, nor even a document, of a substantive ideational position; it makes itself felt only as the expression of an adventitious state. [...] The utterance has virtually ceased to be an object for serious ideational consideration. The categorical word, the word 'from one's own mouth,' the declaratory word remains only alive in scientific writings. In all other fields of verbal-ideological creativity, what predominates is not the 'outright' but the 'contrived' word. All verbal activity in these cases amounts to piecing together 'other persons' words' and 'words seemingly from other persons.' [...] All this bespeaks an alarming instability of the ideological word.
>
> (*MPL* 158–59)

Here we see the other face of the liberation of modernity: instability, insincerity, inauthenticity, anxiety, a crippling of the faculties of expression and an 'adventitious state' of flux. Voloshinov's emphasis on dialogue and unfinalizability is, then, merely a precondition of and clearing of the ground for the categorical and final utterance of proletarian revolution. His use of a quotation from Lorck makes this clear. 'There is only one possibility for [language's] rejuvenation: the proletariat must take over command of the word from the bourgeoisie' (*MPL* 154). In Voloshinov's view, dialogue is the precondition of the silencing of all dialogue by the authoritative word of revolution; open form is the precondition of a future completion.[27]

In Voloshinov's philosophy of language, a form of negative politics is at work. Voloshinov does not himself explicitly call for the proletariat to come to voice, but leaves this to his quotation. Similarly, his concentration is on the provisional, if liberating, form of dialogization, not on the forms that will be taken by the authoritative word of the proletariat. Despite the fact that he is writing 12 years after the October Revolution, he seems not to allow himself to speculate about a future that ought to be so close at hand. In this, he stands in accord with Hegel, for whom 'the owl of Minerva begins its flight only with the onset of dusk',[28] and also in accord with Trotsky. For Trotsky, writing in 1923:

There is no revolutionary art as yet. There are the elements of this art, there are hints and attempts at it [. . .]. Revolutionary art which inevitably reflects all the contradictions of a revolutionary social system, should not be confused with Socialist art for which no basis has as yet been made. [. . .] Not for nothing did Engels speak of the Revolution as a leap from the kingdom of necessity to the kingdom of freedom. The revolution itself is not as yet the kingdom of freedom. On the contrary, it is developing the features of necessity to the greatest degree. Socialism will abolish class antagonisms, as well as classes, but the Revolution carries the class struggle to its highest tension. [. . .] Revolutionary literature cannot but be imbued with a spirit of hatred, which is a creative historical factor in an epoch of proletarian dictatorship. Under Socialism, solidarity will be the basis of society. Literature and art will be tuned to a different key.[29]

The signs of freedom are to be found in the development of their opposites: the realm of freedom is prefigured by the intensification of necessity and the establishment of dictatorship; classlessness is prefigured by the intensification of class struggle; solidarity is prefigured by the intensification of hatred. Just as Trotsky predicts that culture will be 'tuned to a different key' and yet does not claim to be able to sing in it, and just as he sees signs of solidarity in the development of hatred, so Voloshinov sees in the decadent, open forms of indirect speech the signs of a future final word. Other critics, such as Emerson and Morson, have made similar points about Voloshinov's thought:

Whereas Bakhtin celebrates intense dialogization and double-voicing, Voloshinov, writing as a Marxist, describes such phenomena disapprovingly. The forms so central to Bakhtin's ideas of unfinalizability and so characteristic of his prosaic approach to the cultural world are regarded by Voloshinov as symptoms of decadent 'relativistic individualism'. Voloshinov expects and calls for the decay, if not the abolition, of these forms of speech, and he believes that the triumph of the working class is the death knell of these forms.[30]

Nevertheless, it is possible to see a compatibility rather than divergence between Bakhtin and Voloshinov. It is possible to discern a similar notion of open form as the necessary precondition of a future completion that, however, operates within the context of a different narrative, and hence according to a radically different temporal model. Where the future, final word, in Voloshinov's account, is to resound within history as the utterance of the victorious proletariat, one can speculate that in Bakhtin's thought the future, final word is to come from without history as the word of God.

It is possible to argue, more or less in accordance with Coates, that the overall shape of Bakhtin's thought may be conceived of as follows: in the early work (*Toward a Philosophy of the Act*, 'Author and Hero'), the author exists as a figure who, from a position of outsidedness, lovingly bestows form upon the hero as an act of benign consummation. Subsequently, however, beginning with the Dostoevsky book and culminating most radically in the essays on the novel, Bakhtin adopts an aesthetic of radical openness. Here, the author gives up his privileged position outside the world of his heroes and descends onto their plane as an equal participant in the dialogue of the novel:

> The new artistic position of the author with regard to the hero in Dostoevsky's polyphonic novel is a fully realized and thoroughly consistent dialogic position, one that affirms the internal freedom, unfinalizability, and indeterminacy of the hero. For the author the hero is not 'he' and not 'I' but a fully valid 'thou', that is, another and autonomous 'I' (thou art) [...] And this 'great dialogue' of the novel [...] is no stenographer's report of a finished dialogue, from which the author has already withdrawn and over which he is located as if in some higher decision-making position: that would have turned an authentic and unfinished dialogue into an objectivized and finalized image of dialogue, of the sort usual for every monologic novel.
>
> (*DP* 63)

Now, the gift that the author grants his heroes is not the gift of finalization but the gift of the sacrifice of her or his being as a higher principle. Through this gift, her or his heroes are set free. Critics like Coates have usefully pointed out the similarity of Bakhtin's thought here with the Christian theological doctrine of kenosis.[31] This doctrine is expressed in the Christ-hymn cited by Paul in Philippians:

> Let the same mind be in you that was in Christ Jesus who, though he was in the form of God, did not regard equality with God as something to be exploited but emptied himself [*alla heauton ekenosen*], taking the form of a slave [*morphhn doulou labwn*], being born in human likeness. And being found in human form he humbled himself and became obedient to the point of death – even death on a cross. Therefore God also highly exalted him and gave him the

name that is above every name, so that at the name of Jesus every knee should bend, in heaven and on earth and under the earth, and every tongue should confess that Jesus is Lord, to the glory of God the Father.

(Philippians 2: 6–11)

In the incarnation, the word gives up its equality with God; it empties itself of its divine plenitude. This abasement in kenosis, however, is merely the precondition for Christ's rising again to higher glory. Similarly, the abasement and emptying of the word (as, for example, in Benjamin's conception of allegory), its temporary enslavement in earthly conditions, is the precondition for its exaltation in an eternal song of praise.

Kenosis in Bakhtin may be seen as analogous to Benjamin's negative theology of destruction. In the following passage from the Dostoevsky book, Bakhtin struggles to express the apparent paradox of kenosis in relation to the author of the polyphonic novel:

This interaction [of several consciousnesses in the polyphonic novel] provides no support for the viewer who would objectify an entire event according to some ordinary monologic category [...] – and this consequently makes the viewer also a participant. Not only does the novel give no firm support outside the rupture-prone world of dialogue for a third, monologically all-encompassing consciousness – but on the contrary, everything in the novel is structured to make dialogic opposition inescapable. Not a single element of the work is structured from the point of view of a nonparticipating 'third person.' In the novel itself, nonparticipating 'third persons' are not represented in any way. There is no place for them, compositionally or in the larger meaning of the work. And this is not a weakness of the author but his greatest strength. By this means a new authorial position is won and conquered, one located above the monologic position.

(*DP* 18)

The polyphonic novel is a negation of the closed world of the monologic novel. The author has given up his position above the world of the novel as a third, all-compassing consciousness. This is a negation of the closed, monologic form. The monologic author is all-encompassing and leaves no space unoccupied; he is like Kraus's image of George: the poet who occupies the temple. By contrast, like Benjamin's destructive character, the polyphonic author clears space for a future and higher intervention. Thus, in a kenotic vein, the apparent weakness expressed in the author's abdication of his authority constitutes his greatest strength: for this abdication of the authorial outsidedness clears space for a higher-level authorial position that is not presently occupied but can be occupied in the future.[32]

Bakhtin develops a spatial metaphor predicated on definite temporal relations in a fashion remarkably similar to that of Benjamin. Like Benjamin, Bakhtin's conception of open form is of a form that makes space for future completion. The spatial metaphor that Bakhtin develops is expressed most clearly in the image of the threshold: 'The great dialogue in Dostoevsky is organized as an unclosed whole of life itself, life poised on the threshold' (*DP* 64). Open form leaves a door ajar through which consummating intervention may come from the outside. Bakhtin remarks in his notes made in 1961 towards a revision of the Dostoevsky book: 'The threshold, the door, the stairway. The chronotopic significance. The possibility of transforming hell into a paradise in a single instant (that is, passing from one to the other, cf. "the mysterious visitor")' (*DP* 299). The 'mysterious visitor' in this fragment is a reference to a figure in *The Brothers Karamazov*. Reminiscing about his youth on his deathbed, the *starets* Zosima tells how he was visited unexpectedly at night by a strange gentleman. ('There I was, sitting at home the next evening, when all of a sudden the door opened and this very same gentleman entered.'[33]) After a series of such visits, the mysterious visitor confesses to the murder, many years before, of a woman with whom he had fallen unrequitedly in love, a murder of which he was never suspected. It is the act of opening himself in confession – above all, to his fellow human beings – that can transform the hell of guilt into paradise. In the words of the mysterious visitor:

> 'Paradise', he said, 'is concealed within each one of us, it is hidden in me too at this very moment, and I need only to wish it, and it will come about the very next day and remain with me the rest of my life. [...] In order to refashion the world, it is necessary for people themselves to adopt a different mental attitude. [...] You ask when this will come about. It will come about, but first there must be an end to the habit of self-imposed isolation of man.'[34]

Paradise, understood here as the radical refashioning of the world, is dependent on the ending of the closedness of isolation, on the unblocking of passing points, on the leaving clear of thresholds, and on the possibility that doors may be opened from outside. Such intervention from outside might, as Bakhtin suggests in the Dostoevsky book, take the form of a Christ who is to bring about the end of dialogue itself in an act of consummation and subjugation:

> What unfolds before Dostoevsky [...] is a world of consciousnesses mutually illuminating one another [...]. Among them Dostoevsky seeks the highest and most authoritative orientation, and he perceives it not as his own true thought, but as another authentic human being and his discourse. The image of the ideal human being or the image of Christ represents for him the resolution of ideological quests. This image or this highest voice must crown the world of voices, must organize and subdue it.
>
> (*DP* 97)

This end to dialogue, as Bakhtin implies in the notes towards a revision, may, as in Benjamin's conception of messianic happening, come as catastrophe:

> The problem of catastrophe. Catastrophe is not finalization. It is the culmination, in collision and struggle, of points of view (of equally privileged consciousnesses, each with its own world). Catastrophe does not give these points of view resolution, but on the contrary reveals their incapacity of resolution under earthly conditions; catastrophe sweeps them all away without having resolved them. Catastrophe is the opposite of triumph and apotheosis. By its very essence it is denied even elements of catharsis.
>
> (*DP* 298)

This is the catastrophe that clears away the ground and makes space for a resolution that is not earthly in its origin.

The theological metaphor that underlies Bakhtin's philosophy of the novel consists in positing a negative relation between the fallen world (a world that is provisional and open) and the world of salvation (a world of completion).[35] It follows then, that, as Hirschkop comments, 'the double-voicedness of language, its three-dimensionality, is therefore not the cue for some generalized scepticism about all ideology, but the mark of the "future, lodged in the negated present"'.[36] The openness of dialogue is not a *telos* in itself, rather it is the precondition for a truly just final word.[37] Thus, Bakhtin's theory of the polyphonic novel retains negative traces of his early work's emphasis on completion. The polyphonic author is aware that his form-giving word is not the final word, and hence, according to Bakhtin, he gives to its hero a space: what Bakhtin terms a 'loophole'. As Coates comments:

> It should again be stressed that as far as human or authorial final-isation is concerned, Bakhtin is its resolved opponent after 'Author and Hero'. However, he clearly reserves a space, his 'loophole' as it were, for surrender to the loving authority of an absolute Other, a peculiarly spiritual, and radical, solution, to an otherwise apparently hopeless existential situation.[38]

The 'loophole' is the space that makes the entry of the messiah possible. It is in this that consists Bakhtin's messianism, a messianism that stands close to that of Benjamin.[39] Both display the ability to see signs of future completion and future wholeness in the midst of an incomplete and fragmented world.

The temporal orientation of artistic form

For all that aesthetic activity might preserve the integrity of the life upon which it bestows form, a transformation also occurs. This dialectical transformation acts – perhaps most fundamentally – upon the temporal structure of the material of life. Aristotle, in the *Eudemean Ethics*, notes the importance of *stasis* in the work of art – the cessation of happening and the arrest of attention that occur as the artist points to all the things that are happening at one particular moment.[40] *Stasis* may be understood as follows: the moment is lifted out of the flow of time of which it was a part. In this process, it is preserved and dignity is conferred upon it. It is not merely an arbitrary point of passing from one moment to another but a coherent constellation of competing forces and possibilities in its own right.[41] Such is, for example, the moment of decision which the tragic hero enacts on stage. Time, here, stands still, as the hero grapples with all the possible paths of action that seem to be available to him and which present themselves to him as alternative futures. Through *stasis*, art has in its power the ability of rescuing the lived moment in its fullness from the indifferent passing of time that otherwise reduces the lived moment to an insignificant and empty instant of its own flow.

We have already seen in Chapter 2 Bakhtin's and Benjamin's emphasis on remembrance and the transformation of the structure of time that remembrance enacts. In Bakhtin's 'Author and Hero', totalizing aesthetic experience adopts the structure of memory and commemoration. Aesthetic activity, as *stasis*, does not pass over the moment indifferently but rather is able to 'slow down and linger over an object, to hold and sculpt every detail and particular in it, however minute' (*TPA* 64). In so doing, aesthetic activity is able to honour and confer meaning on the totality of the mortal subject. 'Author and Hero' develops the connection between memory and art further:

> My memory of the other and of the other's life differs radically from my contemplating and remembering my own life. Memory sees a life and its content in a different way formally; only memory is aesthetically productive [...]. Memory of someone else's finished life (although anticipation of its end is possible as well) provides the golden key to the aesthetic consummation of a person. An aesthetic approach to a *living* person forestalls his death, as it were – predetermines his future and renders his future redundant, as it were; immanent to any determinateness of inner life is fate. Memory is an approach to the other from the standpoint of his axiological consummatedness. In a certain sense, memory is hopeless; but on the other hand, only memory knows how to value – independently of purpose and meaning – an already finished life, a life that is totally present-on-hand.
>
> (*AH* 107)

Aesthetically productive memory is able to transfigure the total individual life. It confers upon life weight and roundedness. Nevertheless, in so doing it imbues it with a certain hopelessness in the face of death. Benjamin's essay 'The Storyteller', contains a similar insight:

> 'A man who dies at the age of thirty-five,' Moritz Heinemann once said, 'is at every point of his life a man who dies at the age of thirty-five.' Nothing is more dubious than this sentence – but for the sole reason that the tense is wrong. A man – so says the truth that was meant here – who died at the age of thirty-five will appear to remembrance at every point of his life as a man who dies at the age of thirty-five. In other words, the statement that makes no sense for real life becomes indisputable for remembered life.
>
> (*GS II* 456; *SW III* 156)

Bakhtin and Benjamin both imply that totality is only accessible in the shadow of death. A totalizing art is only possible, in Bakhtin's words, as 'the perception of the other under the token of death' (*AH* 107). Or, as Benjamin puts it in his description of the benignly totalizing figure of the storyteller: 'Death is the sanction of everything that the storyteller can tell; he has borrowed his authority from death' (*GS II* 450; *SW III* 151).

The totalization which the artist appears to achieve through memory, then, is bought at a price: 'The deeper and the more perfect the embodiment, the more distinctly do we hear in it the definitive completion of death and at the same time the aesthetic victory over death' (*AH* 131). On the one hand, the artist declares the everlasting meaning of individual deaths in defiance of the abstract, biological and historical fact of death; aesthetic consummation seems to proclaim a promise of eternal life. On the other hand, the artist underlines the inevitability of death and the transience of human existence; aesthetic consummation only offers the prospect of death.[42] In this fashion, aesthetic consummation sets up a complex relationship between history and eternity, between joy and hopelessness:

> Throughout the entire course of an embodied hero's life, one can hear the tones of a requiem. Hence that distinctive hopelessness of rhythm as well as its sorrowfully joyful lightness, that is, its relievedness of the pressure exerted by the irresolvable seriousness of meaning. Rhythm takes possession of a life that *has been lived*: the requiem tones at the end were already heard in the cradle song at the beginning. In art, however, this lived-out life is saved, justified, and consummated in eternal memory; hence the kind, cherishing hopelessness of rhythm.
>
> (*AH* 131)

Perception under the token of death is redemptive. It rescues the life portrayed by conferring upon it the eternal life of memory. Nevertheless, it is peculiarly hopeless, in so far as all the questions of the particular life in consideration have already been answered; all its hopes have already been fulfilled or unfulfilled. The life thus consummated is marked by a resigned knowing-in-advance which is both joyful and melancholy. Paraphrasing the passage from 'The Storyteller' once again: such is our approach in remembrance to the man who dies at thirty-five, who remains forever young, but forever fated to die young.

It is possible to discern an analogous relationship between transience and eternity, effected by an orientation towards the past, in the sonnet which forms a central pillar of Benjamin's interpretation of Baudelaire: 'À une Passante':[43]

> La rue assourdissante autour de moi hurlait.
> Longue, mince, en grand deuil, douleur majestueuse,
> Une femme passa, d'une main fastueuse
> Soulevant, balançant le feston et l'ourlet;
>
> Agile et noble, avec sa jambe de statue.
> Moi, je buvais, crispé comme un extravagant,
> Dans son oeil, ciel livide où germe l'ouragan,
> La douceur qui fascine et le plaisir qui tue.
>
> Un éclair... puis la nuit! – Fugitive beauté
> Dont le regard m'a fait soudainement renaître,
> Ne te verrai-je plus que dans l'éternité?
>
> Ailleurs, bien loin d'ici! trop tard ! jamais peut-être!
> Car j'ignore où tu fuis, tu ne sais où je vais,
> Ô toi que j'eusse aimée, ô toi qui le savais!

[The street around me roared, deafening. / Tall, slender, in deep mourning, majestic in her grief, / A woman passed – with imposing hand / Gathering up a scalloped hem –

Agile and noble, her leg like a statue's. / And as for me, twitching like one possessed, I drank / From her eyes – livid sky brewing like a storm – / The sweetness that fascinates and the pleasure that kills.

A lightning flash...then night! – Fugitive beauty, / Whose gaze has suddenly given me life, / Will I see you again before the close of eternity?

Elsewhere, very far from here! Too late! Perhaps *never*! / For where you're off to I'll never know, nor do you know where I'm going – / O you whom I could have loved, O you who knew it too!]

In the widow's veil mysteriously and mutely borne along by the crowd, an unknown woman crosses the poet's field of vision. What this sonnet communicates is simply this: far from experiencing the crowd as an opposing, antagonistic element, the city dweller discovers in the crowd what fascinates him. The delight of the urban poet is love – not at first sight, but at last sight. It is an eternal farewell which coincides in the poem with the moment of enchantment. Thus, the sonnet deploys the figure of shock, indeed of catastrophe.

(*GS I* 622–23; *SW IV* 323–24)

First, it should be noted that Baudelaire's poem is structured in the same way as the image of the angel of history in 'On the Concept of History'. The poet's regard is a glance backwards, since, as the woman approaches him, she is already receding into the past. The poet longs to stay and address her, but the jostling movement of the roaring street around him and the storm that brews in her eyes propel him into the future and away from her. The fragmentary and fragmenting experience of urban modernity is portrayed as the accumulation of catastrophe. Second (in an instant that is accessible only to art) the poem achieves *stasis*. For one moment, the 'rue assourdissante' is counterposed to the implied quiet of the widow's 'grand deuil' and 'douleur majestueuse'. From being one of the faceless and objectified figures of the crowd, the woman is transformed into a subject; for, in this auratic moment, she looks back at the poet. It is the transience of her appearance that transforms her into a 'fugitive beauté'. And yet, it is this very transience that makes the poet feel reborn and project this moment into eternity. In the linking of the transient and the eternal, Baudelaire summons up an image of totality that is hopeless and joyous. The poet's slowing down, his attention to the fullness of the moment that is passing, reveals all the possibilities in that moment ('Ô toi que j'eusse aimée, ô toi qui le savais!'), and at the same time reveals all their hopelessness ('trop tard! jamais peut-être!'). Benjamin's description of this as shock and catastrophe is apt: these are the result of the collision of joy ('the poet's delight') and his hopelessness (his awareness of the futility of transience).[44] This catastrophe is summed up as 'love at last sight', a phrase that might also describe Bakhtin's aesthetics of consummation.[45]

Bakhtin rejects the conception of aesthetic memory that we have seen in 'Author and Hero', not least because it produces a world that is beautiful but given, and hence dead:

Artistic vision presents us with the *whole* hero, measured in full and added up in every detail; there must be no secrets for us in the hero with respect to meaning; our faith and hope must be silent. From the very outset, we must experience all of him, deal with the whole of him: in respect to meaning, he must be dead for us, formally dead.

(*AH* 131)

This is unacceptable to the later Bakhtin. On the one hand, during the course of his career, Bakhtin's fear of false totalizing grows to such an extent that even the apparently benign totalizing of this sort of aesthetic memory represents a danger. On the other hand, one can also only suggest that the requirement, that in order to become part of aesthetic vision the hero must be 'dead for us', defeats the purpose of aesthetic activity itself: the preserving and benign bestowal of form on life. It is in this light that one must view Bakhtin's conception of the past in his fragment of 1974, 'Towards a Methodology of the Human Sciences':

There is neither a first or last word and there are no limits to the dialogic context (it extends into the boundless past and the boundless future). Even past meanings, that is those born in the dialogue of past centuries, can never be stable (finalized, ended once and for all) – they will always change (be renewed) in the process of subsequent, future development of dialogue. At any moment in the development of the dialogue there are immense, boundless masses of forgotten contextual meaning, but at certain moments of the dialogue's subsequent development along the way they are recalled and invigorated in renewed form (in a new context). Nothing is absolutely dead: every meaning will have its homecoming festival. The problem of great time.

(*SG* 170)

In this formulation, the attitude taken towards the past is towards a past in which nothing is absolutely dead. Here, there always remains the possibility of remembering what has been forgotten, of recalling and invigorating the unfulfilled hopes of the past.[46] Here, any orientation towards the past is a form of memory that draws the past into the living present and hence makes way for a redeemed future.

Such a temporal orientation will make space for what, already in 'Author and Hero', Bakhtin defines as the absolute future:

The absolute future, the future of meaning. That is, not into the future which will leave everything in its place, but into the future which must finally fulfil, accomplish everything, the future which we oppose to the present and the past as a salvation, transfiguration, and redemption. That is, the future not as a bare temporal category, but as a category of meaning – as that which axiologically does not yet exist; that which is still undetermined; that which is not yet discredited by existence.

(*AH* 118)

It follows, then, that, for all the attraction of artistic forms of benign completion, such as the aesthetic finalization in memory of 'Author and Hero' or the auratic mode of storytelling, Bakhtin and Benjamin must give these up and seek out artistic forms that are, on the contrary, open: the polyphonic novel, montage and cognate forms. For these forms do not consign their material to the past but retain a connection to a living present and an ever-open, if dangerous future. The polyphonic novel draws its material into an expanded present. On the one hand, the present of the novel reaches into the past: 'characteristic for the historical novel is a positively weighted modernizing, an erasing of temporal boundaries, the recognition of an eternal present' (*DI* 365). On the other hand, the present of the novel points into the future:

It is precisely the zone of contact with an inconclusive present (and consequently with the future) that creates the necessity of this incongruity of a man with himself. There always remain in him unrealized potential and unrealized demands. The future exists, and this future ineluctably touches on the individual, has its roots in him. [...] There always remains an unrealized surplus of humanness; there always remains a need for the future, and a place for this future must be found.

(*DI* 37)

This temporal orientation towards an open present is different from memory. Aesthetic memory consists in the attempt to slow time down, to hold on to the particular moment in the face of the eroding stream of time. The temporal orientation described here, however, remains in the present. Its aim is to thicken and spatialize time and to bring into being an expanded present in which competing and divergent possibilities might coexist. This is the form of *stasis* that Bakhtin discerns in Dostoevsky:

The fundamental category in Dostoevsky's mode of artistic visualizing was not evolution but coexistence and interaction. He saw and conceived his world primarily in terms of space, not time. Hence his deep affinity for the dramatic form. Dostoevsky strives to organize all available meaningful material, all material of reality into one time-frame, in the form of dramatic juxtaposition. [...] Dostoevsky attempted to perceive the very stages themselves in their simultaneity, to juxtapose and counterpose them dramatically, and not to stretch them out into an evolving sequence. For him, to get one's bearing on the world meant to conceive all its contents as simultaneous, and to guess at their interrelationships in the cross-section of a single moment.

(*DP* 28)

In this temporal orientation, 'reality [...] is only one of many possible realities; it is not inevitable, not arbitrary, it bears within itself other possibilities' (*DP* 37).

Benjamin's aesthetics also propose forms of *stasis* of this nature, analogous to Bakhtin's 'dramatic juxtaposition'. As we have seen, montage substitutes diachronic relations of sequence with synchronic relations of juxtaposition. Similarly, the effect of mechanical reproduction is the spatialization of time. In the destruction of aura, the unique object's historical testimony *through* time is replaced by the simultaneous coexistence of its many reproductions *in* time. As in Bakhtin, these moments of *stasis* that interrupt the flow of events reveal to the contemplator the alternative possibilities in the present. The dragging of the artwork from the cultic and ritual past into the present liberates it for new purposes in the future. Similarly, in Benjamin's analysis of Brecht's epic theatre, interruption, through *Verfremdungseffekte*, creates an expanded present in which the distracted audience can reflect on how events might be different, in which the claims of competing viewpoints can coexist and be evaluated. As in Bakhtin's polyphonic novel, reality reveals itself here as 'one of many possible realities', 'not arbitrary', and as bearing within itself 'many possibilities'. It is, however, in Benjamin's concept of dialectics at a standstill and the dialectical image that this idea receives its most powerful expression:

Thinking involves both thoughts in motion and thoughts at rest. When thinking reaches a standstill in a constellation saturated with tensions, the dialectical image appears. This image is the *caesura* in the movement of thought. Its locus is of course not arbitrary. In short it is to be found wherever the tension between dialectical oppositions is greatest. The dialectical image is, accordingly, the very object constructed in the materialist presentation of history. It is identical with the historical object; it justifies its being blasted out of the continuum of the historical process.

(GS V 595; *AP* 475)

The dialectical image, what Andrew Benjamin describes as a form of 'temporal montage', is a means of bringing the material of the past into a relationship with the present in such a fashion that a pathway to a redeemed future is opened up.[47] Similarly, the expanded present of the polyphonic novel contains 'tension between dialectical oppositions'.[48] The force of present and unresolved oppositions in the dramatic juxtapositions of dialogic discourse gives such discourse an urgency – ready at any moment to blast open the continuum of the historical process and spring over the threshold into the future.

For both Bakhtin and Benjamin, provisional openness and an orientation towards the present and future are ultimately preferable to premature and possibly false completion. The latter presents a world that is given in advance. It runs the danger that men and women attempt to speak the last word that, in truth, belongs only to God. The former make room for the possibility that something utterly unexpected might happen. They present a world that is more alive since it can be changed at any moment. They do not block the threshold but rather leave a loophole open. They make it possible that the present moment might be the 'small gateway in time though which the Messiah might enter' *(GS I* 704; *SW IV* 397).

Notes

Introduction

1. See Jameson's comments on this in Frederic Jameson, *Marxism and Form*, Princeton NJ, 1974, p. 352, and the long quotation he gives there from Hegel's *Aesthetics* concerning the 'prose of the world', pp. 352–53.
2. The final chapter of Hirschkop's study provides a subtle analysis of the implications of Bakhtin's conception of fear for political theory, focusing on the official seriousness and fear inherent in the everyday as an instrument of hegemony. Completed in 1999, the book does not deal with our new culture of fear. See Ken Hirschkop, *Mikhail Bakhtin: An Aesthetic for Democracy*, Oxford, 1999, pp. 272–98.
3. Mouffe articulates her theory of an agonistic democracy, drawing on Schmitt's definition of the political as the sphere of the friend versus enemy distinction, in, *inter alia*, Chantal Mouffe, *On the Political*, London, 2005. I do not wish, however, to deny the undoubted and real connection between Schmitt and Benjamin. This is the subject of substantial controversy in Benjamin scholarship. See Samuel Weber, 'Taking Exception to Decision: Walter Benjamin and Carl Schmitt', *Diacritics*, 22, 1992, 3–4, pp. 5–19, and Horst Bredekamp, 'From Walter Benjamin to Carl Schmitt via Thomas Hobbes', Special edition: 'Angelus Novus: Perspectives on Walter Benjamin', *Critical Inquiry*, 25, 1999, 2, pp. 247–66.
4. Žižek claims that the gesture of a return to Lenin allows us to think beyond post-ideological coordinates and suspend the *Denkverbot* of consensus. Slavoj Žižek, 'A Plea for Leninist Intolerance', *Critical Inquiry*, 28, 2002, 2, pp. 542–66.
5. There have been various attempts to turn Bakhtinian and Benjaminian theory towards the new forms emerging in information technology. See, for example, Bostad's essay that analyses the new public sphere of the Internet and the forms of dialogue it both enables and inhibits: Finn Bostad, 'Dialogue in Electronic Public Space: the Semiotics of Time, Space and the Internet', in Bostad, Brandist, Evensen and Faber (eds), *Bakhtinian Perspectives on Language and Culture: Meaning in Language, Art and New Media*, London, 2004, pp. 167–84. Köpenick attempts to rethink Benjamin's concept of the aura for an age of digital reproducibility in Lutz Köpenick, 'Aura Reconsidered: Benjamin and Contemporary Visual Culture', in Gerhard Richter (ed.), *Benjamin's Ghosts: Interventions in Contemporary Literary and Cultural Theory*, Stanford CA, 2002, pp. 95–117. Ziarek maps an extension to Benjamin's 'Work of Art' essay for an age of Internet interactivity, where reproductions can be altered by their recipients, in Krzysztof Ziarek, 'The Work of Art in the Age of Electronic Mutability', in Andrew Benjamin (ed.), *Benjamin and Art*, London, 2005, pp. 209–26.
6. Barry Sandywell, 'Memories of Nature in Bakhtin and Benjamin', in Craig Brandist and Galin Tihanov (eds), *Materializing Bakhtin: The Bakhtin Circle and Social Theory*, London, 2000, pp. 94–118.

7. See Terry Eagleton, *Walter Benjamin or Towards a Revolutionary Criticism*, London, 1981. Eagleton is also limited by the fact that Bakhtin's early works were not available to him at the time of writing.

8. Pierre (Petr) V. Zima, 'L'Ambivalence dialectique: entre Benjamin et Bakhtine', *Revue d'esthétique*, 1, 1981, 1, pp. 131–40 (136). Zima describes the conception of ambivalence, which he finds in both thinkers and which structures his essay, as follows: 'The obverse of official culture which recognizes only absolute difference and monologue, carnival presents the conjunction of opposites and the plurality of voices: polyphony. [...] In carnival, the absolute difference of values is abolished by the conjunction of opposing values which brings forth laughter. [...] By way of parallel, Benjamin starts out from the notion that opposites touch each other and that their conjunction produces the dialectical shock of recognition and criticism. Shock destroys monovalent contemplation by revealing the ambivalence of reality and the equality (but not identity) of opposing values' (p. 131).

9. Zima is also limited by the range of texts that he refers to. He appears to use French translations of Bakhtin. At the time of writing, the texts translated into French were the Rabelais Book, the Dostoevsky book, 'Discourse in the Novel', 'Epic and Novel', and (under the name of Bakhtin) Voloshinov's *Marxism and the Philosophy of Language*. See the bibliographical appendix to Mikhail Bakhtine (V. N. Volochinov), *Le Freudisme*, trans. Guy Verret, Lausanne, 1980, pp. 214–25.

10. One might mention in passing Schleifer's study which marshals both Bakhtin and Benjamin, devoting substantial portions of text to a comparison of the two thinkers, in support of an ambitious reassessment of the temporality of the post-Enlightenment age. Confused and inaccurate with relation to both thinkers, Schleifer's work, however, itself confuses the problem. For example, he wilfully misreads out of context Bakhtin's use of the word 'aura' to imply a point of equivalence between the two thinkers (p. 211). Ronald Schleifer, *Modernism and Time: The Logic of Abundance in Literature, Science and Culture 1880–1930*, Cambridge, 2000. Cohen's tendentious study, 'a transformative mode of reading I will not quite call *allographics*' that 'operates as a form of (perhaps post post-Marxist) ideology critique' (p. 2), lacks scholarly values and calls for the little boy who points out that the emperor has no clothes. Tom Cohen, *Ideology and Inscription: 'Cultural Studies' after Benjamin, de Man, and Bakhtin*, Cambridge, 1998.

11. Tihanov comments similarly of his own comparison of Bakhtin and Lukács: 'the comparison of [Bakhtin and Lukács] necessarily presupposed a selective redefinition and reconstitution of the objects of our attention: not Lukács as such, but the Lukács who emerges when placed next to Bakhtin; not Bakhtin on his own, but rather the Bakhtin who becomes visible only in the light of Lukács'. Galin Tihanov, *The Master and the Slave: Lukács, Bakhtin, and the Ideas of their Time*, Oxford, 2000, pp. 10–11. As Saussure put it, to an important extent, 'it is the viewpoint adopted that creates the object'. Ferdinand de Saussure, *Course in General Linguistics*, trans. Roy Harris, London, 1983, p. 8.

12. The entry appeared in volume 16 of the *Great Soviet Encyclopaedia* in 1929. See Wolfgang Kassack's textual analysis of its relationship to Benjamin's manuscript in *GS II*, pp. 1472–75. Benjamin's original text can be found in *GS II*, pp. 705–39, *SW II*, pp. 161–93.

13. Brandist and Tihanov have performed the task of discovering, reconstructing and elucidating the many sources and ideas that Bakhtin draws on: Bergson, Cassirer, Scheler, Simmel, Walzel, Marty and so forth. In the case of Brandist in particular, however, this can result in a reductionism that presents Bakhtin's thought as little more than an admittedly imaginative combination of these sources. Thus, taking one of many possible examples, in connection with Bakhtin's theory of laughter in the novel, Brandist demonstrates that Bakhtin's two main influences are Bergson and Cassirer. It is debatable whether his subsequent comments add anything to Bakhtin's theory of laughter other than a sophisticated and convincing argument that Bakhtin draws on Bergson and Cassirer. Craig Brandist, *The Bakhtin Circle: Philosophy, Culture and Politics*, London, 2002, pp. 126–28.

14. This is a frequent claim, made, for example, by Ewen. Frederick Ewen, *Bertolt Brecht: His Life, his Art, his Times*, New York, 1992, p. 224. Jameson is more circumspect: 'Brecht offered many definitions of this term [*Verfremdung*], which seems to have migrated from the "ostranenie" or "making-strange" of the Russian Formalists via any number of visits to Berlin by Soviet modernists like Eisenstein or Tretiakov.' Fredric Jameson, *Brecht and Method*, London, 1998, p. 39.

15. Whilst the relationship between the Bakhtin Circle's thought and Russian Formalism is a matter of debate, the Bakhtin Circle's critique of Formalism has, nevertheless, much in common with the object of its attack. See M. M. Bakhtin/P. N. Medvedev, *The Formal Method in Literary Scholarship: A Critical Introduction to Sociological Poetics* (1928), trans. Albert J. Wehrle, London, 1985. Morson and Emerson chart with great subtlety Bakhtin's complex dialogue with Formalism throughout Gary Saul Morson and Caryl Emerson, *Mikhail Bakhtin: Creation of a Prosaics*, Stanford CA, 1993.

16. As Adlam puts it: 'Bakhtin was given an enthusiastic welcome for ostensibly both anticipating and providing the means for a resolution of the impasses of structuralism and post-structuralism.' Carol Adlam, 'Critical Work on the Bakhtin Circle: A New Bibliographical Essay', in Ken Hirschkop and David Shepherd (eds), *Bakhtin and Cultural Theory*, 2nd edn, Manchester, 2001, pp. 241–65 (247). Kristeva's essay 'Word, Dialogue, Novel' brought a Bakhtinian perspective to the French (post)Structuralist theory of literary production as radical intertextuality, initiated by Roland Barthes. See Julia Kristeva, 'Word, Dialogue, Novel', in Toril Moi (ed.), *The Kristeva Reader*, Oxford, 1986, pp. 34–61. The position in which Bakhtin becomes a liberal alternative to and yet still an articulation of post-structuralist themes is expressed most clearly in the work of Michael Holquist and Katerina Clark. See Katerina Clark and Michael Holquist, *Mikhail Bakhtin*, London, 1984, and for the crudest example of this ideology at work, Michael Holquist, *Dialogism: Mikhail Bakhtin and his World*, London, 1990.

17. Eagleton, for example, finds in Benjamin's thought support for a Derridean theory of writing with a Marxist edge. See Eagleton, *Benjamin*. Eagleton takes Benjamin's notion of reading 'against the grain' as the title of his collection of essays, Terry Eagleton, *Against the Grain: Selected Essays 1975–1985*, London, 1986. This collection also contains an essay on Bakhtin. The most interesting Derridean appropriation of Benjamin is by Derrida himself. In his essay 'The Force of Law', Derrida turns his attention to Benjamin's 'Critique

of Violence', reading into it a conception of law as the deferral of divine judgement. See Jacques Derrida, 'Force of Law: The "mystical foundation of authority" ', in Drucilla Cornell, Michael Rosenfeld and David Gray Carlson (eds), *Deconstruction and the Possibility of Justice*, London, 1992, pp. 3–68. Brandist, without reference to Derrida, sees a similar conception of law in Bakhtin, and also points in passing to a similarity with Benjamin. See Craig Brandist, 'Law and the Genres of Discourse: The Bakhtin Circle's Theory of Language and the Phenomenology of Right', in Bostad, Brandist, Evensen and Faber (eds), *Bakhtinian Perspectives*, pp. 23–45, especially pp. 39–40. The area of jurisprudence (that Brandist has opened up for Bakhtin scholarship) is another area in which analogies between Bakhtin and Benjamin might usefully be followed up.

18. Voloshinov and Medvedev have exerted a profound influence on thinkers of the British left, such as Raymond Williams, Tony Bennett and, once again, Terry Eagleton. See Raymond Williams, *Marxism and Literature*, Oxford, 1977, and Tony Bennett, *Formalism and Marxism*, London, 1979.

19. Momme Brodersen, *Walter Benjamin: A Biography*, London, 1996, p. 4.

20. Tihanov discerns a certain 'anachronistic' aspect to Bakhtin in his discussion of Bakhtin's concept of 'seeing' in the work on the *Bildungsroman*. He notes that for Bakhtin 'seeing' remains something unproblematic, whereas for Benjamin – for example in the work on Baudelaire – the impact of modern experience problematizes the notion of 'seeing': 'thus Bakhtin entertains hopes which appear utopian and perhaps somewhat anachronistic in comparison with other approaches to the culture of seeing in the 1930s, for example Walter Benjamin's bitter premonition that, with the advance of modernity, the act of seeing itself becomes a focal point of contradictions rather than a means of disentangling them'. Tihanov, *Master and Slave*, p. 238.

21. Clark and Holquist comment: 'One of the many enigmas about Bakhtin is that he makes no mention in *Rabelais* of James Joyce's *Ulysses*, a book that might be described as a celebration of heteroglossia and of the body as well.' Clark and Holquist, *Bakhtin*, p. 317. Much literary-orientated Bakhtin scholarship makes an unacknowledged attempt to project Bakhtin into a far more modern world than that of Dostoevsky by engaging in Bakhtinian readings of modernist and post-modernist texts, as if, thereby, Bakhtin were being relocated in what should be his spiritual home. The theorist of postmodernism Linda Hutcheon is one such critic who enlists Bakhtin as a theorist of parody for a postmodernity which she defines in terms of the proliferation of parody. Linda Hutcheon, 'Modern Parody and Bakhtin', in Gary Saul Morson and Caryl Emerson (eds), *Rethinking Bakhtin: Extensions and Challenges*, Evanston IL, pp. 87–103.

22. Tihanov emphasizes the Hegelian element in Bakhtin's thought which previously had often remained obscured by scholars' preoccupation with Bakhtin's roots in neo-Kantianism. Tihanov also points to the tension between a sociological theory of the novel and a metaphysical, primarily Hegelian, theory of novelness that exists in Bakhtin's writings. See Tihanov, *Master and Slave*, especially, on this latter point, pp. 148–49.

23. Morson and Emerson comment: 'the most vulnerable side of dialogue, Bakhtin may have sensed, is its benevolence'. Morson and Emerson, *Bakhtin*,

pp. 469–70. My point here is that Benjamin's position highlights this side of Bakhtin particularly starkly.

24. Scholem's image of Benjamin, the melancholic, has been hugely influential. Gary Smith, in his introductory paragraph to the English publication of Gershom Scholem's 'Walter Benjamin and his Angel', claims that Scholem's biography is 'by far the most cited secondary source in the critical literature'. Gary Smith (ed.), *On Walter Benjamin: Critical Essays and Reflections*, London, 1988, p. 51. See Gershom Scholem, *Walter Benjamin. Die Geschichte einer Freundschaft*, Frankfurt/Main, 1975.

25. Scholem, 'Walter Benjamin and his Angel', in Smith (ed.), *On Walter Benjamin*, pp. 51–89 (86).

26. Leslie draws attention to the depoliticizing tendency of melancholic memory to 'fetishize the act of remembering and not the remembrance of acting'. Esther Leslie, *Walter Benjamin: Overpowering Conformism*, London, 2000, pp. 213–14.

27. Benjamin's review, 'Left-wing Melancholia', was so venomous that the *Frankfurter Zeitung*, which had commissioned it, refused to publish it. Benjamin's review concludes in an almost Nietzschean fashion: 'The rumbling in these lines certainly has more to do with flatulence than subversion. Constipation and melancholy have always gone together. But since the juices began to dry up in the body social, stuffiness meets us at every turn. Kästner's poems do not improve the air [*machen die Luft nicht besser*]' (*GS III* 283; *SW II* 426). This quotation, and particularly the pun in the last sentence, is an example of a Benjaminian joke.

28. One question that lends itself, however, only to speculation is the influence on Benjamin of his close friend, the conservative intellectual, Florens Christian Rang, and his theory of carnival. Rang's lecture of 1909, which Benjamin knew in manuscript form, develops a theory of carnival that, in its heavily Nietzschean tone, reads like a dark obverse to Bakhtin's thought. The key to Rang's conception of carnival is scornful laughter (*Hohngelächter*) which tears down spiritual hierarchies as the 'first blasphemy'. Carnival laughter is also, as in Bakhtin, a means of combating fear: in ancient carnival man got intoxicated 'until he finally did not take himself seriously; until he cast off his cares and the spectre became comical; he abandoned God, as well as the false God of being a good man; he drank away his fear with scorn and laughter'. Florens Christian Rang, 'Historische Psychologie des Karnevals', in Lorenz Jäger (ed.) *Karneval*, Berlin, 1983, pp. 7–45 (18).

29. Graeme Gilloch, *Walter Benjamin: Critical Constellations*, Cambridge, 2002, p. 159. Gilloch also points out that such laughter has nothing in common with the laughter of the entertainment industry. Adorno's criticisms of Benjamin's enthusiasm for popular cinema emerged, in part, from a view of the cruelty of laughter in popular culture: 'The laughter of the audience at a cinema [...] is anything but good and revolutionary; instead, it is full of the worst Sadism.' Theodor W. Adorno, 'Letters to Benjamin', trans. Harry Zohn, in Ernst Bloch *et al.*, *Aesthetics and Politics*, London, 1977, pp. 110–33 (123). Adorno may have in mind the violent buffoonery of early cinematic slapstick.

30. Benjamin's conception of barbaric laughter in 'Experience and Poverty' (1933) is similar in its effect: 'In its buildings, pictures, and stories, mankind

is preparing to outlive culture, if need be. And the main thing is that it does so with a laugh. This laughter may occasionally sound barbaric. Well and good. Let us hope that from time to time the individual will give a little humanity to the masses, who one day will repay him with compound interest' (*GS II* 219; *SW II* 735). Likewise, as well as seeing in Baudelaire an heir to Baroque melancholy, Benjamin also celebrates his 'satanic laughter' (*GS I* 680; *SW IV* 182).

31. Eagleton notes: 'the melancholy of Western Marxism, bred largely by a history of proletarian defeat, represents the massive loss of an essential dimension of historical materialism. No greater contrast in the annals of Marxist writing could be provided than that between Benjamin's *Theses on the Philosophy of History* and Mikhail Bakhtin's *Rabelais and his World*.' Eagleton, *Benjamin*, p. 144. Whilst persisting with the image of Benjamin, the melancholic, Eagleton nevertheless implies what a Bakhtinian standpoint of laughter can bring to our image of Benjamin.

32. The English translation of Bakhtin's work on Rabelais, *Rabelais and his World*, is of Bakhtin's *Tvorchestvo Fransua Rable i narodnaia kul'tura srednevekov'ia i renessansa* (The Art of François Rabelais and the Popular Culture of the Middle Ages) which was published in 1965. This was a revised version of a text composed during 1940–46 which had its basis in Bakhtin's doctoral dissertation. I shall refer to the book as 'the Rabelais book'.

33. Averintsev is healthily sceptical towards Bakhtin's claim in the Rabelais book that 'violence never lurks behind laughter', commenting: 'Is it true that violence never, ever lurks behind laughter? Well, violence seldom lurks behind laughter, but announces its presence through laughter at the top of its voice.' Sergei S. Averintsev, 'Bakhtin and the Russian Attitude to Laughter', in David Shepherd (ed.), *Bakhtin, Carnival and Other Subjects*, Special edition of *Critical Studies*, 3–4, 1993, pp. 13–19 (16). Bernstein also takes Bakhtin to task on this point, noting that 'in Rabelais it seems to me that we never respond to all the killings, maimings, humiliations and catastrophes as if they happened to human beings', implying that Bakhtin's reading of Rabelais contains a 'very un-Bakhtinian' indifference to the human. Michael André Bernstein, 'When the Carnival Turns Bitter: Reflections on the Abject Hero', in Gary Saul Morson (ed.), *Bakhtin: Essays and Dialogues on his Work*, London, 1986, pp. 99–121 (117).

34. Clark and Holquist, *Bakhtin*, p. 318.

35. Ibid., p. 320.

36. I am referring to the distinction made by Arendt. See Hannah Arendt, *On Revolution*, London, 1991. As quoted by Emerson, Sergei Averintsev, in his article, 'Bakhtin, smekh, khristianskaia kul'tura', in *Rossia/Russia*, 1988, 6, makes a similar point, also, it seems, drawing on this distinction: 'Laughter is always experienced as movement "from a certain unfreedom to a certain freedom," which is to say that laughter is "not freedom, but liberation." As such, there is an inevitable mechanical and involuntary aspect to it, the initiating gesture of a person who is not yet free.' Caryl Emerson, *The First Hundred Years of Mikhail Bakhtin*, Princeton NJ, 1997, p. 181.

37. Ruth Coates, *Christianity in Bakhtin: God and the Exiled Author*, Cambridge, 1998, p. 23.

38. M. M. Bakhtin, 'Dopolneniia i izmeneniia k Rable' (Additions and amendments to 'Rabelais'), in S. G. Bocharov and L. A. Gogotishvili (eds), *Sobranie sochinenii*, Vol. 5, Moscow, 1996, pp. 80–129 (81). Hirschkop discusses this distinction in Hirschkop, *Bakhtin*, pp. 275–78. In the Rabelais book, Bakhtin also approves of Greek tragedy which is fused with the 'spirit of creative destruction', and later genres of 'deep and pure, open seriousness' are likewise praised for being 'always ready to submit to death and renewal' (*Rabelais* 121–22).

39. There are two variants of this book, one from 1929 and one from 1963. Difficulties lie with the fact the published English translation of Bakhtin's Dostoevsky book, *Problems of Dostoevsky's Poetics*, is based on the revised edition of 1963 (*Problemy Poetiki Dostoevskogo*) with passages from the original 1929 edition (*Problemy tvorchestva Dostoevskogo*) included in an appendix. I refer to the text as 'the Dostoevsky book'. Emerson, the editor of the English translation, explains this mode of presentation and its curious rationale in a note in *DP*, p. 275. Tihanov carefully elucidates the divergences between the two versions in Tihanov, *Master and Slave*, pp. 207–15.

40. Karl Marx and Friedrich Engels, 'The Communist Manifesto' (1848), in David McClellan (ed.), *Karl Marx: Selected Writings*, Oxford, 1977, pp. 221–47 (224).

41. Aristotle, *The Poetics of Aristotle*, ed. and trans. Stephen Halliwell, London, 1987, p. 37.

42. Eagleton's comments, whilst inexact at the level of detail, intuit some of the lines of thought that are opened up when one considers Bakhtin and Benjamin together in terms of the commensurability of Marxism and theology: 'Nor can Bakhtin be merely appropriated as a materialist. It would now appear that behind his work lies a Judaeo-Christian mysticism in some ways akin to Benjamin's – that *Marxism and the Philosophy of Language* contains as its secret code a theological devotion to the incarnational unity of word and being similar to that which marks Benjamin's own mediations.' Eagleton, *Benjamin*, pp. 154–55.

43. Leslie's study of Benjamin, written from a hard-left position, exhibits an extraordinary will to push Benjamin's theological motifs to the sidelines. She only deals with Benjamin's writings after 1923–24 in order to discuss his thought only after what she discerns as the beginnings of his conversion to materialism. See Leslie, *Benjamin*. Likewise, Brandist's work on Bakhtin combines a denial of the existence of religious motifs in Bakhtin as anything more than rhetorical tropes with a tendency to play up those aspects of Bakhtin and his collaborators that share affinities with Marxism. See Brandist, *The Bakhtin Circle*, particularly, on what he sees as no more than religious terminology, pp. 23–24.

44. In the case of Benjamin, the work of Scholem, as already indicated, is an example of this. In the case of Bakhtin, one might note, in particular, the work of Mihailovic in which a focus on the incarnational origin of the word obscures the social and political import of Bakhtin's thought. See Alexandar Mihailovic, *Corporeal Words: Mikhail Bakhtin's Theology of Discourse*, Evanston IL, 1997.

45. According to Schmitt, all 'significant concepts of the modern theory of the state are secularized theological concepts'; thus the omnipotent God became the omnipotent lawgiver. It is only with the twin development of

Enlightenment rationalism – which banishes miracle – and the theory of the modern constitutional state – which seeks to curtail the power of the sovereign – that this underlying truth has been repressed. Carl Schmitt, *Political Theology* (1922), trans. George Schwab, Cambridge MA, 1985, p. 36. The notion of Israel as God's chosen people is the source of the close connection between theology and politics in Jewish thought.

46. One might suggest, with Münster, that the end of class struggle might be marked by a 'double happening both religious and political' in which the 'social revolution, as realization of the reign of liberty and suppression of universal alienation, necessarily coincides with the act of the redemption of humanity, of oppression, of exploitation and injustice'. Arno Münster, *Progrès et catastrophe: Walter Benjamin et l'histoire. Réflexions sur l'itinéraire philosophique d'un marxisme mélancolique*, Paris, 1996, p. 53.

47. Leslie, *Benjamin*, pp. 224–25.

48. See Jürgen Habermas, 'Walter Benjamin: Consciousness-Raising or Rescuing Critique', in Smith (ed.), *On Walter Benjamin*, pp. 90–128 (109).

49. Coates's arguments, for example, are persuasive, although I qualify some of them later. See the chapter, 'Was Bakhtin a Marxist?', in Coates, *Christianity in Bakhtin*, pp. 57–83.

1   Habit and tradition

1. Hirschkop starts his work of debunking Bakhtin legends in Ken Hirschkop, 'Bakhtin Myths, or Why we all need Alibis', *Bakhtin/'Bakhtin': Studies in the Archive and Beyond*, Special edition of *The South Atlantic Quarterly*, 97, 1998, 3–4, pp. 579–98 and continues in his *Bakhtin*, where he refers to the myth of the *Bildungsroman* text going up in smoke (p. 113). This enduring story about Bakhtin has even made its way into fiction in Paul Auster's *The New York Trilogy* and from there to Wayne Wang's film of 1995, *Smoke*, the screenplay also by Paul Auster. See Paul Auster, 'The Locked Room', *The New York Trilogy*, London, 1987, pp. 199–314 (254).

2. Hirschkop, *Bakhtin*, p. 113.

3. Clark and Holquist, *Bakhtin*, p. 336. Clark and Holquist refer to the importance of tea and cigarettes to Bakhtin with great frequency in their biography.

4. Clark and Holquist, *Bakhtin*, p. 1.

5. Morson and Emerson make a similar point in their comments on habit in Bakhtin: 'Because of mental habits, intellectual traditions, and centripetal cultural forces, we often lose a sense of the dialogic quality of an event. The live medium becomes dead. [...] Bakhtin uses a variety of terms for this deadening process. In his earliest writings, he calls it "transcription"; later, he speaks of "finalization" and "monologization", depending on which kind of loss concerns him.' Morson and Emerson, *Bakhtin*, p. 56.

6. Kant discusses the relationships between heteronomy and autonomy, natural necessity and moral freedom in the following words which may help us understand Bakhtin's ideas: 'Natural necessity was a heteronomy of efficient causes, since every effect was possible only in accordance with the law that something else determines the efficient cause to causality; what, then, can freedom of the will be other than autonomy, that is, the will's property

of being a law to itself? But the proposition, the will is in all its actions a law to itself, indicates only the principle, to act on no other maxim than that which can also have as object itself as a universal law. This, however, is precisely the formula of the categorical imperative and is the principle of morality; hence, a free will and a will under moral laws are one and the same.' Immanuel Kant, *Groundwork of the Metaphysics of Morals* (1785), ed. and trans. Mary Gregor, Cambridge, 1998, pp. 52–53.

7. The reference is to Kant's formulation in Immanuel Kant, *The Critique of the Power of Judgement* (1790), ed. Paul Guyer, trans. Eric Matthews, Cambridge, 2000, pp. 111–13.

8. On the connection between beauty and morality, see section 59, 'On Beauty as a Symbol of Morality', in Kant, *The Critique of the Power of Judgement*, pp. 225–28.

9. Willem van Reijen and Herman van Doorn, *Aufenthalte und Passagen: Leben und Werk Walter Benjamins*, Frankfurt/Main, 2001.

10. Theodor W. Adorno, 'Benjamin the Letter Writer', in Smith (ed.), *On Walter Benjamin*, Cambrige, 1991, pp. 329–37 (330–31).

11. Jameson has discerned in Benjamin's writings on modern art an underlying emphasis on the habit and the 'rhythm of recurrences'. For Jameson, the ability to synthesize habit in the midst of modern disorder and create the appearance of familiarity is a hallmark of Benjamin's artistic heroes. See Jameson, *Marxism and Form*, pp. 63–64. In life, like Bakhtin, Benjamin was smoker. As one of his aphorisms has it: 'If the smoke from my cigarette and the ink from the nib of my pen flowed with equal ease, I should be in the Arcadia of writing' (*GS IV* 112–13; *SW I* 263). Benjamin was punctiliously observant of the rituals of politeness. Lisa Fittko, a German refugee who accompanied Benjamin on the trek over the Pyrenees to Port-Bou, the site of his suicide, gives her account of Benjamin's last days: ' "*Gnädige Frau*," he said, "please accept my apologies for this inconvenience." The world was coming apart, I thought, but not Benjamin's *politesse*.' Lisa Fittko, 'The Story of Old Benjamin', in *GS V*, pp. 1184–94 (1185), in English in the original.

12. Henceforth, referred to in the text as 'The Work of Art'. See my comments below on the versions of this text and their dates.

13. Howard Caygill, *Walter Benjamin: The Colour of Experience*, London, 1998, p. 26.

14. I am using a periodization of Bakhtin's works that consists of an early stage (*Toward a Philosophy of the Act*, 'Author and Hero in Aesthetic Activity'), a substantial middle stage (the Dostoevsky book, the essays on the novel, the Rabelais book) and a late stage (represented by the texts collected in *Speech Genres*). Morson and Emerson's *Bakhtin* analyses in great detail the question of periodization in Bakhtin's work and is a useful guide.

15. The first version of 'The Work of Art' was published in the journal of the Institute for Social Research in 1936. At Horkheimer's instigation from the institute's headquarters in New York, Benjamin's text was significantly altered by the toning-down of its overtly Marxist terminology. The second version of 'The Work of Art' represents the version in which Benjamin intended to see the essay published. The third version, widely known because of its inclusion in collections of Benjamin's essays after his death, was composed

in either in the spring of 1936 or April 1939. It reflects Adorno's criticisms and comments. My references are to this third version.

16. Bakhtin comments: 'The novel, after all, has no canon of its own. It is, by its very nature, not canonic. It is plasticity itself' (*DI* 39). Todorov notes that Bakhtin's description of the novel amounts, in this sense, to a 'contradiction of the very notion of genre'. He also points out Bakhtin's debt in this conception of the novel as the modern anti-genre to the early German Romantics and to Friedrich Schlegel in particular. Tsvetan Todorov, *Mikhail Bakhtin: The Dialogical Principle*, trans. Wlad Godzich, Minneapolis MN, 1984, p. 86. Tihanov makes the similar comment that the novel's 'generic identity is paradoxically couched in terms of non-identity and constant modification'. Tihanov, *Master and Slave*, p. 145.

17. Ken Hirschkop, 'A Response to the Forum on Mikhail Bakhtin', in Morson (ed.), *Bakhtin: Essays and Dialogues*, pp. 73–79 (76).

18. Susan Buck-Morss, *The Origin of Negative Dialectics*, New York, 1977, pp. 160–61.

19. I discuss this in detail in the final chapter.

20. Tihanov notes the problem in Bakhtin's analysis, of the historical place of Dostoevsky, that arises from Bakhtin's identification of *both* monologism and dialogism as expressions of modernity: 'Rather than appear as the product of specific capitalist developments affecting the fate of a particular class in Russia, Dostoevsky's *oeuvre* now has to be interpreted as the rejection of an all-pervasive and vague cultural pattern.' Tihanov, *Master and Slave*, p. 194.

21. Russian reference to M. M. Bakhtin, *Problemy Poetiki Dostoevskogo*, Moscow, 1972, p. 465.

22. This image makes one think of the opening scenes of Fritz Lang's 1927 film, *Metropolis*, in which a group of workers stand in front of an enormous machine, pulling levers. As the machine speeds up, the workers are forced to jerk their limbs faster and faster. Eventually, an accident occurs and many of the workers are killed. From the point of view of the hero of the film, who witnesses the events, the machine is transformed into the face of a giant monster, which the hero identifies with the Semitic god Moloch, and which devours the workers in the fiery furnace which it has in place of a mouth. There is no evidence that Benjamin saw this film. More directly, Benjamin may draw here on Lukácsian themes of reification and its impact on consciousness. See Georg Lukács, 'Reification and the Consciousness of the Proletariat', trans. Rodney Livingston, in *History and Class Consciousness* (1923), London, 1971, pp. 83–222. Benjamin brings to Lukács's ideas, however, an extra insight into the impact of commodity production on physical experience. Leslie gives a detailed analysis of Benjamin's use of Lukács's concept of reification and Marx's concept of commodity fetishism (the source on which Lukács draws) in Leslie, *Benjamin*, especially pp. 8–10 and 105–16. She also notes Benjamin's treatment of the effect of reification on the body: 'The body annihilated, petrified, subjected to attack, deformed by war weaponry, the body as alien, the skin of the self hardening, inorganic matter. A thing: such images litter Benjamin's work. This person under onslaught is a person subject to commodification.' p. 9.

23. In this essay, 'Experience and Poverty', Benjamin opposes the cluttered bourgeois interior, stuffed full of *collected* objects, to the Modernist glass building of Loos and Le Corbusier that is more exterior than interior and whose functional minimalism is hostile to the collecting of objects.

24. Stoessel comments on Benjamin's formulation that the aura is 'die einmalige Erscheinung einer Ferne so nah sie sein mag' (the unique appearance of a distance no matter how close it may be), noting that the word *einmalig* contains a number of senses: '*Einmalig* has a double meaning: the appearance of aura does not last, and it is unrepeatable [...]. It is independent of the conscious will of the subject. What appears may well appear again, but it cannot be captured by the subject or be consciously conjured up again.' Marleen Stoessel, *Aura: Das vergessene Menschliche: Zu Sprache und Erfahrung bei Walter Benjamin*, Munich, 1983, p. 47, quoted in Charles W. Haxthausen, 'Reproduction/Repetition: Walter Benjamin/Carl Einstein, in *October*, 107, 2004, pp. 47–74 (54). This is another way in which the aura exerts power over the perceiver.

25. Mieszkowski's comments are useful in elucidating the point that Benjamin is making, but does not elaborate on in great detail, about social and political hierarchies of perception: 'Benjamin describes an encounter with the authority that the work's presence acquires from its position in the highly ritualized network that organizes models of tradition and cultural heritage. [...] In these terms, the experience of the authenticity of the work of art is as much a factor of how the presence of the work is framed or situated as it is an immediate experience of that presence; it is in essence a social experience, and for this reason is always open to a political cooption over which the individual viewer may have little control.' Jan Mieszkowski, 'Art forms', in David S. Ferris, *The Cambridge Companion to Walter Benjamin*, Cambridge, 2004, pp. 35–53 (39–40).

26. Whilst Benjamin notes that tradition may be 'itself thoroughly alive and extremely changeable' (*GS I* 480; *SW IV* 256), in auratic transmission, the 'authenticity of a thing' and its 'historical testimony' remain untouched (*GS I* 477; *SW IV* 254).

27. This notion is closely related to the defamiliarization/*Verfremdungseffekt* of the Formalists and Brecht.

28. As Taussig puts it, through the opening of the optical unconscious 'we become aware of patterns and necessities that had previously ruled our lives'. Michael Taussig, *Mimesis and Alterity: A Particular History of the Senses*, London, 1993, p. 25.

29. The importance that Benjamin lends to distraction is evidence of his debt to Brecht's theory of epic theatre. Compare Benjamin's 'What is Epic Theatre' with Bertolt Brecht, 'Das moderne Theater ist das epische Theater', in *Schriften zum Theater*, Frankfurt/Main, 1977, pp. 13–28.

30. Benjamin comments of the world of storytelling where those who listen are also those who retell: 'the more self-forgetful the listener is, the more deeply is what he listens to impressed upon his memory' (*GS II* 447; *SW III* 149).

31. So Wolin: 'The exuberant acceptance of the process whereby traditional aesthetic genres are sacrificed to the all-encompassing onslaught of rationalization, characteristic of "The Work of Art" essay, a process credited with opening up tremendous, heretofore untapped possibilities for the political

employment of art, is a sentiment totally absent from "The Storyteller". In the Leskov essay, Benjamin has come round to a diametrically opposite assessment of this trend.' Richard Wolin, *Walter Benjamin: An Aesthetic of Redemption*, London, Berkeley CA, 1994, p. 224.

32. Gilloch makes remarks that point to this sense of the term 'possession' in Benjamin's thought. See Gilloch, *Benjamin*, pp. 183–84.

33. Eiland comments: 'The opposition now would seem to be between *mere* distraction and, shall we say, productive distraction – between distraction as a skewing of attention, or as an abandonment to diversion, and distraction as a spur to new ways of perceiving.' Howard Eiland, 'Reception in Distraction', in Andrew Benjamin (ed.), *Benjamin and Art*, pp. 3–13 (9).

34. Taussig, *Mimesis and Alterity*, p. 25.

35. In the context of a discussion of Marx's aesthetics, Eagleton provides a useful insight into what might be meant by this sort of 'body politics': 'Marx is most profoundly "aesthetic" in his belief that the exercise of human senses, powers and capacities is an absolute end in itself, without need of utilitarian justification; but the unfolding of this sensuous richness for its own sake can be achieved, paradoxically, only through the rigorously instrumental practice of overthrowing bourgeois social relations. Only when the bodily drives have been released from the despotism of abstract need, and the object has been similarly restored from functional abstraction to sensuously particular use-value, will it be possible to live aesthetically.' Terry Eagleton, *The Ideology of the Aesthetic*, Oxford, 1990, p. 202. Benjamin's point reverses the chain of causes: bodily innervation is itself a necessary source of revolutionary energy. Hitchcock uses Eagleton's reading of Marx's aesthetic politics to argue for the political and materialist orientation of Bakhtin's aesthetics in Peter Hitchcock, 'The World according to Globalization and Bakhtin', in Brandist and Tihanov (eds), *Materializing Bakhtin*, pp. 3–19 (10– 13). The point of convergence between Bakhtin and Benjamin on this matter might be that both think that aesthetics and politics must fully integrate the body.

36. There is an echo here of Erasmus' epigram in the *Diliculum*: 'Clavus clavo pellitur, consuetudo consuetudine vincitur' (one nail is driven out by another nail; habit is overcome by habit).

37. In the context of a discussion of Benjamin's theory of mimesis, Leslie suggests a precedent for Benjamin's theory of different sorts of imitation: 'In the *Kritik der Urteilskraft* Kant makes a distinction between two types of imitation: "nachfolgen" and "nachahmen". The first type of imitation is creative, the second merely reproductive.' Leslie, *Benjamin*, p. 117. This concept may also be a precedent for Bakhtin's and Benjamin's ideas of repetition. There are also echoes of Bakhtin and Benjamin in the later French tradition. In their attitude to repetition, Bakhtin and Benjamin reveal a proximity to both Jacques Lacan and Gilles Deleuze. As Weber comments of Lacan: 'The processes studied by psychoanalysis almost always involve repetition, not however as a return of the same, in any simple sense, but rather as the recurrence of a difference separating that which is repeated from its repetition.' Samuel Weber, *Return to Freud: Jacques Lacan's Dislocation of Psychoanalysis*, Cambridge, 1991, p. 5. Lacan understands his own 'retour' to Freud as a repetition that produces difference. Similarly, Deleuze consistently argues that

difference and repetition are linked in their hostility to the notion of identity. See Ronald Bogue, *Deleuze and Guattari*, London, 1989, pp. 45–80. One might argue that Bakhtin, Benjamin and Deleuze coincide in their resistance to the hegemony of identity.

38. The extreme poles of Benjamin's thought are to be found in the study of Goethe's *Wahlverwandtschaften* (composed 1919–22) and in the essay 'Experience and Poverty'. In the former, Benjamin argues that the destruction of tradition does not result in emancipation and a clearer vision of the world, but rather in new forms of blindness: 'Where does their freedom lead those who act in such a manner [who break with tradition]? Far from opening new perspectives for them, it blinds them to the reality that inhabits their fears' (*GS I* 132; *SW I* 303). In the latter, Benjamin asks us, in the words of Brecht's slogan, to 'Erase the traces!' as part of a new Barbarism.

39. Arendt neatly expresses the relationship between tradition and authority: 'In so far as the past has been transmitted as tradition, it possesses authority; in so far as authority presents itself historically, it becomes tradition.' Hannah Arendt, Introduction, in Walter Benjamin, *Illuminations*, trans. Harry Zohn, London, 1992, pp. 9–55 (43).

40. John McCole, *Walter Benjamin and the Antinomies of Tradition*, London, Ithaca NY, 1993, p. 2.

41. This second form of tradition is what Düttmann describes when he states that 'a tradition which would have already set its standards once for all time would be one which delivered itself to oblivion'. Alexander Garcia Düttmann, 'Tradition and Destruction: Walter Benjamin's Politics of Language', in Andrew Benjamin and Peter Osborne (eds), *Walter Benjamin's Philosophy: Destruction and Experience*, London: Routledge, 1994, pp. 32–58 (45). Düttmann's article discusses Benjamin's conception of destruction and tradition in relation to the essays 'On Language as Such and on the Language of Man' and 'The Work of Art' and with a particular focus on the fight against fascism. He also sets these themes into the context of a discussion of the ideas of Jacques Derrida and Maurice Blanchot.

42. Hirschkop comments: 'The problem with authority, so far as Bakhtin is concerned, is not that it shuts people up, presents the false as true, or imposes an otherwise neutral language on downtrodden subjects; the problem with authority or power is that it distorts the natural intersubjectivity of language, giving us meaning without voices.' Hirschkop, *Bakhtin*, p. 87.

43. Benjamin's materialism is, nevertheless, far from convincing and certainly not very dialectical or orthodoxly Marxist. Criticisms of this kind form an important part of Adorno's approach to Benjamin's writings on Baudelaire in the Adorno/Benjamin correspondence, 1936–38. The key letters of the exchange are collected in Bloch *et al.*, *Aesthetics and Politics*, pp. 110–14. Nägele has made a careful analysis of Benjamin's materialism in relation to the Adornian negative dialectics of the Frankfurt School and Brechtian method, conducted largely through a biographical prism. Rainer Nägele, 'Body Politics: Benjamin's Dialectical Materialism between Brecht and the Frankfurt School', in Ferris (ed.), *Companion to Benjamin*, Cambridge, 2004, pp. 152–76.

44. Speaking of these two forces, Tihanov comments: 'Bakhtin never attaches a clearly defined social group or class to either force, any more than he

presents the concrete historical dynamics of this conflict, and this makes for the metaphysical resonance of his account.' Tihanov, *Master and Slave*, p. 143.

45. Geulen has argued against an understanding of 'The Work of Art' as a piece that describes a materialistically and technologically determined process, reading it instead as a programmatic piece: 'One ought to view the text less as a *description* than as the *production* of a crisis in art. The essay on the work of art is not a descriptive text, not an analysis of the status quo. Rather its theses are themselves the result of that which, in a purely thematic perspective, appears to be its program.' Eva Geulen, 'Under Construction: Walter Benjamin's "The Work of Art in the Age of Mechanical Reproduction"', in Richter (ed.), *Benjamin's Ghosts*, pp. 121–41 (123). Hirschkop discerns a similar oscillation between description and prescription in Bakhtin's theory of dialogue, as I note later. Leslie has also argued strongly against what she terms a 'techno-determinist' reading of Benjamin. Her arguments, based on the distinction that Benjamin makes in the second version of the essay between a 'first' and 'second' *Technik*, are convincing. Nevertheless, the *appearance* of material and technological determination, which undoubtedly exists in Benjamin, continues to set him apart from the *appearance* of metaphysics in Bakhtin. See Leslie, *Benjamin*, pp. 161–62.

46. The simultaneity of montage is another variant of Benjamin's notion of 'dialectic at a standstill'. Andrew Benjamin treats Benjamin's notion of simultaneity and his 'opening of the present' in Andrew Benjamin, 'Time and Task: Benjamin and Heidegger showing the Present', in Andrew Benjamin and Osborne (eds), *Benjamin's Philosophy*, pp. 216–50. I return to this theme in the final chapter. The spatialization of time that is treated by both Benjamin and Bakhtin is also an important feature of avant-garde poetics, since it is both a revision of tradition and a site for the reformulation of the subject. The founding gesture of simultaneity as an aesthetic principle is perhaps Apollinaire's 'Zone' where 'même les automobiles ont l'air d'être anciennes'. Guillaume Apollinaire, 'Zone' (1913), in *Alcools*, London, 1993, pp. 39–44 (39).

47. Osborne also notes the similar temporal and spatial logic of the novel and of montage: 'And if, as Bakhtin argued, all literary genres have increasingly been subject to novelization as a process of linguistic familiarization and the creation of a certain semantic open-endedness, so, we might argue, all genres of communication (including the novel) have subsequently been subject to cinematization, the logic of montage and the image, and an intensification of that "revolution in the hierarchy of times" whereby "the present becomes the center of human orientation in time and in the world", which Bakhtin associated with the novel.' Peter Osborne, *The Politics of Time: Modernity and Avant-Garde*, London, 1995, p. 197. Leslie tacitly points to an affinity between Benjamin's theory of montage and Bakhtin, as well as noting that montage is an assault on habit. She writes: 'Two seemingly dissimilar things, word and image, are forced together in a montage, clashing and dialogically relaying back and forth. [...] This unfamiliar perspective [of montage], as imagined by the Russian constructivists, freezes the real, protecting it from habit and alienating the alienated.' Leslie, *Benjamin*, p. 60.

48. This is despite Benjamin's scathing assertion in *One-Way Street* that 'the critic has nothing in common with the interpreter of past cultural epochs' (*GS IV* 108; *SW I* 460).

49. What Tihanov terms Bakhtin's 'metageneric' theory of the novel, that comes to dominate in the 1963 version of the Dostoevsky book, is, with its historical and sociological vagueness, something of a straw man. See Tihanov, *Master and Slave*, pp. 209–15.

50. See Umberto Eco, *Foucault's Pendulum*, trans. William Weaver, London, 1990.

51. Benjamin, with the Romantics, seems to assert that criticism stands prior to literature. In this recognition, Benjamin and the German Romantics pre-empt the reversal of the traditional prioritization of author and critic by French thinkers such as Roland Barthes, whose 'birth of the reader' might better be glossed as the 'birth of the critic' who makes the *scriptible* text possible. See Roland Barthes, 'La Mort de l'auteur', in *Le Bruissement de la langue: Essais critiques IV*, Paris, 1984, pp. 63–69.

52. As Comay comments of Schlegel (on whose thought Benjamin draws heavily for his conception of criticism): 'For Schlegel, the "essence of critique" is to link history and philosophy through the reconstruction, reinterpretation, and retransmission of lost, damaged, incomplete, inaccessible or otherwise absent (neglected, unread, unreadable) objects.' Rebecca Comay, 'Benjamin and the Ambiguities of Romanticism', in Ferris, *Companion to Benjamin*, pp. 134–51 (140).

53. One can compare this position to Benjamin's comments: 'The survival of artworks should be represented from the standpoint of the struggle for existence. Their true humanity consists in their unlimited adaptability' (*GS VII* 678; *SW III* 141).

54. It is possible to discern here the influence of late Formalist theories of literary evolution and their notion that great works' survival through time can be attributed to their formal complexity which enables repeated processes of deautomatization. See J. N. Tynjanov, 'On Literary Evolution' (1927), in Ladislav Matejka and Krystyna Pomorska (eds), *Readings in Russian Poetics: Formalist and Structuralist Views*, Cambridge MA, 1971, pp. 66–78. Bakhtin is particularly close here to Czech Structuralism and Mukařovský's notion of the renewal of the literary series. See Jan Mukařovský, 'Estetická funkce, norma a hodnota jako sociální fakty', in *Studie I*, ed. Miroslav cervenka and Milan Jankovič, Brno, 2000, pp. 81–148. Many areas of connection between Bakhtin and Mukařovský still need to be fully explored, Mukařovský's conception of dialogue not least among them. Holquist's brief treatment of the matter thoroughly misrepresents Mukařovský's thought for the sake of preserving what he presents as the unique brilliance of Bakhtin. See Holquist, *Dialogism*, pp. 57–59. Bakhtin's 'Response', however, should also be seen as a contemporary engagement with the Structuralism of the Tartu School.

55. Benjamin describes criticism as 'another, if a lesser, factor in the continued life of literary works' (*GS IV* 15; *SW I* 256). His comments on the translations of the Romantics in this essay point back to 'The Concept of Criticism in German Romanticism'.

56. It is here that Bakhtin and Benjamin depart, at least in emphasis, from the late Formalist and Czech Structuralist view of literary evolution which,

whilst arguing that the semantic and structural complexity of great works is an important factor in their capacity for artistic survival, tends to put greater emphasis on the historical and social context of reception as the necessary background for re-defamiliarization. Nevertheless, Mukařovský again comes close to Bakhtin's and Benjamin's position. In his work of the 1940s, Mukařovský rehabilitates the notion of intentionality in (Czech) Structuralist literary history, thereby diminishing what had previously been seen as the overriding importance of the context of reception. Jan Mukařovský, 'Záměrnost a nezáměrnost v umění', in *Studie I*, pp. 353–88.

2   Experience

1. Georg Wilhelm Friedrich Hegel, *Elements of the Philosophy of Right*, ed. Allen W. Wood, trans. H. B. Nisbet, Cambridge, 1991, p. 161.
2. Hegel, *Philosophy of Right*, p. 195.
3. Ibid.
4. Hegel's distinction between *Sittlichkeit* and *Gewöhnlichkeit* is comparable to the distinction that I have introduced in the previous chapter between integrated and alienated habit.
5. '*Gemeinschaft* [community] should be understood as a living organism, *Gesellschaft* [society] as a mechanical aggregate and artefact.' Friedrich Tönnies, *Community and Association*, trans. Charles P. Loomis, London, 1955, p. 39.
6. See, for example, Max Weber, 'Science as Vocation' (1917), in ed. and trans. H. H. Gerth and C. Wright Mills, *From Max Weber: Essays in Sociology*, London, 1991, pp. 129–56.
7. For details of this and of Benjamin's youthful admiration for Simmel, see Brodersen, *Benjamin*, p. 46.
8. Smith argues for the substantial influence of Simmel on Benjamin in Gary Smith, 'Thinking through Benjamin: An Introductory Essay', in Gary Smith (ed.), *Benjamin: Philosophy, History, Aesthetics*, London, 1983, pp. vii–xlii (xxxii).
9. Susan Buck-Morss, *Dialectics of Seeing: Walter Benjamin and the Arcades Project*, London, Cambridge MA, 1989, pp. 71–72.
10. See Benjamin's use of Simmel's comments on fashion in *The Arcades Project* in *GS V*, p. 127; *AP*, pp. 76–77.
11. Adorno criticizes this aspect of 'Paris of the Second Empire in Baudelaire', pointing out that the essay 'not entirely by accident uses a quotation from Simmel'. Adorno, 'Letters to Benjamin', p. 129. The quotation survives Adorno's criticism and reappears in the text of 'On Some Motifs in Baudelaire' as published by the Institute of Social Research (*GS I* 539–40; *SW IV* 19–20). Benjamin's vigorous response to Adorno provides an interesting suggestion that, despite the distance between Simmel and Marx, Simmel's thought could be rescued for the purposes of leftist cultural politics: 'You look askance at Simmel: might it not be time to respect him as one of the ancestors of cultural bolshevism [*Kulturbolshevismus*]?' (*Briefe* 808). Benjamin, nevertheless, seems to have taken on board some of Adorno's criticisms of Simmel. In his encyclopaedia article on 'Jews in German

Culture', Benjamin makes the following, in general negative, assessment: 'His characteristic dialectic is employed in the service of *Lebensphilosophie* and attempts a form of psychological impressionism which devotes itself – in a fashion that is hostile to systematic thought – to the analysis of the being [*Wesenserkenntnis*] of particular mental [*geistiger*] phenomena and tendencies' (*GS II* 810). Frisby suggests that Adorno's hostility to Simmel's writing may have stemmed from the fact that the essayistic form of Simmel's writing, which Benjamin highlights in the above passage, might have been 'rather too close to that of Adorno's'. David Frisby, *Simmel*, London, 1992, p. 148. The tendency of writers of the left either to criticize Benjamin for his association with Simmel or to minimize this association persists. Leslie all but ignores Simmel's influence, despite the fact that at its heart is a study of Benjamin's treatment of commodity capitalism, an area where, as I have argued, Simmel's influence is unmistakable. Simmel receives only two references, one of which refers to him, in passing, disparagingly as 'the money-critic Georg Simmel'. Leslie, *Benjamin*, p. 9.

12. Tihanov and Brandist are foremost amongst these critics. See Tihanov, *Master and Slave*, and Brandist, *The Bakhtin Circle*. See also Greg Nielsen, 'Looking Back on the Subject: Mead and Bakhtin on Reflexivity and the Political', in Brandist and Tihanov (eds), *Materializing Bakhtin*, London, 2000, pp. 142–63 (161–62). Bonetskaia also treats the connection between Simmel and Bakhtin. Natal'ia Bonetskaia, 'Bakhtin's Aesthetics as a Logic of Form', in David Shepherd (ed.), *The Contexts of Bakhtin: Philosophy, Authorship, Aesthetics*, Amsterdam, 1998, pp. 83–94. Vorokhov seems to have been one of the first to have treated the connection. P. N. Vorokhov, 'M. M. Bakhtin i G. Zimmel', in N. I. Voronina *et al.* (eds), *M. M. Bakhtin i gumanitarnoe myshlenie na poroge XXI veka*, 2 vols, Précis from the Third Saransk International Bakhtin Readings, 1995, referred to in Emerson, *The First Hundred Years*, p. 213.

13. See Michael F. Bernard-Donals, *Mikhail Bakhtin: Between Phenomenology and Marxism*, Cambridge, 1994, especially pp. 18–46. Clark and Holquist's substantial biographical study, *Bakhtin*, pays attention to neo-Kantianism, especially pp. 57–61, but does not mention Simmel or *Lebensphilosophie*. In a similar vein, Roberts speaks of 'Bakhtin's early "neo-Kantian" period'. Matthew Roberts, 'Poetics Hermeneutics Dialogics: Bakhtin and Paul de Man', in Morson and Emerson (eds), *Rethinking Bakhtin*, Evanston IL, 1989, pp. 115–34 (118).

14. *MPL*, p. 39. I analyse Voloshinov's use of Simmel in the next chapter.

15. *Logos* was published simultaneously in Russian and German editions in Tübingen and Moscow. Hirschkop notes that it had on its joint editorial board figures such as Husserl, Weber, F. F. Zelinsky, Peter Struve and Heinrich Rickert, and that it published, amongst other things, articles by Simmel and Husserl's 'Philosophy as a Strict Science'. The appearance of articles by Simmel and Husserl in a journal that was meant to be an organ of neo-Kantianism displays the dialogue and convergence of neo-Kantianism, *Lebensphilosophie* and phenomenology at the time. See Hirschkop, *Bakhtin*, p. 100.

16. See Bonetskaia, 'Bakhtin's Aesthetics', p. 94.

17. None the less, as Léger points out, Simmel sees the tragedy of culture as a result not merely of modernity but also as an epistemological constant as a

result of the transformation – exacerbated by the conditions of modernity, nevertheless – that life undergoes when it creates a cultural value. See François Léger, *La Pensée de Georg Simmel*, Paris, 1989, p. 326. This process, however, is an eternal phenomenon. Simmel's ahistoricism here is the target of Adorno's criticism.

18. Georg Simmel, 'Die Gross-Städte und das Geistesleben', in *Das Individuum und die Freiheit*, ed. Michael Landmann and Margarete Susman, Frankfurt/Main, 1993, pp. 192–204 (202). See also Georg Simmel, 'Der Begriff und die Tragödie der Kultur', in *Aufsätze und Abhandlungen 1909–1918, Gesamtausgabe* Vol. 12, ed. Otthein Rammstedt, Frankfurt/Main, 2001, pp. 194–223.

19. In essence, Simmel transfers to the sphere of culture and history the Kantian dualism of subject and object.

20. Simmel, 'Die Gross-Städte', p. 203.

21. Kai Hammermeister, *The German Aesthetic Tradition*, Cambridge, 2002, p. 161. Here, we may also consider the figure of Nietzsche. In his authoritative study, Schacht argues that Nietzsche is perhaps best understood as one of the inaugurators of *Lebensphilosophie*. Richard Schacht, *Nietzsche*, London, 1983, p. 531. Nietzsche's image of the world as a state of flux in which tendencies to coagulation contend with the dynamism of the will-to-power stands in close proximity to the themes of this chapter. Amongst the many of Nietzsche's ideas that would also be relevant to this chapter are his criticism of mechanism and causalism and his treatment of Kant in *The Will to Power* (notes from the 1880s, published posthumously), and the distinction between Apollonian art of image and form and Dionysian art of direct experience and intoxication in *The Birth of Tragedy* (1872). See Friedrich Nietzsche, *The Will to Power*, ed. and trans. Walter Kaufmann and R. J. Hollingdale, New York, 1968, and Friedrich Nietzsche, *The Birth of Tragedy*, ed. Michael Tanner, trans. Shaun Whiteside, London, 1993.

22. Sandywell comments: 'One reaction to [the] totalization [of objective culture] is the revolt against form as such and the reversion to an imaginary state of formlessness – leading Simmel to the resigned conclusion that formlessness was itself the appropriate form of modernity.' This statement is something of a caricature but captures well the opposition of form and culture and formlessness and life. Sandywell, 'Memories of Nature', p. 96.

23. 'Experience consists in the synthetic connection of appearances (perceptions) in a consciousness, in so far as this connection is necessary.' Furthermore, necessity is a concept that pertains only to *a priori* knowledge. Immanuel Kant, 'Prolegomena to any Future Metaphysics' (1783), in *Prolegomena to any Future Metaphysics with Selections from the Critique of Pure Understanding*, ed. and trans. Gary Hatfield, Cambridge, 1997, pp. 3–137 (58).

24. Kant, 'Prolegomena', pp. 53–54.

25. See Immanuel Kant, *Critique of Pure Reason* (1781), ed. Vasilis Politis, trans. J. M. Meiklejohn, London, 1993, p. 165.

26. Any tendencies in Kant to abstraction do not occlude the importance of empirical perception. As Köhnke notes: 'Kant indicates again and again that every act of the subject in the process of cognition can only be effectual through an actual application to real or in the event thinkable experience.'

Klaus Christian Köhnke, *The Rise of Neo-Kantianism: German Academic Philosophy between Idealism and Positivism*, Cambridge, 1991, p. 181.

27. Kant, 'Prolegomena', p. 58.

28. The basic dualism from which the opposition of *Erlebnis* and *Erfahrung* proceeds is Kant's distinction between concepts and sensible representations or intuitions. See J. Michael Young, 'Functions of Thought and the Synthesis of Intuitions', in Paul Guyer (ed.), *The Cambridge Companion to Kant*, Cambridge, 1992, pp. 101–22.

29. For details of Hegel's rejection of Kantian dualism, see Paul Guyer, 'Absolute Idealism and the Rejection of Kantian Dualism', in Karl Ameriks (ed.), *The Cambridge Companion to German Idealism*, Cambridge, 2000, pp. 37–56. Fichte's *Wissenschaftslehre* (1794), with its doctrine of the absolute ego which includes, through reflection, both self and not-self, is an equally important moment in the rejection of the Kantian bifurcation of experience that is influential for the early Benjamin. See Johann Gottlieb Fichte, *The Science of Knowledge*, ed. and trans. Peter Heath and John Lachs, Cambridge, 1982.

30. Rousseau's influence was also important. Rousseau had argued that the transition from the happy state of nature to a state of inequality and servitude is made possible only by the development of calculation and abstraction, particularly through the invention of language. A theory of experience constructed on the basis of Rousseau's thinking here bears strong similarities to the position of *Lebensphilosophie*. See Jean-Jacques Rousseau, 'A Discourse on the Origin of Inequality' (1754), in *The Social Contract and Discourses*, ed. P. D. Jimack, trans. G. D. H. Cole, London: Everyman, 1993, pp. 31–126 (63–70). Rousseau's revolutionary investigation of his own inner experience in the *Confessions* had a profound influence on Dilthey.

31. Wilhelm Dilthey, *Poetry and Experience: Selected Works* (1906), Vol. 5, ed. Rudolf A. Makkreel and Frithjof Rodl, Princeton NJ, 1996.

32. See Edmund Husserl, 'Philosophy and the Crisis of European Man' (1935), in *Phenomenology and the Crisis of Philosophy*, trans. Quentin Lauer, New York, 1965, pp. 149–92. Husserl's objections to Kant are similar to those raised by Bakhtin that I discuss below. 'According to Kant, transcendental subjectivity is a transpersonal abstractly deduced principle of justification, whereas for Husserl it is a concrete and finite subject.' Dan Zahavi, *Husserl's Phenomenology*, Stanford CA, 2003, p. 108.

33. Martin Jay, 'Experience without a Subject: Walter Benjamin and the Novel', in Laura Marcus and Lynda Nead, *The Actuality of Walter Benjamin*, London, 1998, pp. 194–211 (195).

34. In this context one should not ignore Bakhtin's place within the Russian philosophical tradition (and particularly in relation to trends emerging from Slavophilism), with its tendency to oppose a (Western, rationalist) concern with 'abstract' truth to a (Russian, irrationalist) concern with 'lived' truth. Emerson notes possible affinities between Bakhtin and the thought of Soloviev and Ivanov and their 'blurring and rubbing out of fundamental categories of rationality' in Emerson, *The First Hundred Years*, p. 258. Similarly, Emerson and Morson locate Bakhtin in a tradition of Russian 'anti-ideological' thinkers such as Herzen, Tolstoy and Chekhov who see the answers to life's questions in life itself rather than in abstract thought. See Emerson and Morson, *Bakhtin*, pp. 23–24.

35. Bergson is a reference point for Bakhtin in *Toward a Philosophy of the Act*. Benjamin engages intensively with Bergson in his reading of Proust and Baudelaire.
36. Henri Bergson, 'Introduction à la métaphysique', in *La Pensée et le mouvant* (1907), Paris, 1999, pp. 177–227 (211).
37. Henri Bergson, 'De la position des problèmes', in *La Pensée et le mouvant*, pp. 25–98 (31).
38. Bergson, 'De la position des problèmes', p. 30.
39. Ibid., p. 76.
40. The string that holds the pearls together alludes to Kant's investigation of the transcendental categories.
41. Bergson, 'De la position des problèmes', p. 69.
42. Bergson, 'Introduction à la métaphysique', p. 212.
43. 'Transfiguration' (*Verklärung*) is a Benjaminian term, a Bakhtinian analogy of which is 'transcription' as he uses it in *Toward a Philosophy of the Act* (for example, *TPA* 39), or in M. M. Bakhtin, 'The Problem of Content, Material, and Form in Verbal Art', in *Art and Answerability*, pp. 257–325 (285). I discuss Benjamin's use of the term 'transfiguration' in my final chapter.
44. Filippo Marinetti, 'The Founding and Manifesto of Futurism' (1909), in Vassiliki Kolocotroni, Jane Goldman and Olga Taxidou (eds), *Modernism: An Anthology of Sources and Documents*, Edinburgh, 1998, pp. 249–53 (251).
45. On the connection between Bergson, Italian Futurism and war, see Mark Antliff, *Inventing Bergson: Cultural Politics and the Parisian Avant-garde*, Princeton NJ, 1993, pp. 157–66. A similar connection between Bergson and war can be seen in Vorticism. See Natan Zach, 'Imagism and Vorticism', in Malcolm Bradbury and James McFarlane (eds), *Modernism: A Guide to European Literature 1890–1930*, Harmondsworth, 1991, pp. 228–42.
46. Ernst Jünger, *Der Kampf als inneres Erlebnis*, Berlin, 1926, p. 41.
47. *Dannyi* and *zadannyi* are the Russian equivalents of *gegeben* (given) and *aufgegeben* (set as a task), standard terms in the German tradition which go back to Kant.
48. Coates, *Christianity in Bakhtin*, p. 27.
49. Holquist is correct in observing that *Toward a Philosophy of the Act* is concerned more with Kant than with neo-Kantianism. Michael Holquist, 'Foreword', in *TPA*, pp. vii–xv (ix).
50. This is the essence of Kant's categorical imperative which focuses only on what tends to universal validity in a particular act. As Kant formulates it: 'I ought never to act except in such a way that I could also will that my maxim should become a universal law.' Kant, *Metaphysics of Morals*, p. 15. *Toward a Philosophy of the Act* contains a sustained critique of Kantian ethics. Bakhtin argues as follows: 'The categorical imperative determines the performed act as a universally valid law, but as a law that is devoid of a particular, positive content.' As a consequence, this 'law of conformity-to-the-law' becomes an 'an empty formula of pure theoreticism' that 'excludes the actual – individual and historical – self-activity of the performed act' (*TPA* 25–26).
51. For Kant's discussion of the possibility of experience, see Kant, *Critique of Pure Reason*, pp. 151–53.
52. Roberts seems wide of the mark when he argues that Bakhtin was following the lead of Dilthey and his conception of subjective *Verstehen* (under-

standing), which he opposes to the objective knowledge of the sciences. *Verstehen*, like Bergson's intuition, prioritizes immediate experience. See Roberts, 'Poetics Hermeneutics Dialogics', p. 119.

53. Bakhtin's reading presents a somewhat caricatured and reductionist notion that does not do justice to Nietzsche's understanding of the interdependence of Apollonian and Dionysian modes. Bakhtin is more on target in his assessment of then modish Dionysianism: 'The aspiration of Nietzsche's philosophy reduces to a considerable extent to this possessedness by Being (one-sided participation); its ultimate result is the absurdity of contemporary Dionysianism' (*TPA* 49).

54. Bakhtin is close here to the thought of Aristotle and his understanding of man as the *zoon politikon* whose essence is to be found in activity and participation in a plural, public sphere. Furthermore, Bakhtin's thought would bear comparison with Hannah Arendt who draws substantially on Aristotle. Many of her key themes – her preference for activity over contemplation, for becoming over being, her emphasis on participation in the public sphere and on the nexus between freedom and speech – resonate with Bakhtin's ideas. See Hannah Arendt, *The Human Condition*, London, 1998. Attention to Arendt might usefully supplement Hirschkop's analysis of Bakhtin as a thinker of the public sphere in Hirschkop, *Bakhtin*.

55. Here Hirschkop's comments on the similar lack of clarity over the status of the notion of dialogue are relevant: '[Dialogism] is both the natural state of being of language as such and a valorized category of certain discourses. It has a role in the theoretical critique of Saussurean linguistics and in the evaluative literary history Bakhtin narrates. When these two senses of the term are conflated, the specific form dialogism takes in the novel is assumed to be the manifestation of the true essence of language, an essence somehow repressed in the monological. In fact it is the status of monologism which is most problematic: if dialogism is the nature of all language, then what gives rise to monologism? For monologism is not merely an illusion or an error, it is a form of discourse with real, if mystifying, effects, which must be accounted for in a theory of language. It is this reality, or effectivity, of an illusionary or mystifying language which is evaded when the monological is treated as a theoretical error.' Hirschkop, 'A Response to the Forum on Mikhail Bakhtin', p. 75. Hirschkop develops this and related ideas in order to highlight the political dimension of Bakhtin's thought as one of the central themes of his later monograph. See Hirschkop, *Bakhtin*, for example, pp. 55–57. Hirschkop's 'Is Dialogism for Real?' also explores the double nature of dialogue as description and political imperative. Ken Hirschkop, 'Is Dialogism for Real?', in Shepherd (ed.), *The Contexts of Bakhtin*, Amsterdam, 1998, pp. 183–95.

56. Tihanov also effects a certain historicization of Bakhtin by virtue of the comparative angle gained from his study of Lukács. General historicization is not, however, his major aim. Hirschkop's work, by contrast, in its desire to present the 'actuality of Mikhail Bakhtin' considers historicization to be one of its major tasks. See Tihanov, *Master and Slave*, and Hirschkop, *Bakhtin*.

57. For example, 'modern science' is his consistent and infelicitous gloss on Kantian theoreticism.

58. Hirschkop, *Bakhtin*, p. 51.

59. Tihanov, *Master and Slave*, p. 293.
60. Simmel's philosophy of money shares substantial ground both with Marx's theory of alienation and with Lukács's theory of reification. For a detailed analysis of this, see Gianfranco Poggi, *Money and the Modern Mind: Georg Simmel's Philosophy of Money*, Berkeley CA, 1993.
61. The indifference that he attributes to money is linked to the blasé character of the modern city-dweller that he describes in 'The Metropolis and Mental Life'. Simmel, 'Die Gross-Städte', pp. 192–204.
62. Georg Simmel, *Philosophie des Geldes*, ed. David Frisby and Klaus Christian Köhnke Frankfurt/Main, 1989, pp. 594–95.
63. Bakhtin's insight into the connection between (Kantian) theoreticism and the exchange-economy is echoed by Eagleton: 'The qualities of the Kantian moral law are those of the commodity form. Abstract, universal and rigorously self-identical, the law of Reason is a mechanism which, like the commodity, effects formally equal exchanges between isolated individual subjects, erasing the difference of their needs and desires in its homogenizing injunctions.' Eagleton, *The Ideology of the Aesthetic*, p. 83.
64. Brandist suggests that 'this Bakhtin presumably saw manifested in the wars and revolutions that had gripped Russia and much of Europe in the years before the composition of his essay'. Brandist, *The Bakhtin Circle*, pp. 36–37.
65. Elias gives an account of the development of the antithesis of culture and civilization in Norbert Elias, *The Civilizing Process*, Oxford, 1994, especially, 'Part One: On the Sociogenesis of the Concepts of "Civilization" and "Culture" ', pp. 5–42. One source of this distinction is Kant: 'We are *cultivated* to a high degree by art and science. We are *civilised* to the point of excess in all kinds of social courtesies and proprieties. But we are still a long way from the point where we could consider ourselves morally mature. For while the idea of morality is indeed present in culture, an application of this idea which only extends to the semblances of morality, as in love of honour and outward propriety, amounts merely to civilisation.' Immanuel Kant, 'Ideas on a Universal History with a Cosmopolitan Purpose' [1784], in Kant, *Political Writings*, ed. Hans Reiss, trans. H. B. Nisbet, Cambridge, 2002, pp. 41–53 (49). Another source is Rousseau. Both Rousseau and Kant, in their negative description of civilization, emphasize the way in which it induces men and women to act insincerely. Rousseau's comments on this matter raise a number of themes of relevance here: custom, ritual, system and insincerity: 'Before art had moulded our behaviour, and taught our passions to speak an artificial language, our morals were rude but natural [...]. In our day, now that more subtle study and a more refined taste have reduced the art of pleasing to a system, there prevails in modern manners a servile and deceptive conformity; so that one would think every mind had been cast in the same mould. Politeness [...] decorum [...] ceremony [...] fashion [...] these we must always follow, never the promptings of our own nature.' Jean-Jacques Rousseau, 'A Discourse on the Moral Effects of the Arts and Sciences' (1750), in *The Social Contract and Discourses*, pp. 1–29 (6). Similarly, Bakhtin stresses the link between ritual and insincerity as a mark of deadened, theoretical being with his notion of the impostor: 'In attempting to understand [...] every act we perform – as a ritual act, we turn into impostors or pretenders' (*TPA* 52).

66. See Spengler's comments on the writing of his book and its connection with the war in Oswald Spengler, *Der Untergang des Abendlandes*, 2 vols, Munich, 1923, Vol. 1, pp. 62–67. On the reception of Spengler in Germany, Hawthorn comments: '[German] wartime propaganda had portrayed the battle as an heroic struggle between culture and civilization, between the high ideals of Germany and the crass materialism of England. The defeat appeared to mean that culture and with it the whole humanist *Weltanschauung* had apparently gone down [...] to civilization. The despair which this induced accounted immediately after 1918 for the extraordinary popularity of Spengler's *The Decline of the West* in which the distinction between culture and civilization was most dramatically drawn and in which the transition from the one to the other, from the summer to the autumn of Faustian culture, was projected in a way that even now one has to admit, for all its faults, is remarkably plausible.' Geoffrey Hawthorn, *Enlightenment and Despair: A History of Social Theory*, Cambridge, 1976, pp. 178–79.

67. Spengler, *Untergang*, p. 41.

68. Spengler's ideas on the cyclical nature of history contain strong echoes of the thought of Vico and Herder. See Isaiah Berlin, *Three Critics of the Enlightenment: Vico, Hamann, Herder*, Princeton, 2000.

69. Brandist argues that Bakhtin's ethics in *Toward a Philosophy of the Act* come about, in part, through the appropriation of Simmel's critique of the categorical imperative: 'Simmel had transformed the Kantian concept of duty [...] into the structure of individual experience. Rationally discerned obligation was now replaced by the *sentiment*, or feeling of obligation. This allowed Simmel to argue that what one is morally obliged to do is dependent on historical circumstances and that the "sentiment of obligation", conscience, is the internalized promptings of social discipline.' Brandist, *The Bakhtin Circle*, p. 37. Bakhtin's objections to the abstract nature of the categorical imperative for the concrete individual echo Simmel when the latter speaks of the 'the indifference of the law for the individual'. Georg Simmel, 'Das individuelle Gesetz: Ein Versuch über das Prinzip der Ethik', in *Aufsätze und Abhandlungen 1909–1918*, Frankfurt/Main, 2001, pp. 417–70 (425). Bakhtin also stresses the situational nature of ethics. It should, nevertheless, be clear that Bakhtin would object to the idea that the *lebensphilosophische* notion of empathetic sentiment (*Einfühlung*) could be the basis of ethics or that ethical obligation could be given by internalized social norms. This last suggestion would be an abdication of responsibility. Responsibility is a principle, even if it is not one that tends towards universal laws.

70. An interpretation of Bakhtin's conception of love from a theological standpoint runs though Coates, *Christianity in Bakhtin*. Coates also discusses Kagan's conception of love and its relation to Bakhtin in Ruth Coates, 'Two of a Small Fraternity? Points of Contact and Departure in the Work of Bakhtin and Kagan up to 1924', in Shepherd (ed.), *The Contexts of Bakhtin: Philosophy, Aesthetics, Authorship*, Amsterdam, 1998, pp. 17–28. Palmieri discusses Bakhtin's conception of love and notes its debt to Scheler in Giovanni Palmieri, ' "The Author" According to Bakhtin... And Bakhtin the Author', in Shepherd (ed.), *The Contexts of Bakhtin*, pp. 45–56 (54–55). Brandist also reveals the extent of the influence of Max Scheler on Bakhtin as regards the conception of self-other relations. Brandist makes frequent

reference to this, particularly the conception of self-other relations, but does not say very much about Bakhtin's conception of love. He is even able to refer to the notes that Bakhtin made on Scheler's work. See Brandist, *The Bakhtin Circle*, pp. 36–52. Certainly, Scheler's influence was strong. Scheler objects to those trends that see the essence of loving as a merging with the loved object. Instead, he describes love as an intersubjective act. The following, for example, is his interpretation of Augustine which also reflects his own views: 'The appearance of an image or meaning in the intellectual act, even in the simplest perception, is for him not merely an activity of the knowing subject that penetrates the completed object. Rather an image is simultaneously an answering reaction of the *object* itself, a "giving of itself" or a "self-revealing" of the object. An image is a consequence of a "question" asked with "love" that the world answers and in so doing reveals itself. In this revelation the world *comes to its full existence and value*.' Max Scheler, 'Love and Knowledge', in *On Feeling, Knowing and Valuing*, ed. and trans. Harold Bershady, Chicago, 1992, pp. 147–65 (163–64).

71. Bakhtin's conception of love is not subordinated to morality. Morality may be understood as a grouping of general categories. The maxim, 'I love him not because he is good but he is good because I love him', allows the possibility that love might not conform to standard moral categories.

72. Once again, Arendt offers a point of comparison with Bakhtin's thought. Arendt argues in *The Human Condition* that human beings should not limit themselves to the abstraction of contemplation but rather at cultivating a *vita activa*, since it is only in participation and action that we are capable of moral responsibility. Understood in this fashion, her account of Adolf Eichmann shows that the banality of evil is possible when human beings do not participate actively. For Arendt, Eichmann allowed what Bakhtin would term the pride of ritualism to overcome his individuality and hence he never thought critically – or did anything – about his complicity in the murder of millions. See Arendt, *The Human Condition*, and Hannah Arendt, *Eichmann in Jerusalem: A Report on the Banality of Evil*, London, 1998. Mihailovic performs a more immediate contextualization of *Toward a Philosophy of the Act* and the link between theoreticism and indifference to death, noting that it was written 'in the aftermath of the Russian Civil War when thousands perished or gave their own lives for inflexibly held political principles'. Mihailovic, *Corporeal Words*, p. 64.

73. It is the disinterested nature of aesthetic activity, in the sense meant by Kant with the term *interessenlos*, that brings it close to loving activity.

74. This is one of the points where Bakhtin parts company with the existentialist ethics with which – in, for example, his emphasis on authentic being – he may seem to share common ground. Coates notes, for example, that 'Bakhtin's description of the pretender bears a striking resemblance to Sartre's person living in bad faith.' Coates, 'Bakhtin and Kagan', p. 23. Sartre, however, conceives of love (on the analogy of sexual love) as the desire to possess, hence he conceives of love as an oscillation between love and hatred, of the desire to be possessed and to possess. See Jean-Paul Sartre, *Being and Nothingness: An Essay on Phenomenological Ontology*, New York, 1954, pp. 339–430. For a discussion of this and, in particular, the lack of a Sartrean conception of shame in Bakhtin, as well as an assessment of hierarchy

in 'Author and Hero', see Ann Jefferson, 'Bodymatters: Self and Other in Bakhtin, Sartre and Barthes', in Hirschkop and Shepherd (eds), *Bakhtin and Cultural Theory*, pp. 152–57. The ultimate point of conflict between Bakhtin and Sartre must be, however, as Clark and Holquist point out, Sartre's maxim that 'hell is other people'. Clark and Holquist, *Bakhtin*, p. 94.

75. Coates, *Christianity in Bakhtin*, for example, pp. 32–35. The whole of Mihailovic's *Corporeal Words* reads Bakhtin with reference to the notion of incarnation. He deals with *Toward a Philosophy of the Act* on pp. 51–85.

76. Emerson and Morson dismiss a theological reading of *Toward a Philosophy of the Act*: 'In contrast to those Russian – and Russian Orthodox – admirers of Bakhtin (including his editor Sergei Bocharov, and those Western commentators who have seen Bakhtin's thought as essentially religious) the work barely touches on theology, except in one passage. [...] It would seem hard to justify the notion that Bakhtin's works are, at least in the Western sense of the term, really a theology in code.' Gary Saul Morson and Caryl Emerson, 'Introduction: Rethinking Bakhtin', in Morson and Emerson (eds), *Rethinking Bakhtin*, pp. 1–60 (6). Nevertheless, Bakhtin's secular Christian ethics are plain to see here and not in code.

77. The link that Hobbes makes between authorship and authority, in Chapter XVI, 'Of Persons, Authors and Things Personated', finds a resonance in Bakhtin's thinking on the same themes in 'Author and Hero in Aesthetic Activity'. Thomas Hobbes, *Leviathan*, ed. Richard Tuck, Cambridge, 1996, pp. 111–15. One might also argue for the importance of Hobbes's philosophy of language to Bakhtin and, perhaps, Voloshinov. Using arguments that bear comparison with Voloshinov's distinction between theme and meaning (a distinction that I discuss in the next chapter), Hobbes argues that meaning is not a fixed property of words but rather that speakers' evaluative judgements, based on their desire for power and their own gain, are the basis of signification. See Hobbes, Chapter IV, 'Of Speech', *Leviathan*, pp. 24–31.

78. Such is Hobbes's 'naturall condition of mankind' in which we find 'three principall causes of quarell. First, Competition; Secondly, Diffidence; Thirdly, Glory'; these result in life being characterized by 'continuall fear, and danger of violent death; And the life of man, solitary, poore, nasty, brutish, and short.' Hobbes, *Leviathan*, Chapter XIII, pp. 88–89. Like Bakhtin, Hobbes makes his argument entirely on an ahistorical analysis of experience. Like Bakhtin, however, one can easily contextualize Hobbes's thought in terms of contemporary concerns – in Hobbes's case the crisis of authority in the English Civil War period – rather than Bakhtin's Russian civil war. See Johann P. Sommerville, *Thomas Hobbes: Political Ideas in Historical Contexts*, London, 1992.

79. Hobbes, *Leviathan*, Chapter XVIII, 'The Establishment of the Commonwealth'.

80. Ibid., Chapter XIV, p. 92.

81. For a discussion of the relationship between Hobbes's theology and what Overhoff terms his materialism, examining the antagonism between materialist philosophy and traditional Christian eschatology, see Jürgen Overhoff, 'The Theology of Thomas Hobbes's *Leviathan*', *Journal of Ecclesiastical History*, 51, 2000, 3, pp. 527–55.

82. See, for example, Beatrice Hansen, 'Language and Mimesis in Walter Benjamin's Work', in Ferris (ed.), *Companion to Benjamin*, pp. 54–72 (70–71);

Thomas Weber, 'Erfahrung', in Michael Opitz and Erdmut Wizisla (eds), *Benjamins Begriffe*, Frankfurt/Main, 2000, pp. 230–59; taking one example: in his generally perspicacious study, McCole devotes seven pages to the question of 'just what is actually responsible for the mutual exclusivity of *Erlebnis* and *Erfahrung*', without exploring the intellectual-historical context of the 'tragedy of culture' which would provide much in the way of an answer. McCole, *Benjamin*, pp. 272–79.

83. Jay, 'Experience without a Subject', p. 195. Plate is another critic who, apparently independently of Jay, recognizes this aspect of Benjamin's thought and its debt to the confrontation of Kantianism and *Lebensphilosophie*: 'Benjamin was not content with either [*Erfahrung* or *Erlebnis*] – the former being too rationalistic and pragmatically impossible to render in a modern age of shock, the latter being too immediate and individualistic – and so instead he sets up a dialectic between the two varieties of experience, attempting to overcome the subject-object distinction.' S. Brent Plate, *Walter Benjamin, Religion and Aesthetics: Rethinking Religion through the Arts*, London, 2005, p. 4.

84. Benjamin was one of the founder members of the 'Detachment for School Reform', on the committee of the Free Students' Union, lecturing on behalf of the 'League for Free School Communities' and still in regular contact with his mentor, the educational reformer, Gustav Wyneken (1875–1964). See Brodersen, *Benjamin*, pp. 46–49.

85. The themes of childhood, youth and the nature of experience – which seem not to have a parallel in Bakhtin's writings – are a feature of Benjamin's entire career. They occur, for example, in his writings on toys, on children's literature, on mimesis and in his autobiographical texts.

86. See Friedrich Nietzsche, 'The Genealogy of Morals', in *Basic Writings of Nietzsche*, ed. and trans. Walter Kaufmann, New York, 1992, 451–599, especially pp. 475–80. This is the passage that discusses the infamous *blonde Bestie*. One can discern in Benjamin's text not only the influence of Nietzsche but also perhaps of Decadence. The opposition of the destructive and rejuvenating Barbarian and enervated and sterile civilization is a standard topos of Decadence from Verlaine's 'La Langueur' (1883) onwards.

87. Benjamin revisits the notion of a positive barbarism in the essay of 1933, 'Experience and Poverty'. By this point, however, his ideas have been purged of vitalism. See *GS II* 213–29; *SW II* 731–36.

88. This sense of *Erfahrung* is already implicit in Kant's use of the term: Kant's *Erfahrung* is universal as opposed to the singularity of *Erlebnisse*; hence it must be communicable.

89. Here, then, Benjamin first introduces the idea, to be worked out more fully in the 'The Work of Art', that fascism is the aestheticization of politics. Benjamin points to the connection between Jünger's celebration of experience and an aristocratic standpoint with a quotation: 'With the mobilization of the masses, of worse blood, of those with a bourgeois sensibility, in short of the common man, especially into the ranks of the officers, more and more of the eternally aristocratic elements of the soldierly craft have been destroyed' (*GS III* 240–41; *SW II* 314). As Benjamin comments, this is at best a tactless thing to say in view of the numbers of ordinary soldiers who died.

90. There is also, in the term '*Sklavenaufstand*', an implied reference to Nietzsche.

91. Benjamin here may again echo Lukács's identification of the static and passive attitude of contemplation – which he attributes both to Kant's philosophy and the attitude of the worker in front of a machine – as a defining feature of reified consciousness. See Lukács, 'Reification'.

92. Leslie, *Benjamin*, p. 33. Leslie's study contains a sustained reading of Benjamin's theory of fascism which seeks to explain Benjamin's turn to Marxist materialism. Whilst I agree with Leslie's reading in a number of respects, I seek to emphasize that Benjamin's concern with the concrete nature of experience is more than simply part of a turn to a necessarily Marxist materialism.

93. The passage to which Benjamin refers here is the opening lines of the conclusion to Kant's *Critique of Practical Reason* (1788): 'Two things fill the mind with ever new and increasing admiration and awe, the oftener and the more steadily we reflect on them: the starry heavens above and the moral law within.' The passage continues with a striking description of the way in which the synthetic activity of practical reason conjoins the universal and the particular; on the one hand, in practical reason our sense experience and animal being are validated in universal terms; and on the other, the realm of the universal receives the weight of actual experience. My orientation towards the laws of nature 'begins from the place I occupy in the external world of sense, and enlarges my connection therein to an unbounded extent with worlds upon worlds and systems of systems'. My orientation towards universal moral laws 'exhibits me in a world which has true infinity, but which is traceable only by the understanding, and with which I discern that I am not in a merely contingent but in a universal and necessary connection'. Kant, thus, establishes a harmonious and dynamic relationship of communication between the realm of universal laws of nature, the realm of universal laws of morality and the individual cognizing consciousness that inhabits a sensual world. Immanuel Kant, *Critique of Practical Reason and Other Moral Writings* (1788), trans. Lewis White Beck, Chicago IL, 1948, p. 351.

94. Another source of this insight is Simmel's theory of the modern, urban *blasé* attitude in 'The Metropolis and Mental Life'. See Simmel, 'Die Gross-Städte'.

95. Wolin makes this point in Wolin, *Benjamin*, p. 218.

96. Gasché, however, makes a case for the presence of Kantian motifs in the 'The Work of Art', commenting: 'Benjamin's borrowings from Kant [in the 'The Work of Art'] do not exclude his rejection of major aspects of Kant's doctrine. [...] The contention that Benjamin objected to the unifying gesture of transcendental deduction, to what he called Kant's despotism, in other words, to his transcendentalism, is highly suggestive of what sort of Kant – a ant folded back into the empirical, a criticist economy without transcendentalism – is operative in Benjamin's work.' Rodolph Gasché, 'Objective Diversions: On Some Kantian Themes in Benjamin's "The Work of Art in the Age of its Mechanical Reproduction"', in Andrew Benjamin and Osborne (eds), *Benjamin's Philosophy*, London, 1994, pp. 183–204 (201–02).

97. Hirschkop mentions, in passing, the similarity between Bakhtin and Benjamin's 'On the Programme of the Coming Philosophy' in Hirschkop, *Bakhtin*, p. 100.

98. McCole, *Benjamin*, p. 76.

99. Hermann Cohen, the leading Marburg neo-Kantian, whose *Kants Theorie der Erfahrung* (1918) was a source for both Bakhtin and Benjamin, only underlined the Kantian mathematical bias. In Jennings's words: 'Cohen attempted to confirm the continuing validity of Kant's description of the structure of the understanding. For Cohen, however, modern philosophy could "delineate in a positive manner the horizons of knowledge" only by severely restricting "the concept of the possibility of experience," for example, by limiting the data of experience to a model of the world based solely on verifiable mathematical and scientific evidence.' Michael W. Jennings, *Dialectical Images: Walter Benjamin's Theory of Literary Criticism*, Ithaca NY, 1987, p. 84. For Cohen's influence on the early Bakhtin, see Nikolai Nikolaev, 'The Nevel School of Philosophy (Bakhtin, Kagan and Pumpianskii) between 1918 and 1925: Materials from Pumpianskii's Archives', in Shepherd (ed.), *The Contexts of Bakhtin*, pp. 29–41. Brandist also deals frequently with Bakhtin's debt to Cohen in Brandist, *The Bakhtin Circle*.

100. Wolin reads 'On the Programme of the Coming Philosophy' as a proto-Surrealist text that points to Benjamin's later work, and there is no doubt that this passage can be read as an example of that tendency. It shows Benjamin's continuing preoccupation with phenomena which cannot be subsumed to a Western rationalist viewpoint. See Richard Wolin, 'Benjamin, Adorno and Surrealism', in Tim Huhn and Lambert Zuidervaart (eds), *The Semblance of Subjectivity: Essays in Adorno's Aesthetic Theory*, London, 1999, pp. 93–122. Nevertheless, Benjamin is not proposing irrationalism; his concern is that philosophy's understanding of the rational must expand to take into account what is normally dismissed as irrational.

101. Rochlitz sums up the debate over the ethical dimension of Benjamin's thought as follows: 'In Benjamin's work, the contemporary debate on ethics is confronted with a mode of thought situated to one side of what seems to have become its immutable framework, the opposition between Kantians and Aristotelians or Hegelians. Here again, Benjamin occupies a peculiar place: he is claimed both by thinkers who, like Ricoeur, lean toward a neo-Aristotelian philosophy and an anchoring of ethics in narration, and by those who, like Habermas, defend a procedural ethics of narration. How are such contradictory claims possible? We find very little moral theory in Benjamin; thus the two sides can draw support only from his intuitions and implicit presuppositions.' Rainer Rochlitz, *The Disenchantment of Art: The Philosophy of Walter Benjamin*, trans. Jane Marie Todd, London, New York: Guildford, 1996, p. 253.

102. Wohlfarth describes Benjamin's notion of actuality as the utopian mean between journalism and philosophy: 'The philosopher's spurious claim "to master from lofty vantage-point, the intellectual horizon of the times", does no more justice to true actuality, in Benjamin's view, than does the journalist's unconditional surrender to passing fashion.' Irving Wohlfarth, 'The Measure of the Possible, the Weight of the Real and the Heat of the Moment: Benjamin's Actuality Today', in Marcus and Nead (eds), *The Actuality of Walter Benjamin*, pp. 13–39 (17).

103. I am proposing here that the conjunction of Bakhtin and Benjamin might help us to discern a greater degree of politics in Bakhtin and a greater degree

of ethics in Benjamin. The question of whether Bakhtin should be read as primarily an ethical thinker or a political thinker is contested. Bakhtin has certainly provided a rich source for the many thinkers of the recent 'ethical turn'. In particular the comparison of Bakhtin and Emmanuel Lévinas has been fruitful. See, for example, Michael J. Gardiner, 'Alterity and Ethics: A Dialogical Perspective', *Theory, Culture and Society*, 13, 1996, 2, pp. 121–43, and Jeffrey T. Nealon, 'The Ethics of Dialogue: Bakhtin and Lévinas', *College English*, 59, 1997, 2, pp. 129–48. Nevertheless, some scholars, notably American liberals, have displayed a tendency to focus on the ethical aspect of Bakhtin's thought with the result that they depoliticize it entirely. Representative of this trend is Emerson's comment: 'It could be argued that the most enduring lesson Bakhtin offered his Soviet era was this: Do not conflate the ethical with the political [...] for the time honoured reason that the ethical realm, if politicised, is prevented from functioning as an autonomous *check* on the political.' Emerson, *The First Hundred Years*, p. 22. Brandist has argued powerfully against this collapsing of the political into the ethical in his work, particularly in Craig Brandist, 'Ethics, Politics and the Potential of Dialogism', *Historical Materialism*, 5, 1999, 1, pp. 231–53.

3   Language

1. An intriguing point of comparison is provided by the Viennese Circle of logical positivists and their desire to reduce language and knowledge to a series of mathematical propositions. There is a reversal here, in Bakhtin's assertion that logical purity is unutterable, of Wittgenstein's definition of silence and the utterable at the end of the *Tractatus*. It is not clear whether Bakhtin would have known this work at this time. See Ludwig Wittgenstein, *Tractatus Logico-philosophicus* (1921), London, 1999, pp. 187–89.
2. In their periodization of Bakhtin's work, Morson and Emerson see the period 1924–29 as the period in which Bakhtin shifts towards a more explicitly linguistically orientated philosophy. Morson and Emerson, *Bakhtin*, pp. 83–86. This is also the period in which, after the Bakhtin group's move to Leningrad, Voloshinov studies with the linguist Lev Iakubinskii. See Brandist, *The Bakhtin Circle*, pp. 9–11.
3. Matejka points out the dialectical structure of *Marxism and the Philosophy of Language* and interprets it as Voloshinov's attempt to be or at least to appear to be a good Marxist dialectician. Nevertheless, as noted above, one can observe an analogous dialectical approach in *Toward a Philosophy of the Act*, where Bakhtin is making no attempt to appear to be a Marxist. Ladislav Matejka, 'On the First Prolegomena to Semiotics', Appendix I, in *MPL*, pp. 161–74 (169).
4. This reversal of the liberal, Anglo-American account of the relationship between individual and society where individuals come together and constitute society aligns Voloshinov with the broad tradition of French Structuralism from Durkheim to Lacan, Althusser and Foucault. According to this tradition, 'collective representations' (Durkheim), 'langue' (Lacan), 'ideology' (Althusser) and 'discourse' (Foucault) are the fundamental social

unities out of which the individual constructs her- or himself. In particular, the parallels with Lacan have been used by Bakhtin scholars as a means to present Bakhtin and the Bakhtin Circle as ethical proto-deconstructionists. See, for example, William Handley, 'The Ethics of Subject Creation in Bakhtin and Lacan', in Shepherd (ed.), *Bakhtin, Carnival and Other Subjects*, 3–4, 1993, pp. 144–62. Williams seizes on Voloshinov's prioritizing of the collective over the individual in order to support his notion of the collective nature of 'structures of feeling' in Williams, *Marxism and Literature*, pp. 35–43. For a critique of this on the grounds of Williams's misreading of Voloshinov's notion of consciousness, with reference to Althusser and Lacan, see Antony Easthope, 'The Bakhtin School and Raymond Williams: Subject and Signifier', in Shepherd (ed.), *Bakhtin, Carnival and Other Subjects*, pp. 115–24.

5. See *MPL*, pp. 45–63. Voloshinov's reading of Saussure is polemical and produces an image of his thought that is reduced to the abstracting gesture that distinguishes between *langue* and *parole*. Thibault argues against the understanding of the opposition of *langue* and *parole* as an inert binary in Paul J. Thibault, *Re-reading Saussure: The Dynamics of Signs in Social Life*, London, 1997. He demonstrates some of the reductionist character of Voloshinov's reading of Saussure, particularly in Voloshinov's treatment of Saussure's doctrine of the arbitrary nature of the sign, pp. 251–54.

6. Humboldt holds that the primary and original aspect of language was *energeia*, activity. As languages develop and stabilize, however, linguistic forms accrue to language and it takes on the aspect of *ergon*, an inert product. Humboldt describes the individual speaker and the relationship of *energeia* to *ergon* as follows: 'in the influence exerted on him lies the regularity of language and its forms; in his own reaction, a principle of freedom'. Wilhelm von Humboldt, *On Language: The Diversity of Human Language-Structure and its Influence on the Mental Development of Mankind* (1836), trans. Peter Heath, Cambridge, 1989, p. 37. Humboldt notes the tendency of languages to develop in terms of the complexity of grammatical forms with the result that the quality of language as *ergon* comes to predominate over *energeia*. Whilst Humboldt noted that this could lead to degeneracy of a linguistic culture, he also saw this in terms of a narrative of progress whereby a language develops from the poetry-dominated state of primitive cultures to the prose-dominated state of culture capable of philosophical discourse. These ideas are pertinent not only to Voloshinov but also to Bakhtin's theory of the novel.

7. Gilles Deleuze and Félix Guattari, *A Thousand Plateaus: Capitalism and Schizophrenia*, trans. Brian Massumi, London, 1992, p. 84. Deleuze and Guattari make explicit the extent to which Voloshinov's ideas attack (in Derrida's term) the 'logocentrism' of Western culture that views the individual speaking subject as the guarantor of meaning. The paradox that direct speech follows indirect speech is analogous to Derrida's assertion that speech follows writing. Both Derrida and Voloshinov elevate what Derrida terms a 'supplement' (writing, indirect discourse) to the position of primary term. Likewise, both use their theory of their respective 'supplements' to make an assault on Western culture's rigid modes of subject construction. See Jacques Derrida, *Of Grammatology*, trans. Gayatri Chakravorty Spivak, London, 1998.

8. Williams, *Marxism and Literature*, p. 37.

9. Émile Benveniste, 'Active and Middle Voice in the Verb', in *Problems in General Linguistics*, trans. Mary E. Meek, Coral Gables FL, 1971, pp. 145–51. Lock provides an account of the development of the theory of free indirect speech and its connection to the Bakhtin Circle in Charles Lock, 'Bakhtin's Dialogism and the History of the Theory of Free Indirect Discourse', in Jørgen Bruhn and Jon Lundquist (eds), *The Novelness of Bakhtin*, Copenhagen, 2001, pp. 71–87.

10. Jacques Derrida, 'Différance', in *Margins of Philosophy*, trans. Alan Bass, London, 1984, pp. 1–28 (9).

11. Jay, 'Experience without a Subject', p. 205.

12. Ibid.

13. Ibid., p. 206.

14. Friedrich Hölderlin, 'Being Judgement Possibility' (also known as 'The Thalia Fragment'), in J. M. Bernstein (ed.), *Classical and Romantic German Aesthetics*, Cambridge, 2003, pp. 191–92. Whilst his German etymology is doubtful here, he is thinking of the meanings of the Greek *kritein*: to separate and to judge.

15. Hölderlin, 'Being Judgement Possibility', p. 191.

16. Friedrich Hölderlin, letter to Schiller of September 4, 1795, in Michael Knaupp (ed.) Friedrich Hölderlin, *Sämtliche Werke und Briefe*, 3 vols, Munich, 1992, pp. 595–96 (595).

17. Friedrich Hölderlin, 'Empedokles' (1797), in Hölderlin, *Sämtliche Werke und Briefe*, Munich, 1992, pp. 763–881 (870).

18. Bakhtin's reference to Heidegger is surely to the Heidegger who draws his inspiration from Hölderlin. See Heidegger's reading of Hölderlin's poetry and the relation of language and being in Martin Heidegger, '... poetically, man dwells...', trans. Albert Hofstadter, in Martin Heidegger, *Philosophical and Political Writings*, ed. Manfred Stassen, London, 2003, pp. 265–78. In 'The Origin of the Work of Art', Heidegger writes: 'Projective saying is poetry: the saying of the world and earth. Poetry is the saying of the unconcealment of beings... Projective saying is saying which, in preparing the sayable, simultaneously brings the unsayable as such into the world.' Martin Heidegger, 'The Origin of the Work of Art', in D. F. Krell (ed.), *Basic Writings*, London, 1993, pp. 140–212 (198–99). Steiner comments: 'Heidegger finds in Hölderlin one of those very rare, immeasurably important expressions of man's fallenness, of his ostracism from Being and the gods, and, simultaneously, a statement of this very condition, whose truth and lyric power give assurance of rebirth.' George Steiner, *Heidegger*, London, 1992, pp. 141–42.

19. Larmore points out, however, that poetry is not omnipotent in this respect and is restricted in its temporal dimension: 'Strain as it may against the division between subject and object, poetry remains an act of reflection. The poet must step back from whatever inkling he has of the unity of being in order to put it into words. For Hölderlin, the moments of vision are therefore never in the present. They are always past or future, remembered or anticipated.' Charles Larmore, 'Hölderlin and Novalis', in Ameriks (ed.), *Companion to German Idealism*, pp. 141–60 (152). As I argue in the final chapter, a similar temporal restriction of true experience is echoed in Benjamin's work.

20. For a detailed study of Benjamin's relationship to the German tradition of language mysticism and Hamann in particular, see Winfried Menninghaus, *Walter Benjamins Theorie der Sprachmagie*, Frankfurt/Main, 1995, pp. 9–50.

21. As Münster comments: 'At the moment when logical positivism starts out during the 1920s, this essay of Benjamin's might be considered to be the very last expression of the philosophical idealism of language of the 18th and 19th centuries.' Münster, *Progrès et catastrophe*, p. 124. Münster also discusses Benjamin's reading of Carnap and attempts to construct a possible dialogue of Benjamin with the Vienna Circle, pp. 139–41.

22. Pensky and Menninghaus make similar points. Max Pensky, *Melancholy Dialectics: Walter Benjamin and the Play of Mourning*, Amherst MA, 1993, pp. 47–48; Menninghaus, *Benjamins Theorie der Sprachmagie*, p. 16. Benjamin himself also implies as much: 'If in what follows the nature of language is considered on the basis of the first chapter of Genesis, the object is neither biblical interpretation, nor subjection of the Bible to objective consideration as revealed truth, but the discovery of what emerges of itself from the biblical text with regard to the nature of language; and the Bible is only *initially* indispensable for this purpose because the present argument follows it in presupposing language as an ultimate reality, perceptible only in its manifestation, inexplicable and mystical' (*GS II* 147; *SW I* 67). The Bible is essential to Benjamin because only through its myth of origin is language explicable as the 'ultimate reality'.

23. Pensky suggests that Benjamin simply lacks a linguist's conceptual vocabulary, and that this might be an additional explanation for his recourse to mysticism: 'Benjamin's earliest systematic attempt to ground the objectively existing truth elements residing within quotidian language takes the form of theological doctrine because the arbitrary–nonarbitrary distinction upon which such attempts must test themselves could not, at least in 1916, be itself grounded without resort to axiomatic, and hence indisputable theology.' Pensky, *Melancholy Dialectics*, p. 56.

24. Pressler, whose study consists of a close reading and contextualization of Benjamin's review article, is forced, time and time again, to acknowledge Benjamin's wilful misreading of his material. For example, on Bühler: 'Benjamin does not show the least inclination to deal with the rich empirical proofs for Bühler's axioms nor to work through the axioms themselves.' Günter Karl Pressler, *Vom mimetischen Ursprung der Sprache: Walter Benjamins Sammelreferat 'Probleme der Sprachsoziologie' im Kontext seiner Sprachtheorie*, Frankfurt/Main, 1992, p. 34.

25. In his notes from 1970–71, however, Bakhtin has recourse to a nature mysticism that is not dissimilar to Benjamin's thinking, speculating that 'when consciousness appeared in the world (existence) and, perhaps, when biological life appeared (perhaps not only animals, but trees and grass also witness and judge) the world (existence) changed radically' (*SG* 137). Morson and Emerson interpret this passage as Bakhtin's development of a Stoical conception of freedom. Morson and Emerson, *Bakhtin*, p. 453.

26. Voloshinov claims, in 1929, that 'the majority of Russian thinkers in linguistics are under the determinative influence of Saussure and his disciples, Bally and Sèchehaye' (*MPL* 59). Alpatov discusses the context of Soviet and pre-Soviet linguistics and Voloshinov's 'marginal' position in Vladimir Alpatov, 'The Bakhtin Circle and Problems in Linguistics', in Craig Brandist, David Shepherd and Galin Tihanov (eds), *The Bakhtin Circle: In the Master's Absence*, Manchester, 2004, pp. 70–96. The full story of Russian

linguistics of the period will only become clear upon the completion of the Bakhtin Centre's project, 'The Rise of Sociological Linguistics in the Soviet Union, 1917–1938: Institutions, Ideas and Agendas'. See http://www.shef.ac. uk/uni/academic/A-C/bakh/sociolinguistics.html, accessed 4 January 2007.

27. A comparison with Voloshinov's work that engages in thorough and well-informed detail with material similar to the material of Benjamin's article makes this clear. Nevertheless, Alpatov raises doubts over Bakhtin and Voloshinov's credentials in his examination of the early notes for *Marxism and the Philosophy of Language*. (Alpatov views Bakhtin and Voloshinov as co-authors.) See Alpatov, 'The Bakhtin Circle and Problems in Linguistics', pp. 75–83.

28. In the remainder of this chapter I shall follow Benjamin's (biblical) diction in using the term 'Man' to speak of humanity in general.

29. Rochlitz, *The Disenchantment of Art*, p. 218.

30. Bröcker gives a parallel explanation for nature's subjectivity which relies on the fusion of creation and naming which is inherent in the creation of things through the word: 'because God did not first create mere matter which he then called something, but rather expressed the things [of creation] in the word, the cognition of these things cannot be reduced to subject–object relations'. Michael Bröcker, 'Sprache', in Opitz and Wizisla (eds), *Benjamins Begriffe*, Frankfurt/Main, 2000, pp. 740–73 (745).

31. Michel Foucault, *Les Mots et les choses*, Paris, 1966, p. 51.

32. Bröcker, 'Sprache', pp. 746–47.

33. My argument here, then, differs from that of Thornhill who contends that 'influenced by both Klages and Cassirer, Benjamin conceives the initial period of history as a state of undifferentiation, a state of unruptured mimesis in which no distinction is made between subject and object. This is for Benjamin the state of *Erfahrung*, continuous ontological experience, a form of experience which is replaced by the sporadic, fractured *Erlebnis* of modern existence.' Christopher Thornhill, *Walter Benjamin and Karl Kraus: Problems of a Wahlverwandschaft*, Stuttgart, 1996, p. 87.

34. Hofmannsthal's 'Chandos Letter' expresses a crisis of and a rejection of conventional language, as well as its narrator's frustrated desire to discover a new form of language in which the mute objects of creation would speak to him. See Hugo von Hofmannsthal, 'Ein Brief', in Hofmannsthal, *Gesammelte Werke in Einzelausgaben: Prosa II*, ed. by Herbert Steiner, Frankfurt/Main, 1951, pp. 7–22. Rochlitz points out Benjamin's affinities with George and Mallarmé, arguing that their 'aesthetic aristocratism' helps us understand Benjamin's use of the term, 'bourgeois', which has, as yet, nothing to do with Marxism. Rochlitz, *The Disenchantment of Art*, p. 12. McCole discusses the ambivalent attitude of Benjamin to George in McCole, *Benjamin*, pp. 79–80. As I show in the next chapter, Benjamin criticizes what he terms George's *Sprachkultus* (cult of language) in his essay on Kraus. Bröcker also points out the influence of Wyneken's youth movement and its anti-modern stance on Benjamin's 'anti-bourgeois' conception of language: 'The concept of the "divine", the "absolute" which is free from empirical aims and motivations and which stands in opposition to the notion of language as a system of instrumentally oriented signs, points back to the intellectual *milieu* of the Youth movement which must be understood not only as a limited reaction to the crisis of the Gymnasium

and the University but also as a resistance to the modernization of German society.' Bröcker, 'Sprache', p. 742.

35. Benjamin draws here on Hamann in whose 'Aesthetica in nuce' we read: 'Speak, that I may see Thee! This wish was answered by the Creation, which is an utterance to created things through created things [...] The fault may lie where it will (outside us or within us): all we have left in nature is fragmentary verse and *disjecta membra poetae*. To collect these together is the scholar's modest part; the philosopher's to interpret them; to imitate them, or – bolder still – to adapt them, the poet's. To speak is to translate – from the tongue of angels into the tongue of men, that is to translate thoughts into words – things into names – images into signs.' J. G. Hamann, 'Aesthetica in Nuce: A Rhapsody in Cabbalistic Prose', in J. M. Bernstein (ed.), *Classical and Romantic German Aesthetics*, Cambridge, 2003, pp. 1–23 (4).

36. Fenves comments that this means that 'the original [...] is derivative at the origin'. Peter Fenves, 'The Genesis of Judgement: Spatiality, Analogy, and Metaphor in Benjamin's "On Language as Such and on Human Language"', in David S. Ferris (ed.), *Walter Benjamin: Theoretical Questions*, Stanford CA, 1996, pp. 75–93 (88).

37. Rochlitz points out the extent to which Benjamin draws on modern creeds of *l'art pour l'art*, quoting Diderot: 'If in drawing a picture, one imagines a beholder, all is lost.' Rochlitz, *The Disenchantment of Art*, p. 23.

38. See my comments above on the tension between description and prescription in Bakhtin's thought.

39. Benjamin's conception of aura, then, has attributes of Bakhtin's conception of dialogue.

40. Habermas, 'Walter Benjamin: Consciousness-Raising or Rescuing Critique', p. 107.

41. Typically, however, Benjamin is able to see seeds of hope, even in a degraded phenomenon such as bad translation. His notes read: 'The value of bad translations – productive misunderstandings' (*GS VI* 159; *SW III* 250). Whilst bad translation (in Benjamin's special sense) objectifies and does not produce the newness of a good translation, errors in bad translations (here, 'bad' I take to imply the conventional sense of containing errors) can help create something new.

42. Benjamin refers here to Romain Rolland's 10-volume novel, *Jean-Christophe*, published between 1904 and 1912. The story of a German musician, Jean-Christophe Krafft, this is a novel that draws on German as much as French literary traditions and could have been, so to speak, written in German.

43. Caygill, *Benjamin*, p. 19.

44. This is the analysis of different forms of discourse from direct unmediated discourse, through objectified discourse to various forms of discourse with an orientation towards someone else's discourse. Bakhtin gives a diagrammatic presentation of the scheme that results. See *DP*, p. 199.

45. Benjamin's incessant self-quotation has practical grounds. Given that for much of his life he was a freelance writer and critic, often in acute financial difficulties, self-quotation proved a means of producing more copy. This can be seen in his recycling of fundamentally the same material for different commissioners. Nevertheless, this does not go against the fact that Benjamin sees (with Bakhtin) the importance of variations of the same material that

produce new formulations and new ideas in their new contexts. This is another area where the themes of repetition and difference emerge in both thinkers.

46. Gardiner has some perspicacious comments on Bakhtin's similarity to Ernst Bloch, someone with whom Benjamin also has many similarities. '[...] one could mention Bloch's fragmentary and elliptical prose style which, by drawing on expressionist techniques (including Brecht's "alienation effect"), attempts to induce a defamiliarization of the taken-for-granted in order to generate an awareness of alternative possibilities. This recalls Bakhtin's confessed "love for variations and for a diversity of terms for a single phenomenon [and the] multiplicity of focuses".' Michael J. Gardiner, 'Bakhtin's Carnival: Utopia as Critique', in Shepherd (ed.), *Bakhtin: Carnival and Other Subjects*, 3–4, 1993, pp. 20–47 (42). Whilst he does not say it explicitly, Gardiner seems to have noticed the kinship between Bloch's Expressionist technique of montage and Bakhtin's method of thinking and writing. For the connections between Bloch and Benjamin, see Wolin, *Benjamin*, pp. 16–17 and 23–27. Brodersen gives biographical details of Benjamin and Bloch's friendship in Brodersen, *Benjamin*, pp. 99–100. Bloch discusses his wary friendship with Benjamin in Ernst Bloch, 'Recollections of Walter Benjamin', in Gary Smith (ed.), *On Walter Benjamin*, London, Cambridge MA, 1991, pp. 338–45. Specifically, he discusses Benjamin's use of montage on pp. 341–42.

47. Both thinkers could be construed as ideologues of plagiarism. Their attitude to quotation resembles the medieval. A good number of the quotations produced by Benjamin in the *Trauerspiel* book cannot be traced to any verifiable sources.

48. Bürger develops his theory of the Avant-garde on the basis of Benjamin's theory of montage, suggesting that montage is the main weapon of the Avant-garde's attack on organic works of art in the name of the sublation of art and life. Despite my criticisms of Bürger below, seeing a theory of montage in Bakhtin allows one to think of him as a much more modernist thinker and writer than he might at first seem, given his apparent lack of interest in the historical Avant-garde movements of which he was a contemporary. See Peter Bürger, *Theory of the Avant-Garde*, trans. Michael Shaw, Minneapolis MN, 1984, particularly pp. 73–82. The question of Bakhtin's relation to the Avant-garde is contested. I have already made some comments on this in relation to Bakhtin and Russian Formalism. Tiupa implies that Bakhtin's aesthetics are necessarily hostile to the Avant-garde's 'radical pessimism' in Valerii Tiupa, 'The Architectonics of Aesthetic Discourse', in Shepherd (ed.), *The Contexts of Bakhtin*, pp. 95–107. In the same volume, however, Pechey, arguing for Bakhtin's modernity and seeing a possible reincarnation of Bakhtin's Rabelais in James Joyce, contends that 'Bakhtin's modernist critique of modernity [...] is achieved by the simple and yet astonishingly creative gesture of projecting the story of the European avant-garde back into the continent's past.' Graham Pechey, 'Modernity and Chronotopicity in Bakhtin', in Shepherd (ed.), *The Contexts of Bakhtin*, Amsterdam, 1998, pp. 173–82 (180). Benjamin explicitly associates himself with the Avant-garde. Jennings traces in an elegant fashion Benjamin's 'waking up' to the Avant-garde 'sometime in 1924'. Michael

Jennings, 'Walter Benjamin and the European Avant-garde', in Ferris (ed.), *Companion to Benjamin*, Cambridge, 2004, pp. 18–34.

49. Buck-Morss, *Dialectics of Seeing*, p. 74.

50. Both montage and polyphony, then, are forms of mimesis and are not opposed to it, as might be assumed. The deconstruction of traditional mimetic forms is carried out both in response to a radically new reality and for the sake of a new form of mimesis. Adorno makes a similar point in his interpretation of Baudelaire's poetry as a disruption of traditional mimetic forms: 'The new is the aesthetic seal of expanded reproduction, with its promise of undiminished plenitude. Baudelaire's poetry was the first to codify that, in the midst of the fully developed commodity society, art can ignore this tendency only at the price of its powerlessness. [...] Art is modern art through mimesis of the hardened and alienated; only thereby, and not by the refusal of a mute reality, does art become eloquent; this is why art no longer tolerates the innocuous.' Theodor W. Adorno, *Aesthetic Theory*, ed. and trans. Robert Hullot-Kentor, London, 1997, p. 21.

51. Jennings, 'Walter Benjamin and the European Avant-garde', p. 30.

52. Here, we see again the themes of memory and attentiveness, raised at the end of the previous chapter.

53. Bertolt Brecht, 'Vergnügungs-Theater oder Lehrtheater', in *Schriften zum Theater*, pp. 60–74 (61–62). Brecht uses the term 'epic' in a completely different sense from Bakhtin. The opposition of 'epic' and 'dramatic' is the cornerstone of his theory of theatre. Benjamin appropriates and expands this theory in his various writings on Brecht.

54. One might, with Bürger, map Brecht's distinction between dramatic and epic art onto a distinction between organic and inorganic art, a distinction that Bürger develops on the basis of Benjamin's theory of allegory. Bürger describes this distinction as follows: 'Artists who produce an organic work (in what follows we shall refer to them as classicists...) treat their material as something living. They respect its significance as something that has grown from concrete life situations. For avant-gardistes, on the other hand, material is everything. Their activity initially consists in nothing other than in killing the 'life' of the material, that is, in tearing it out of its functional context that gives it meaning. Whereas the classicist recognizes and respects in the material the carrier of a meaning, the avant-gardistes see only the empty sign, to which they can impart significance. The classicist correspondingly treats the material as a whole, whereas the avant-gardiste tears it out of the life totality, isolates it, and turns it into a fragment.' Bürger, *Theory of the Avant-garde*, p. 70. Nevertheless, Bürger seems to miss the point that, for Benjamin, montage preserves the life of its material.

55. Alfred Döblin, *Berlin Alexanderplatz*, Frankfurt/Main, 1980, pp. 92–93. A rough translation, that unfortunately preserves little of the complexity of different registers and dialect forms, reads as follows: 'When all of a sudden the conversation on the neighbouring table grows louder, the one newcomer starts talking big. He wants to sing, it's too quiet for him here. Franz chews, thinks: they mean me. He wouldn't have believed it possible that old Georg Dreske sits with young'uns like that and doesn't even come over to his table. What an old boot, married, a right old boot, and sits by that kid and listens to her nattering.'

56. Döblin himself, however, preferred to call his novel 'homophonic', as opposed to the 'polyphonic' novel of Dos Passos, since his novel is focused on its protagonist, Franz Biberkopf. See 'Alfred Döblin', in Rudolf Raddler *et al.* (eds), *Kindlers neues Literaturlexikon*, 22 vols, Munich, 1988–98, Vol. 4, pp. 739–52 (743).

57. My argument here coincides with that of Coates who notes the withdrawal of the author into silence over the course of Bakhtin's work. See Coates, *Christianity in Bakhtin*, particularly pp. 116–18. Lock also treats the theme of silence in Bakhtin. His focus, however, is on a Derridean reading of the fact that Bakhtin favours the silently read genre of the novel to voiced genres. See Charles Lock, 'Bakhtin and the Tropes of Orthodoxy', in Susan M. Felch and Paul J. Contino (eds), *Bakhtin and Religion: A Feeling for Faith*, Evanston IL, 2001, pp. 97–119 (112–14).

58. One may also consider here Voloshinov's chronology of reported and reporting speech as the increasing decomposition of the authorial context. See *MPL*, pp. 120–23. I discuss Voloshinov's history of language in the next chapter.

59. Benjamin's ingenious response to the question of why the tree of good and evil is planted in the garden runs as follows: 'The tree of knowledge did not stand in the garden in order to dispense information on good and evil, but as an emblem of judgment over the questioner' (*GS II* 154; *SW I* 71).

60. He adds that 'this results later in the plurality of languages'. This point is a reversal of Saussure's argument for the arbitrary nature of the linguistic sign. Saussure argues that the sign must be arbitrary on the basis of the existence of different words in different languages for the same concept. 'No reason can be given for preferring *sister* to *soeur*, *Ochs* to *boeuf*, etc.' Saussure, *Course in General Linguistics*, p. 73. Benjamin argues that different languages have come into being because the sign has become arbitrary.

61. Benjamin sums up his position as follows: 'The immediacy in the communication of abstraction came into being as judgement when in the Fall, man abandoned immediacy in the communication of the concrete, name, and fell into the abyss of the mediatedness of all communication, of the word, as means, of the empty word, into the word of prattle' (*GS I* 154; *SW I* 72).

62. 'Bakhtin claims that to pretend to axiological self-sufficiency is to fall into a state of profound self-contradiction and self-negation, to live a lie: "We may say that this is the fall [*grekhopadenie*] which is immanent to being and experienced from within it; it lies in the tendency of being towards self-sufficiency." ' Coates, *Christianity in Bakhtin*, pp. 44–45. Coates gives her own translation here which makes clear Bakhtin's reference to the theological concept of the Fall, a reference that is obscured in Liapunov's translation.

63. See Craig Brandist, 'The Hero at the Bar of Eternity: The Bakhtin Circle's Juridical Theory of the Novel', *Economy and Society*, 30, 2001, 2, pp. 208–28.

64. Brandist's arguments on this point can be over-dogmatic. He gives, for example, the following reading of Bakhtin's analysis of Dostoevsky: '[Bakhtin] follows the neo-Kantian trend of treating individuals not as concretely singular and embodied beings subjected to material economic and social influences, but as juridical persons who are exclusively considered as bearers of rights and responsibilities. [...] This inevitably imposes a partic-

ular character on work that adopts such a principle and this should be clearly recognized before Bakhtin's categories are employed in literary analysis today.' Brandist, *The Bakhtin Circle*, p. 94.

65. In the formulation of this split we see the influence that Benjamin has on the thought of Adorno. The notion of a dialectic of mimetic behaviour that approximates to, but does not dominate, the object and rejects end-means rationalization that seeks to subsume the object to itself forms the core of Adorno and Horkheimer's *Dialectic of Enlightenment*. As they put it: 'Mimesis imitates the environment but false projection makes the environment like itself.' Theodor W. Adorno and Max Horkheimer, *Dialectic of Enlightenment*, trans. John Cumming, London, 1997, p. 18.

66. The term 'archive of non-sensuous similarities'(*GS II* 209; *SW II* 697) comes from Benjamin's 'The Doctrine of the Similar', part of his writings on mimesis which are closely related to the philosophy of language of 'On Language as Such and on the Language of Man'.

67. See René Descartes, 'Meditations on First Philosophy' (1641), in *Key Philosophical Writings*, ed. Enrique Chavez-Arvizo, trans. Elizabeth S. Haldane and G. R. T Ross, Ware, 1997, pp. 121–90 (144–47).

68. J. M. Bernstein, 'Introduction', in Bernstein (ed.), *German Aesthetics*, Cambridge, 2003, pp. vii–xxxiii (ix).

4   Totalities

1. Following the theological strand that runs through both Bakhtin's and Benjamin's thought, one might describe the task that Bakhtin and Benjamin set themselves as the task of discerning how the restoration of totality and the redemption of a fallen world might best be served. Habermas highlights the importance of the concept of *Rettung* (rescuing, redemption) in Benjamin's thought with the complex of theological associations that such a concept brings to mind. Habermas sees Benjamin's rescuing-critique as orientated towards a restoration of what he described as 'unmutilated experience', a 'continuum of experience'. Habermas, 'Walter Benjamin: Consciousness-Raising or Rescuing Critique', especially p. 106.

2. Gilloch, *Benjamin*, p. 237.

3. Andrew Benjamin and Osborne's comment is valid as much for Bakhtin as it is for Benjamin: 'It was in works of art that Benjamin found the self-contained form of totality he thought necessary for experience to participate in truth.' Andrew Benjamin and Osborne, 'Introduction', p. ix.

4. Hirschkop argues that Bakhtin's philosophy of art 'appears to be the old wine of German idealist aesthetics in a new intersubjective bottle': 'As in Kant, aesthetic form heals the rift between the lawfulness of that which we know through natural science (which Bakhtin calls cognition) and the orientation towards ends characteristic of morality: in art we experience something both sensual and apparently purposeful: in Bakhtin's words, existence as "beautiful givenness", self-sufficient and needing no justification.' Hirschkop, *Bakhtin*, p. 58.

5. Friedrich Schiller, *On the Aesthetic Education of Man* (1794), ed. and trans. E. M. Wilkinson and L. A. Willoughby, Oxford, 1967, p. 43.

6. Tihanov has drawn attention to the importance of the notion of aesthetic *Bildung* in Bakhtin's work, particularly in Bakhtin's texts on Goethe and in the first version of the Dostoevsky book. For both thinkers, the *Bildung* of aesthetic experience acts equally on both creators and contemplators of art. As Bakhtin notes: 'In form I find myself, find my own productive, axiologically form-giving, activity, I feel intensely my own movement that is creating the object, and I do so not only in primary creation, not only during my own performance, but also during the contemplation of the work of art. I must to some extent experience myself as the creator of form, in order to actualize the artistically valid form as such' (*AH* 304). Benjamin's preoccupation with both creator and contemplator is more consistently noticeable.

7. Bakhtin uses the opposition of open and closed; Benjamin prefers the opposition of fragment and whole. Despite this different conceptual vocabulary, both thinkers seem to be concerned with totality and its opposite (openness/fragmentation). The matter is complicated by the fact that one can present the terms of these oppositions positively ('completeness' and 'openness', for example, tend to carry positive associations) or negatively (similarly, 'closedness' and 'incompleteness' tend to carry negative associations).

8. As a result, Bakhtin and Benjamin go beyond what Eagleton terms the 'ideology of the aesthetic'. According to Eagleton, the emergent middle class, wishing to define itself as the universal subject of history without sacrificing the sense of particularity that is part of its individualistic ideology, finds in the aesthetic a 'dream of reconciliation'. Here is a sphere in which individuals are to be 'woven into intimate unity with no detriment to their specificity' whilst the 'abstract totality' of art is 'suffused with all the flesh-and-blood reality of individual being'. The aesthetics of openness and fragmentation that Bakhtin and Benjamin embrace are not to be domesticated into a dream of easy resolution. Eagleton, *The Ideology of the Aesthetic*, p. 25.

9. The German title is *Über den Ursprung des deutschen Trauerspiels*. It has been translated by John Osborne as *The Origin of German Tragic Drama*. '*Trauerspiel*', however, is better translated as 'play of lamentation'. I shall refer to it as the *Trauerspiel* book. Whilst it failed to win Benjamin a university position, the *Trauerspiel* book came out in 1928.

10. Gilloch comments: '[Benjamin's] interest in the *Trauerspiel*, in particular, was sparked by the recognition that the bleak, broken world of the baroque might have a special significance for, an "elective affinity" with his own time, convulsed as it was by the carnage of the Great War, the financial turmoil and inflation of the Weimar years, and a sense of cultural crisis.' Gilloch, *Benjamin*, p. 237.

11. As Leslie points out: 'Benjamin was frequently able to employ the concept of decline (*Verfall*) positively, and to perceive in decay historical truth.' Leslie, *Benjamin*, p. 43. This goes as much for the supposedly degenerate era of the Weimar Republic as for the supposedly degenerate form of *Trauerspiel*.

12. McCole glosses this as follows: '*Verklärung* suggests first of all a transformation in which an object takes on a certain radiance. The object glows; it beams, like a face transfigured by bliss, or shines, as does the beautiful appearance (*schöner Schein*) of the work of art. Transfiguration often involves an exaltation into the transcendent [...]. But finally, *Verklärung* may also mean an idealization of something in the negative sense of distortion or

even falsification [...]. The aesthetic symbol's transgression, in a word, is *Verklärung*, a falsifying transfiguration.' McCole, *Benjamin*, pp. 137–38.

13. This aspect of Benjamin's work has drawn the attention of thinkers of decon-struction. Benjamin's theory of the primacy of script here is similar to that of Derrida in *Of Grammatology*: 'there is nothing subordinate about written script; it is not cast away in reading, like dross. It is absorbed along with what is read as its "pattern"' (*GS I* 388; *OGTD* 215). Likewise, the effect of script-based allegory on the symbol might well be described as deconstructive of a metaphysics of presence. Eagleton's reading of allegory runs along these lines. See Eagleton, *Benjamin*, especially pp. 20–23.

14. In the terms of 'On Language as Such and on the Language of Man', symbol corresponds to name, allegory to fallen sign. We see in the *Trauerspiel* book, Benjamin's re-evaluation of the opposition of name and sign through his discovery of new potentialities in the debased nature of the sign.

15. As Andrew Benjamin and Osborne comment: 'in *The Origin of German Tragic Drama*, allegory is seen to destroy the deceptive totality of the symbol, wrenching it out of context and placing it in new, transparently constructed, configurations of meaning'. Benjamin and Osborne, 'Introduction', p. xi.

16. As Nägele comments: '*Erfahrung* is laid bare as *Erlebnis*. Yet it is the gesture of laying bare the *Erlebnis* without any borrowed robe of *Erfahrung* that gives the *Erlebnis* the weight of *Erfahrung*.' Rainer Nägele, 'The Poetic Ground Laid Bare (Benjamin reading Baudelaire)', in Ferris (ed.), *Benjamin: Theoretical Questions*, pp. 118–38 (138).

17. Hirschkop, *Bakhtin*, p. 87.

18. The phrase, 'the tyranny of a usurper', is reminiscent of Bakhtin's conception of the 'pretender' discussed above.

19. Meschonnic charts this tradition and the utopian images that it contains in biblical texts, medieval Cabalistic literature, as well as in twentieth-century thinkers such as Rosenzweig, Lévinas and Benjamin, to whom the last third of his book is dedicated. Meschonnic also points to the connec-tion between Jewish negative theology and the apophatic tradition which, critics have argued, is influential in Orthodoxy and thus on Bakhtin. See Henri Meschonnic, *L'Utopie du Juif*, Paris, 2001, particularly, on negative theology, pp. 189–227.

20. Scholem notes: 'Beginning at the moment of the deepest catastrophe there exists the chance of redemption.' He goes on to quote the *Midrash Tehillim* to Psalm 43: 'Israel speaks to God: When will you redeem us? He answers: When you have sunk to the lowest level, at that time I will redeem you.' Gershom Scholem, 'Towards an Understanding of the Messianic Idea in Judaism', in *The Messianic Idea in Judaism*, New York, 1971, pp. 1–36 (11–12).

21. Brian Britt, *Walter Benjamin and the Bible*, New York, 1996, p. 105.

22. Fritz Breithaupt, 'History as the Delayed Disintegration of Phenomena', in Richter (ed.), *Benjamin's Ghosts*, Stanford CA, 2002, pp. 191–203 (199). More problematically, Breithaupt goes on to argue: 'this Messiah can only arrive in strict imagelessness. He or She does not need to come because the empty space is the condition of possibility of his or her arrival and that is all that is needed.' This seems to me to be a reduction of Benjamin's serious theological and political meditations to the dimension of mere possibility for its own sake.

23. As Tiedemann and others have pointed out, however, this conception of revolution as catastrophe owes perhaps more to Blanqui and anarchism than it does to Marx. See Rolf Tiedemann, 'Historical Materialism or Political Messianism? An Interpretation of the Theses "On the Concept of History"', in Smith (ed.), *Benjamin: Philosophy, Aesthetics, History*, London, Chicago IL, 1983, pp. 175–209.

24. 'Buying and selling can be separated. They are, then, crises in potential.' Marx, *Theories of Surplus Value*, quoted in Christoph Türcke and Gerhard Bolte, *Einführung in die kritische Theorie*, Darmstadt, 1994, p. 6. Türcke and Bolte provide a lucid account of the relation between commodity and crisis in Marx's thought and the influence of this aspect of his thought in Germany following the First World War.

25. Julia Kristeva, 'Une poétique ruinée', Preface to M. M. Bakhtine, *La Poétique de Dostoievski*, Paris, 1975, pp. 5–27 (14–15).

26. Hirschkop, 'A Response to the Forum on Mikhail Bakhtin', p. 76.

27. It is in this context that we can understand statements such as the one that Voloshinov makes about Freud. In his essay on Freudism, Voloshinov argues that the unconscious is simply the unofficial conscious that bourgeois society cannot accept. He goes on to assert: 'In a healthy social body, just as in a socially healthy individual, everyday ideology, established on the socio-economic basis, is coherent and solid, without any divergence between the official and unofficial consciousnesses.' Valentin Voloshinov, 'Freidism: Kriticheskii ocherk' (Freudism: a criticial sketch) (1927), in *Filosofiia i sotsiologiia gumanitarnykh nauk*, ed. D. A. Iunov, St Petersburg, 1995, pp. 87–189 (167). This statement seems to concord with some of the most extreme Stalinist positions on the need for an absolute convergence between the private and the public.

28. Hegel, *Philosophy of Right*, p. 23.

29. Leon Trotsky, *Literature and Revolution* (1923), trans. Rose Strunsky, London, 1991, pp. 258–59.

30. Morson and Emerson, *Bakhtin*, pp. 124–25.

31. Coates suggests that it is the 'quintessentially Russian concept of kenotic self-humiliation and self-giving love' which inspired Bakhtin. Ruth Coates, 'The First and Second Adam in Bakhtin's Thought', in Felch and Contino (eds), *Religion in Bakhtin*, Evanston IL, 2001, pp. 63–78 (77).

32. Interpreting this passage in terms of different temporalities seems to be the only way to understand what is otherwise an incoherent conception of a 'new, higher authorial position', located above the monologic author's position.

33. Fyodor Dostoevsky, *The Karamazov Brothers*, trans. Ignat Avsey, Oxford, 1998, p. 377.

34. Dostoevsky, *The Karamazov Brothers*, p. 379.

35. Just as Benjamin's thought bears a relation to the Jewish tradition of negative theology, Poole and others have argued that Bakhtin's thought bears a relation to the Christian tradition of apophasis. See Randall Poole, 'The Apophatic Bakhtin', in Felch and Contino (eds), *Bakhtin and Religion*, Evanston IL, 2001, pp. 151–75.

36. Hirschkop, *Bakhtin*, p. 95.

37. As Tihanov comments: 'true dialogue should be resolved, at the end of the day, into a monologue. The task of dialogue is to enact a cathartic deliverance

from the plurality of voices besetting the inner world of the characters.'
Tihanov, *Master and Slave*, pp. 199–200.

38. Coates, *Christianity in Bakhtin*, p. 123.

39. Brandist posits a genealogy of messianic motifs in Bakhtin's thought that
suggests a direct connection to the messianic tradition in which Benjamin
stands. Referring to the superaddressee as the 'ultimate, "loophole" judge',
Brandist argues that 'since the world is nothing but the systematic and
cumulative but perpetually unfinished totality of all representations, the
judgement of the world (Weltgericht) associated with the "superaddressee"
is actually a type of messianism that derives, at least in part, from the Judaic
elements of Marburg neo-Kantianism.' Brandist, 'Law and the Genres of
Discourse', p. 39.

40. See Diane Collinson, 'Aesthetic Experience', in Oswald Hanfling (ed.), *Philosophical Aesthetics*, Oxford, 1992, pp. 111–78 (119–21).

41. *Stasis* in the Classical world meant the stability that is guaranteed by the
coexistence of opposing forces that cancel each other out. Thucydides uses
the term to describe violent civil strife such as occurred in Corcyra during
the Peloponnesian War. See Thucydides, *History of the Peloponnesian War*,
ed. M. I. Finley, trans. Rex Warner, London, 1972, pp. 236–45.

42. This second factor appears to be missing in Coates's account of this passage.
Coates reads Bakhtin here in terms of new birth and eternal life. See Coates,
Christianity in Bakhtin, pp. 50–51. Bonetskaia's contextualizing comments are
also relevant: 'In the early twentieth century the Russian cultural consciousness had developed a notion of the artist as a tragic personality: there was
a belief in the fatal guilt attached to any creative work. The poet's guilt
was considered similar to that of a murderer, in that the creation of artistic
form was always an act of limiting, and in some ways even killing, the vital
impulse behind it. Hence Aleksandr Blok in a poem precisely on this theme
"The Artist" ("Khudozhnik", 1913) uses the image of a cage imprisoning a
free bird. Form in relation to life – this is the perspective in which Bakhtin,
too, poses the problem of the aesthetic. "The problem of the aesthetic
is precisely how the world may be thus paralysed by form."' Bonetskaia,
'Bakhtin's Aesthetics', p. 84. It is unclear to what extent this is a merely
Russian phenomenon or more a phenomenon of the European *Fin de siècle*
as a whole. One thinks of the connection between artistic creation and death
in Huysmans's *A Rebours* (1884).

43. This poem embodies much of the structure of Benjamin's aesthetics, hence
the long quotation and the attention that I devote here to Baudelaire's poem
itself. In both *Toward a Philosophy of the Act* and 'Author and Hero', Bakhtin
illustrates his understanding of aesthetic activity by means of a reading of
Pushkin's poem 'Parting'. This poem, likewise, seems to occupy a privileged
place in Bakhtin's understanding of aesthetic form. It is extraordinary to note
the degree of congruence, in terms of underlying structure, between these two
poems: A woman who recedes; an attempt to stay time; a projection of eternity;
transience and death. See both the poem and its analysis in *TPA*, pp. 65–72.

44. Weber's comments on this passage capture a key aspect of its bitter ambivalence: 'Such love at last sight imposes direction and meaning upon an appar-
ition whose transfiguring power, Benjamin insists, reposes exclusively upon
a mass that as such is never depicted or named. The mass here, invisible and

nameless, is precisely that ambivalent, divergent movement that carries the *passante* even as she appears to emerge out of it.' Samuel Weber, 'Mass Mediauras; or, Art, Aura, and Media in the Work of Walter Benjamin', in Ferris (ed.), *Benjamin: Theoretical Questions*, Stanford CA, 1996, pp. 27–49 (41).

45. One might also note that this poem contains an image of the shadow of death from which it never quite escapes, the shadow cast by the (young?) widow's *feston* and *ourlet*.

46. It must be conceded that 'Epic and Novel', the most deconstructive of Bakhtin's essays, rejects almost entirely the concept of memory in relation to the novel: 'The "modernity" of the novel is indestructible, and verges on an unjust evaluation of the times. Let us recall the re-evaluation of the past that occurred during the Renaissance [...] and that is inherent in positivism (the exposure of myth, legend, heroization, a maximum departure from memory [...]' (*DI* 31). Towards the end of his life, Bakhtin reincorporates some of the insights of his earliest period. This revised conception of memory stems from this period. It may also be usefully related to Bakhtin's thoughts on criticism and tradition, discussed in Chapter 1.

47. Andrew Benjamin, 'Benjamin's Modernity', in Ferris (ed.), *Companion to Benjamin*, pp. 97–114 (111).

48. Gardiner's suggestion seems to hit the mark: 'Like Walter Benjamin, perhaps the Western Marxist he has the most affinity with, Bakhtin therefore exhorts us to probe the gaps and silences, the fractures and the fault lines that expose the operations of a monologism which seeks to effect an ideological closure in order to "blast a specific era out of the homogenous course of history". Only then can the meaning of a suppressed history have its "homecoming festival", that is, be allowed to speak to us, and we in turn have the linguistic capacity and the cultural resources to answer it in a free and familiar manner, without fear of censure or retribution.' Gardiner, *Dialogics of Critique*, p. 194.

Bibliography

Primary texts by Bakhtin and the Bakhtin Circle

Bakhtin, M. M., *Problemy Poetiki Dostoevskogo*, Moscow: Sovetskaia Rossia, 1972.
———., *Art and Answerability: Early Philosophical Essays by M. M. Bakhtin*, ed. Michael Holquist and Vadim Liapunov, trans. Vadim Liapunov, Austin TX: University of Texas Press, 1990.
———., *Rabelais and his World*, ed. and trans. Hélène Iswolsky, Bloomington IN: Indiana University Press, 1984.
———., *Problems of Dostoevsky's Poetics*, ed. and trans. Caryl Emerson, Manchester: Manchester University Press, 1994.
———., *The Dialogic Imagination: Four Essays by M. M. Bakhtin*, ed. Michael Holquist, trans. Caryl Emerson and Michael Holquist, Austin TX: University of Texas Press, 1996.
———., *Toward a Philosophy of the Act*, ed. Michael Holquist and Vadim Liapunov, trans. Vadim Liapunov, Austin TX: University of Texas Press, 1993.
———., *Speech Genres and Other Late Essays*, ed. Caryl Emerson and Michael Holquist, trans. Vern W. McGee, Austin TX: University of Texas Press, 1986.
———., 'Dopolneniia i izmeneniia k Rable' (Additions and amendments to 'Rabelais'), in *Sobranie sochinenii*, Vol. 5, ed. S. G. Bocharov and L. A. Gogotishvili, Moscow: Russkie Slovari, 1996, pp. 80–129.
Bakhtin, M. M./Medvedev, P. N., *The Formal Method in Literary Scholarship: A Critical Introduction to Sociological Poetics*, trans. Albert J. Wehrle, London, Cambridge MA: Johns Hopkins University Press, 1985.
Bakhtine, M. (V. N. Volochinov), *Le Freudisme*, trans. Guy Verret, Lausanne: Editions l'Age d' Homme, 1980.
Vološinov, V. N., *Marxism and the Philosophy of Language*, ed. and trans. Ladislav Matejka and I. R. Titunik, Cambridge MA: Harvard University Press, 1993.
Voloshinov, V. N., 'Freidism: Kriticheskii ocherk', in *Filosofiia i sotsiologiia gumanitarnykh nauk*, ed. D. A. Iulov, St Petersburg: Asta Press, 1995, pp. 87–189.

Primary texts by Benjamin

Benjamin, W., 'What is Epic Theatre? [First Version]', in Walter Benjamin, *Understanding Brecht*, trans. Anna Bostock, London: Verso, 1983, pp. 1–13.
———., *The Origin of German Tragic Drama*, trans. John Osborne, London: Verso, 1985.
———., *Briefe*, ed. Gershom Scholem and Theodor W. Adorno, 2 vols, Frankfurt/Main: Suhrkamp, 1993.
———., *Selected Writings*, ed. Michael W. Jennings and others, trans. Howard Eiland, Rodney Livingstone and others, 4 vols, Cambridge MA: Belknap/Harvard, 1996–2003.

——., *Gesammelte Schriften*, ed. Rolf Tiedmann and Hermann Schweppenhäuser, 7 vols, Frankfurt/Main: Suhrkamp, 1998.
——., *The Arcades Project*, trans. Howard Eiland and Kevin McLaughlin, Cambridge MA: Belknap/Harvard 1998.

Works on Bakhtin and Benjamin

Cohen, T., *Ideology and Inscription: 'Cultural Studies' after Benjamin, de Man, and Bakhtin*, Cambridge: Cambridge University Press, 1998.
Sandywell, B., 'Memories of Nature in Bakhtin and Benjamin', in Craig Brandist and Galin Tihanov (eds), *Materializing Bakhtin: The Bakhtin Circle and Social Theory*, London: Macmillan, 2000, pp. 94–118.
Zima, P. V., 'L'Ambivalence dialectique: entre Benjamin et Bakhtine', *Revue d'esthétique*, 1, 1981, 1, pp. 131–40.

Works on Bakhtin and the Bakhtin Circle

Adlam, C., 'Critical Work on the Bakhtin Circle: A New Bibliographical Essay', in Ken Hirschkop and David Shepherd (eds), *Bakhtin and Cultural Theory*, 2nd edition, Manchester: Manchester University Press, 2001, pp. 241–65.
Alpatov, V., 'The Bakhtin Circle and Problems in Linguistics', in Craig Brandist, David Shepherd and Galin Tihanov (eds), *The Bakhtin Circle: In the Master's Absence*, Manchester: Manchester University Press, 2004, pp. 70–96.
Averintsev, S. S., 'Bakhtin and the Russian Attitude to Laughter', in David Shepherd (ed.), *Bakhtin, Carnival and Other Subjects*, Special edition of *Critical Studies*, 3–4, 1993, pp. 13–19.
Bernard-Donals, M. F., *Mikhail Bakhtin: Between Phenomenology and Marxism*, Cambridge: Cambridge University Press, 1994.
Bernstein, M. A., 'When the Carnival Turns Bitter: Reflections on the Abject Hero', in Gary Saul Morson (ed.), *Bakhtin: Essays and Dialogues on his Work*, London, Chicago IL: Chicago University Press, 1986, pp. 99–121.
Bonetskaia, N., 'Bakhtin's Aesthetics as a Logic of Form', in David Shepherd (ed.), *The Contexts of Bakhtin: Philosophy, Authorship, Aesthetics*, Amsterdam: Harwood, 1998, pp. 83–94.
Bostad, F., 'Dialogue in Electronic Public Space: the Semiotics of Time, Space and the Internet', in Finn Bostad, Craig Brandist, Lars Sigred Evensen and Hege Faber (eds), *Bakhtinian Perspectives on Language and Culture: Meaning in Language, Art and New Media*, London: Palgrave/Macmillan, 2004, pp. 167–84.
Brandist, C., 'Ethics, Politics and the Potential of Dialogism', *Historical Materialism*, 5, 1999, 1, pp. 231–53.
——., 'The Hero at the Bar of Eternity: The Bakhtin Circle's Juridical Theory of the Novel', *Economy and Society*, 30, 2001, 2, pp. 208–28.
——., *The Bakhtin Circle: Philosophy, Culture and Politics*, London: Pluto, 2002.
——., 'Law and the Genres of Discourse: the Bakhtin Circle's Theory of Language and the Phenomenology of Right', in Finn Bostad, Craig Brandist, Lars Sigred Evensen and Hege Faber (eds), *Bakhtinian Perspectives on Language and Culture: Meaning in Language, Art and New Media*, London: Palgrave/Macmillan, 2004, pp. 23–45.

Clark, K., and Holquist, M., *Mikhail Bakhtin*, Cambridge MA, London: Harvard University Press, 1984.

Coates, R., *Christianity in Bakhtin: God and the Exiled Author*, Cambridge: Cambridge University Press, 1998.

——., 'Two of a Small Fraternity? Points of Contact and Departure in the Work of Bakhtin and Kagan up to 1924', in David Shepherd (ed.), *The Contexts of Bakhtin: Philosophy, Authorship, Aesthetics*, Amsterdam: Harwood, 1998, pp. 17–28.

——., 'The First and Second Adam in Bakhtin's Thought', in Susan M. Felch and Paul J. Contino (eds), *Religion in Bakhtin: A Feeling for Faith*, Evanston IL: Northwestern University Press, 2001, pp. 63–78.

Easthope, A., 'The Bakhtin School and Raymond Williams: Subject and Signifier', in David Shepherd (ed.), *Bakhtin, Carnival and Other Subjects*, Special edition of *Critical Studies*, 3–4, 1993, pp. 115–24.

Emerson, C., *The First Hundred Years of Mikhail Bakhtin*, Princeton NJ: Princeton University Press, 1997.

Gardiner, M. J., *The Dialogics of Critique: M. M. Bakhtin and the Theory of Ideology*, London: Routledge, 1992.

——., 'Bakhtin's Carnival: Utopia as Critique', in David Shepherd (ed.), *Bakhtin: Carnival and Other Subjects*, Special edition of *Critical Studies*, 3–4, 1993, pp. 20–47.

——., 'Alterity and Ethics: A Dialogical Perspective', *Theory, Culture and Society*, 13, 1996, 2, pp. 139–61.

Handley, W., 'The Ethics of Subject Creation in Bakhtin and Lacan', in David Shepherd (ed.), *Bakhtin, Carnival and Other Subjects*, Special edition of *Critical Studies*, 3–4, 1993, pp. 144–62.

Hirschkop, K., 'A Response to the Forum on Mikhail Bakhtin', in Gary Saul Morson (ed.), *Bakhtin: Essays and Dialogues on his Work*, London, Chicago IL: Chicago University Press, 1986, pp. 73–79.

——., 'Bakhtin Myths, or Why we all need Alibis', in *Bakhtin/'Bakhtin': Studies in the Archive and Beyond*, Special edition of *The South Atlantic Quarterly*, 97, 1998, pp. 579–98.

——., 'Is Dialogism for Real?', in David Shepherd (ed.), *The Contexts of Bakhtin: Philosophy, Authorship, Aesthetics*, Amsterdam: Harwood, 1998, pp. 183–95.

——., *Mikhail Bakhtin: An Aesthetic for Democracy*, Oxford: Oxford University Press, 1999.

Hitchcock, P., 'The World according to Globalization and Bakhtin', in Craig Brandist and Galin Tihanov (eds), *Materializing Bakhtin: The Bakhtin Circle and Social Theory*, London: Macmillan, 2000, pp. 3–19.

Holquist, M., *Dialogism: Mikhail Bakhtin and his World*, London: Routledge, 1990.

——., Foreword, in M. M. Bakhtin, *Toward a Philosophy of the Act*, ed. Michael Holquist and Vadim Liapunov, trans. Vadim Liapunov, Austin TX: University of Texas Press, 1993, pp. vii–xv.

Hutcheon, L., 'Modern Parody and Bakhtin', in Gary Saul Morson and Caryl Emerson (eds), *Rethinking Bakhtin: Extensions and Challenges*, Evanston IL: Northwestern University Press, pp. 87–103.

Jefferson, A., 'Bodymatters: Self and Other in Bakhtin, Sartre and Barthes', in Ken Hirschkop and David Shepherd (eds), *Bakhtin and Cultural Theory*, Manchester: Manchester University Press, 1989, pp. 152–57.

Kristeva, J., 'Une poétique ruinée', Preface to M. M. Bakhtine, *La Poétique de Dostoievski*, Paris: Seuil, 1975, pp. 5–27.

Kristeva, J., 'Word, Dialogue, Novel', in Toril Moi (ed.), *The Kristeva Reader*, Oxford: Blackwell, 1986, pp. 34–61.

Lock, C., 'Bakhtin and the Tropes of Orthodoxy', in Susan M. Felch and Paul J. Contino (eds), *Bakhtin and Religion: A Feeling for Faith*, Evanston IL: Northwestern University Press, 2001, pp. 97–119.

——., 'Bakhtin's Dialogism and the History of the Theory of Free Indirect Discourse', in Jørgen Bruhn and Jon Lundquist (eds), *The Novelness of Bakhtin*, Copenhagen: University of Copenhagen Press, 2001, pp. 71–87.

Matejka, L., 'On the First Prolegomena to Semiotics', Appendix I, in V. N. Vološinov, *Marxism and the Philosophy of Language*, London, Cambridge MA: Harvard University Press, 1986, pp. 161–74.

Mihailovic, A., *Corporeal Words: Mikhail Bakhtin's Theology of Discourse*, Evanston IL: Northwestern University Press, 1997.

de Man, P., 'Dialogue and Dialogism', in Gary Saul Morson and Caryl Emerson (eds), *Rethinking Bakhtin: Extensions and Challenges*, Evanston IL: Northwestern University Press, 1989, pp. 105–14.

Morson, G. S., 'Who speaks for Bakhtin?', in Gary Saul Morson (ed.), *Bakhtin: Essays and Dialogues on his Work*, London, Chicago IL: Chicago University Press, 1986, pp. 1–19.

——., 'Introduction: Rethinking Bakhtin', in Gary Saul Morson and Caryl Emerson (eds), *Rethinking Bakhtin: Extensions and Challenges*, Evanston IL: Northwestern University Press, 1989, pp. 1–60.

Morson, G. S., and Emerson, C., *Mikhail Bakhtin: Creation of a Prosaics*, Stanford CA: Stanford University Press, 1993.

Nealon, J. T., 'The Ethics of Dialogue: Bakhtin and Lévinas', *College English*, 59, 1997, 2, pp. 129–48.

Nielsen, G., 'Looking Back on the Subject: Mead and Bakhtin on Reflexivity and the Political', in Craig Brandist and Galin Tihanov (eds), *Materializing Bakhtin: The Bakhtin Circle and Social Theory*, London: Macmillan, 2000, pp. 142–63.

Nikolaev, N., 'The Nevel School of Philosophy (Bakhtin, Kagan and Pumpianskii) between 1918 and 1925: Materials from Pumpianskii's Archives', in David Shepherd (ed.), *The Contexts of Bakhtin: Philosophy, Authorship, Aesthetics*, Amsterdam: Harwood, 1998, pp. 29–41.

Palmieri, G., ' "The Author" According to Bakhtin ... And Bakhtin the Author', in David Shepherd (ed.), *The Contexts of Bakhtin: Philosophy, Authorship, Aesthetics*, Amsterdam: Harwood, 1998, pp. 45–56.

Pechey, G., 'Modernity and Chronotopicity in Bakhtin', in David Shepherd (ed.), *The Contexts of Bakhtin: Philosophy, Authorship, Aesthetics*, Amsterdam: Harwood, 1998, pp. 173–82.

——., 'Philosophy and Theology in "Aesthetic Activity" ', in Paul J. Contino and Susan M. Felch (eds), *Bakhtin and Religion: A Feeling for Faith*, Evanston IL.: Northwestern University Press, 2001, pp. 47–62.

Poole, R., 'The Apophatic Bakhtin', in Paul J. Contino and Susan M. Felch (eds), *Bakhtin and Religion: A Feeling for Faith*, Evanston IL: Northwestern University Press, 2001, pp. 151–75.

Roberts, M., 'Poetics Hermeneutics Dialogue: Bakhtin and Paul de Man', in Gary Saul Morson and Caryl Emerson (eds), *Rethinking Bakhtin: Extensions and Challenges*, Evanston IL: Northwestern University Press, 1989, pp. 115–34.

Tihanov, G., *The Master and the Slave: Lukács, Bakhtin, and the Ideas of their Time*, Oxford: Oxford University Press, 2000.

——., 'Culture, Form, Life: The Early Lukács and the Early Bakhtin', in Craig Brandist and Galin Tihanov (eds), *Materializing Bakhtin: The Bakhtin Circle and Social Theory*, London: Macmillan, 2000, pp. 43–69.

Tiupa, V., 'The Architectonics of Aesthetic Discourse', in David Shepherd (ed.), *The Contexts of Bakhtin: Philosophy, Authorship, Aesthetics*, Amsterdam: Harwood, 1998, pp. 95–107.

Todorov, T., *Mikhail Bakhtin: The Dialogical Principle*, trans. Wlad Godzich, Minneapolis MN: University of Minnesota Press, 1984.

Works on Benjamin

Adorno, T. W., 'Letters to Walter Benjamin', in Ernst Bloch *et al.*, *Aesthetics and Politics*, London: Verso, 1977, pp. 110–33.

——., 'Benjamin the Letter Writer', in Gary Smith (ed.), *On Walter Benjamin: Critical Essays and Reflections*, London, Cambridge MA: MIT Press, 1991, pp. 329–37.

——., 'Introduction to Benjamin's *Schriften*', in Gary Smith (ed.), *On Walter Benjamin: Critical Essays and Recollections*, London, Cambridge MA: MIT Press, 1991, pp. 2–17.

Arendt, H., Introduction, in Walter Benjamin, *Illuminations*, trans. Harry Zohn, London: Fontana, 1992, pp. 9–55.

Benjamin, A., 'Time and Task: Benjamin and Heidegger showing the Present', in Andrew Benjamin and Peter Osborne (eds), *Walter Benjamin's Philosophy: Destruction and Experience*, London: Routledge, 1994, pp. 216–50.

——., 'Benjamin's Modernity', in David S. Ferris (ed.), *The Cambridge Companion to Walter Benjamin*, Cambridge: Cambridge University Press, 2004, pp. 97–114.

Benjamin, A., and Osborne, P., Introduction, in Andrew Benjamin and Peter Osborne (eds), *Walter Benjamin's Philosophy: Destruction and Experience*, London: Routledge, 1994, pp. x–xiv.

Bloch, E., 'Recollections of Walter Benjamin', in Gary Smith (ed.), *On Walter Benjamin: Critical Essays and Reflections*, London, Cambridge MA: MIT Press, 1991, pp. 338–45.

Bredekamp, H., 'From Walter Benjamin to Carl Schmitt via Thomas Hobbes', *Critical Inquiry*, Special edition: 'Angelus Novus: Perspectives on Walter Benjamin', 25, 1999, 2, pp. 247–66.

Breithaupt, F., 'History as the Delayed Disintegration of Phenomena', in Gerhard Richter (ed.), *Benjamin's Ghosts: Interventions in Contemporary Literary and Cultural Theory*, Stanford CA: Stanford University Press, 2002, pp. 191–203.

Britt, B., *Walter Benjamin and the Bible*, New York: Continuum Press, 1996.

Bröcker, M., 'Sprache', in Michael Opitz and Erdmut Wizisla (eds), *Benjamins Begriffe*, Frankfurt/Main: Suhrkamp, 2000 pp. 740–73.

Brodersen, M., *Bibliografia critica generale*, Palermo: Centro Internazionale Studi di Estetica, 1984.

——., *Walter Benjamin: A Biography*, London: Verso, 1996.

Buck-Morss, S., *Dialectics of Seeing: Walter Benjamin and the Arcades Project*, London, Cambridge MA: MIT Press, 1989.

Caygill, H., 'Benjamin, Heidegger and the Destruction of Tradition', in Andrew Benjamin and Peter Osborne (eds), *Walter Benjamin's Philosophy: Destruction and Experience*, London: Routledge, 1994, pp. 1–31.

——., *Walter Benjamin: The Colour of Experience*, London: Routledge, 1998.

Cohen, M., *Profane Illumination: Walter Benjamin and the Paris of Surrealist Revolution*, London, Berkeley CA: University of California Press, 1993.

Comay, R., 'Benjamin and the Ambiguities of Romanticism', in David S. Ferris (ed.), *The Cambridge Companion to Walter Benjamin*, Cambridge: Cambridge University Press, 2004, pp. 134–51.

Düttmann, A. G., 'Tradition and Destruction: Walter Benjamin's Politics of Language', in Andrew Benjamin and Peter Osborne (eds), *Walter Benjamin's Philosophy: Destruction and Experience*, London: Routledge, 1994, pp. 32–58.

Eagleton, T., *Walter Benjamin or Towards a Revolutionary Criticism*, London: Verso, 1981.

Eiland, H., 'Reception in Distraction', in Andrew Benjamin (ed.), *Walter Benjamin and Art*, London: Continuum, 2005, pp. 3–13.

Fenves, P., 'The Genesis of Judgement: Spatiality, Analogy, and Metaphor in Benjamin's "On Language as Such and on Human Language" ', in David S. Ferris (ed.), *Walter Benjamin: Theoretical Questions*, Stanford CA: Stanford University Press, 1996, pp. 75–93.

——., 'Tragedy and Prophecy in Benjamin's "Origin of the German Mourning Play" ', in Gerhard Richter (ed.), *Benjamin's Ghosts: Interventions in Contemporary Literary and Cultural Theory*, Stanford CA: Stanford University Press, 2002, pp. 237–59.

Gasché, R., 'Objective Diversions: On Some Kantian Themes in Benjamin's "The Work of Art in the Age of its Mechanical Reproduction" ', in Andrew Benjamin and Peter Osborne (eds), *Walter Benjamin's Philosophy: Destruction and Experience*, London: Routledge, 1994, pp. 183–204.

Geulen, E., 'Under Construction: Walter Benjamin's "The Work of Art in the Age of Mechanical Reproduction" ', in Gerhard Richter (ed.), *Benjamin's Ghosts: Interventions in Contemporary Literary and Cultural Theory*, Stanford CA: Stanford University Press, 2002, pp. 121–41.

Gilloch, G., *Walter Benjamin: Critical Constellations*, Cambridge: Polity, 2002.

Habermas, J., 'Walter Benjamin: Consciousness-Raising or Rescuing Critique', in Gary Smith (ed.), *On Walter Benjamin: Critical Essays and Recollections*, London, Cambridge MA: MIT Press, 1991, pp. 90–128.

Hansen, B., 'Language and Mimesis in Walter Benjamin's Work', in David S. Ferris (ed.), *The Cambridge Companion to Walter Benjamin*, Cambridge: Cambridge University Press, 2004, pp. 54–72.

——., 'Benjamin or Heidegger: Aesthetics and Politics in an Age of Technology', in Andrew Benjamin (ed.), *Benjamin and Art*, London: Routledge, 2005, pp. 73–92.

Haxthausen, C. W., 'Reproduction/Repetition: Walter Benjamin/Carl Einstein', *October*, 107, 2004, pp. 47–74.

Hodge, J., 'The Timing of Elective Affinity: Walter Benjamin's Strong Aesthetics', in Andrew Benjamin (ed.), *Walter Benjamin and Art*, London: Continuum, 2005, pp. 14–31.

Jay, M., 'Experience without a Subject: Walter Benjamin and the Novel', in Laura Marcus and Lynda Nead (eds), *The Actuality of Walter Benjamin*, London: Lawrence and Wishart, 1998, pp. 194–211.

Jennings, M. W., *Dialectical Images: Walter Benjamin's Theory of Literary Criticism*, London, Ithaca NY: Cornell University Press, 1987.

——., 'Walter Benjamin and the European Avant-garde', in David S. Ferris (ed.), *The Cambridge Companion to Walter Benjamin*, Cambridge: Cambridge University Press, 2004, pp. 18–34.

Käther, R. *'Über Sprache überhaupt und über die Sprache des Menschen': Die Sprachphilosophie Walter Benjamins*, Bern, Frankfurt/Main, New York: Peter Lang, 1989.

Köpenick, L., 'Aura Reconsidered; Benjamin and Contemporary Visual Culture', in Gerhard Richter (ed.), *Benjamin's Ghosts: Interventions in Contemporary Literary and Cultural Theory*, Stanford CA: Stanford University Press, 2002, pp. 95–117.

Leslie, E., *Walter Benjamin: Overpowering Conformism*, London: Pluto Press, 2000.

Markner, R., and Weber, T. (eds), *Literatur über Walter Benjamin. Kommentierte Bibliographie 1983–92*, Berlin: Argument-Verlag, 1993.

McCole, J., *Walter Benjamin and the Antinomies of Tradition*, London, Ithaca NY: Cornell University Press, 1993.

Menninghaus, W., *Walter Benjamins Theorie der Sprachmagie*, Frankfurt/Main: Suhrkamp, 1995.

Mieszkowski, J., 'Art forms', in David S. Ferris (ed.), *The Cambridge Companion to Walter Benjamin*, Cambridge: Cambridge University Press, 2004, pp. 35–53.

Münster, A., *Progrès et catastrophe, Walter Benjamin et l'histoire: Réflections sur l'intinéraire philosophique d'un Marxisme 'mélancolique'*, Paris: Editions Kimé, 1996.

Nägele, R., 'The Poetic Ground Laid Bare (Benjamin reading Baudelaire)', David S. Ferris (ed.), *Benjamin: Theoretical Questions*, Stanford CA: Stanford University Press, 1996, pp. 118–38.

——., 'Body Politics: Benjamin's Dialectical Materialism between Brecht and the Frankfurt School', in David S. Ferris, *The Cambridge Companion to Walter Benjamin*, Cambridge: Cambridge University Press, 2004, pp. 152–76.

Pensky, M., *Melancholy Dialectics: Walter Benjamin and the Play of Mourning*, Amherst MA: University of Massachusetts Press, 1993.

Plate, S. B., *Walter Benjamin, Religion and Aesthetics: Rethinking Religion through the Arts*, London: Routledge, 2005.

Pressler, G. K., *Vom mimetischen Ursprung der Sprache: Walter Benjamins Sammelreferat 'Probleme der Sprachsoziologie' im Kontext seiner Sprachtheorie*, Bern, Frankfurt/Main, New York: Peter Lang, 1992.

Raulet, G., *Le Caractère destructeur: Esthétique, théologie et politique chez Walter Benjamin*, Paris: Aubier, 1997.

van Reijen, W., and van Doorn, H., *Aufenthalte und Passagen: Leben und Werk Walter Benjamins*, Frankfurt/Main: Suhrkamp, 2001.

Rochlitz, R., *The Disenchantment of Art: The Philosophy of Walter Benjamin*, trans. Jane Marie Todd, London, New York: Guildford, 1996.

Scholem, G., *Walter Benjamin. Die Geschichte einer Freundschaft*, Frankfurt/Main: Suhrkamp, 1975.

——., 'Walter Benjamin and his Angel', in Gary Smith (ed.), *Walter Benjamin: Critical Essays and Reflections*, London, Cambridge MA: MIT Press, 1991, pp. 51–89.

Smith, G., 'Thinking through Benjamin: An Introductory Essay', in Gary Smith (ed.), *Benjamin: Philosophy, History, Aesthetics*, London, Chicago IL: University of Chicago Press, 1983, pp. vii–xlii.

Tackels, B., *Petite Introduction à Walter Benjamin*, Paris: L'Harmattan, 2001.

Thornhill, C., *Walter Benjamin and Karl Kraus: Problems of a Wahlverwandschaft*, Stuttgart: Verlag Hans-Dieter Heinz, 1996.

Tiedemann, R., *Studien zur Philosophie Walter Benjamins*, Frankfurt/Main: Suhrkamp, 1973.

——, 'Historical Materialism or Political Messianism? An Interpretation of the Theses "On the Concept of History"', in Gary Smith (ed.), *Benjamin: Philosophy, Aesthetics, History*, London, Chicago IL: University of Chicago Press, 1983, pp. 175–209.

Voigts, M., 'Zitat', in Michael Opitz and Erdmut Wizisla (eds), *Benjamins Begriffe*, Frankfurt/Main: Suhrkamp, 2000, pp. 826–50.

Weber, S., 'Taking Exception to Decision: Walter Benjamin and Carl Schmitt', *Diacritics*, 22, 1992, 3–4, pp. 5–19.

——., 'Mass Mediauras; or, Art, Aura, and Media in the Work of Walter Benjamin', in David S Ferris, *Walter Benjamin: Theoretical Questions*, Stanford CA: Stanford University Press, 1996, pp. 27–49.

Weber, T., 'Erfahrung', in Michael Opitz and Erdmut Wizisla (eds), *Benjamins Begriffe*, Frankfurt/Main: Suhrkamp, 2000, pp. 230–59.

Wohlfarth, I., 'The Measure of the Possible, the Weight of the Real and the Heat of the Moment: Benjamin's Actuality Today', in Laura Marcus and Lynda Nead (eds), *The Actuality of Walter Benjamin*, London: Lawrence and Wishart, 1998, pp. 13–39.

Wolin, R., *Walter Benjamin: An Aesthetic of Redemption*, London, Berkeley CA: University of California Press, 1994.

——., 'Benjamin, Adorno and Surrealism', in Tim Huhn and Lambert Zuidervaart (eds), *The Semblance of Subjectivity: Essays in Adorno's Aesthetic Theory*, London, Cambridge MA: MIT press, 1999, pp. 93–122.

Ziarek, K., 'The Work of Art in the Age of Electronic Mutability', in Andrew Benjamin (ed.), *Walter Benjamin and Art*, London: Continuum, 2005, pp. 209–26.

General

'Alfred Döblin', in Rudolf Raddler *et al.*, *Kindlers neues Literaturlexikon*, 22 vols, Munich, 1988–98, Vol. 4, pp. 739–52.

Adorno, T. W., *Aesthetic Theory*, ed. and trans. Robert Hullot-Kentor, London: Athlone, 1997.

Adorno, T. W., and Horkheimer, M., *Dialectic of Enlightenment*, trans. John Cumming, London: Verso, 1997.

Antliff, M., *Inventing Bergson: Cultural Politics and the Parisian Avant-garde*, Princeton NJ: Princeton University Press, 1993.

Apollinaire, G., 'Zone', in *Alcools*, London: Athlone Press, 1993, pp. 39–44.

Arendt, H., *The Origins of Totalitarianism*, London: Harcourt Brace, 1973.

——., *On Revolution*, London: Penguin, 1991.

——., *Eichmann in Jerusalem: A Report on the Banality of Evil*, London: Penguin, 1998.

——., *The Human Condition*, London, Chicago IL: University of Chicago Press, 1998.

Aristotle, *The Poetics of Aristotle*, ed. and trans. Stephen Halliwell, London: Duckworth, 1987.

Auster, P., 'The Locked Room', in *The New York Trilogy*, London: Faber and Faber, 1987, pp. 199–314.

Barthes, R., 'La Mort de l'auteur', in *Le Bruissement de la langue: Essais critiques IV*, Paris: Seuil, 1984, pp. 63–69.

Benjamin, A., *Art, Mimesis, and the Avant-Garde*, London: Routledge, 1991.

Bennett, T., *Formalism and Marxism*, London: Methuen, 1979.

Benveniste, E., *Problems in General Linguistics*, trans. Mary E. Meek, Coral Gables FL: University of Miami Press, 1971.

Bergson, H., 'De la position des problèmes', in *La Pensée et le mouvant*, Paris: Presses Universitaires de France, 1999, pp. 25–98.

——., 'Introduction à la métaphysique', in *La Pensée et le mouvant*, Paris: Presses Universitaires de France, 1999, pp. 177–227.

Berlin, I., *Three Critics of the Enlightenment: Vico, Hamann, Herder*, Princeton NJ: Princeton University Press, 2000.

Bernstein, J. M., Introduction, in J. M. Bernstein (ed.), *Classical and Romantic German Aesthetics*, Cambridge: Cambridge University Press, 2003, pp. vii–xxxiii.

Bloch, E., Adorno, T. W., Benjamin, W., Brecht, B. and Lukas, G., *Aesthetics and Politics*, London: Verso, 1980.

Bogue, R., *Deleuze and Guattari*, London: Routledge, 1989.

Brecht, B., 'Vergnügungs Theater oder Lehrtheater', in *Schriften zum Theater*, Frankfurt/Main: Suhrkamp, 1977, pp. 60–74.

——., 'Das moderne Theater ist das epische Theater', in *Schriften zum Theater*, Frankfurt/Main: Suhrkamp, 1977, pp. 13–28.

Buck-Morss, S., *The Origin of Negative Dialectics*, New York: Free Press, 1977.

Bürger, P., *Theory of the Avant-Garde*, trans. Michael Shaw, Minneapolis MN: University of Minnesota Press, 1984.

Collinson, D., 'Aesthetic Experience', in Oswald Hanfling, *Philosophical Aesthetics*, Oxford: Blackwell, 1992, pp. 111–78.

Deleuze, G., and Guattari, F., *A Thousand Plateaus: Capitalism and Schizophrenia*, trans. Brian Massumi, London: Athlone, 1992.

Derrida, J., 'Différance', in *Margins of Philosophy*, trans. Alan Bass, London, Chicago IL: University of Chicago Press, 1984, pp. 1–28.

——., 'Force of Law: The "mystical foundation of authority" ', in Drucilla Cornell, Michael Rosenfeld and David Gray Carlson (eds), *Deconstruction and the Possibility of Justice*, London: Routledge, 1992, pp. 3–68.

——., *Of Grammatology*, trans. Gayatri Chakravorty Spivak, London: Routledge, 1998.

Descartes, R., 'Meditations on First Philosophy', in *Key Philosophical Writings*, ed. Enrique Chavez-Arvizo, trans. Elizabeth S. Haldane and G. R. T. Ross, Ware: Wordsworth, 1997, pp. 121–90.

Dilthey, W., *Poetry and Experience: Selected Works Vol. 5*, ed. Rudolf A. Makkreel and Frithjof Rodl, Princeton NJ: Princeton University Press, 1996.

Döblin, A., *Berlin Alexanderplatz*, Frankfurt/Main: Suhrkamp, 1980.

Dostoevsky, F., *The Karamazov Brothers*, trans. Ignat Avsey, Oxford: Oxford University Press, 1998.

Eagleton, T., *Against the Grain: Selected Essays 1975–1985*, London: Verso, 1986.

——., *The Ideology of the Aesthetic*, Oxford: Blackwell, 1990.

Eco, U., *Foucault's Pendulum*, trans. William Weaver, London: Vintage, 1990.

Elias, N., *The Civilizing Process*, Oxford: Blackwell, 1994.

Ewen, F., *Bertolt Brecht: His Life, his Art, his Times*, New York: Citadel Press, 1992.

Johann Gottlieb Fichte, *The Science of Knowledge*, ed. and trans. Peter Heath and John Lachs, Cambridge: Cambridge University Press, 1982.

Foucault, M., *Les Mots et les choses*, Paris: Flammarion, 1966.

Frisby, D., *Simmel*, London: Routledge, 1992.

Guyer, P., 'Absolute Idealism and the Rejection of Kantian Dualism', in Karl Ameriks (ed.), *The Cambridge Companion to German Idealism*, Cambridge: Cambridge University Press, 2000, pp. 37–56.

Hamann, J. G., 'Aesthetica in Nuce: A Rhapsody in Cabbalistic Prose', in J. M. Bernstein (ed.), *Classical and Romantic German Aesthetics*, Cambridge: Cambridge University Press, 2003, pp. 1–23.

Hammermeister, K., *The German Aesthetic Tradition*, Cambridge: Cambridge University Press, 2002.

Hawthorn, G., *Enlightenment and Despair: A History of Social Theory*, Cambridge: Cambridge University Press, 1976.

Hegel, G. W. F., *Elements of the Philosophy of Right*, ed. Allen W. Wood, trans. H.B. Nisbet, Cambridge: Cambridge University Press, 1991.

Heidegger, M., '...Poetically, Man dwells...', trans. Albert Hofstadter, in *Philosophical and Political Writings*, ed. Manfred Stassen, London: Continuum, 2003, pp. 265–78.

Heidegger, M., 'The Origin of the Work of Art', in *Basic Writings*, ed. D. F. Krell, London: Routledge, 1993, pp. 140–212.

Hobbes, T., *Leviathan*, ed. Richard Tuck, Cambridge: Cambridge University Press, 1996.

Hofmannsthal, H. von, 'Ein Brief', in Hofmannsthal, *Gesammelte Werke in Einzelausgaben: Prosa II*, ed. Herbert Steiner, Frankfurt/Main: Fischer, 1951, pp. 7–22.

Hölderlin, F., Letter to Schiller of 4 September 1795, in *Sämtliche Werke und Briefe*, ed. Michael Knaupp, 3 vols, Munich: Carl Hauser, 1992, Vol. 2, pp. 595–96.

——., 'Empedokles', in Friedrich Hölderlin, *Sämtliche Werke und Briefe*, ed. Michael Knaupp, 3 vols, Munich: Carl Hauser, 1992, Vol. 1, pp. 763–81.

——., 'Being Judgement Possibility', in J. M. Bernstein (ed), *Classic and Romantic German Aesthetics*, Cambridge: Cambridge University Press, 2003, pp. 191–92.

Humboldt, W. von, *On Language: The Diversity of Human Language-Structure and its Influence on the Mental Development of Mankind*, trans. Peter Heath, Cambridge: Cambridge University Press, 1989.

Husserl, E., 'Philosophy and the Crisis of European Man', in *Phenomenology and the Crisis of Philosophy*, trans. Quentin Lauer, New York: Harper, 1965, pp. 149–92.

Jameson, F., *Marxism and Form*, Princeton NJ: Princeton University Press, 1971.

——., *The Prison-House of Language: A Critical Account of Structuralism and Russian Formalism*, Princeton NJ: Princeton University Press, 1972.

——., *Brecht and Method*, London: Verso, 1998.

Jünger, E., *Der Kampf als inneres Erlebnis*, Berlin: Mittler und Sohn, 1926.

Kant, I., *Critique of Practical Reason and Other Moral Writings*, trans. Lewis White Beck, Chicago CA: University of Chicago Press, 1948.

——., *Critique of Pure Reason*, ed. Vasilis Politis, trans. J. M. Meiklejohn, London: Everyman, 1993.

——., 'Prolegomena to any Future Metaphysics', in *Prolegomena to any Future Metaphysics with Selections from the Critique of Pure Understanding*, ed. and trans. Gary Hatfield, Cambridge: Cambridge University Press, 1997, pp. 3–137.

——., *Groundwork of the Metaphysics of Morals*, ed. and trans. Mary Gregor, Cambridge: Cambridge University Press, 1998.

——., *Critique of the Power of Judgment*, ed. Paul Guyer, trans. Eric Matthews, Cambridge: Cambridge University Press, 2000.

——., 'Ideas on a Universal History with a Cosmopolitan Purpose', in *Political Writings*, ed. Hans Reiss, trans. H. B. Nisbet, Cambridge: Cambridge University Press, 2002, pp. 41–53.

Köhnke, K. C., *The Rise of Neo-Kantianism: German Academic Philosophy between Idealism and Positivism*, Cambridge: Cambridge University Press, 1991.

Larmore, C., 'Hölderlin and Novalis', in Karl Ameriks (ed.), *The Cambridge Companion to German Idealism*, Cambridge: Cambridge University Press, 2000, pp. 141–60.

Léger, F., *La Pensée de Georg Simmel*, Paris: Editions Kimé, 1989.

Lukács, G., 'Reification and the Consciousness of the Proletariat', in *History and Class Consciousness*, trans. Rodney Livingstone, London: Merlin, 1971, pp. 83–222.

——., *The Theory of the Novel*, trans. Anna Bostock, London: Merlin, 1971.

Marinetti, F., 'The Founding and Manifesto of Futurism', in Vassiliki Kolocotroni, Jane Goldman and Olga Taxidou (eds), *Modernism: An Anthology of Sources and Documents*, Edinburgh: Edinburgh University Press, 1998, pp. 249–53.

Marx, K., and Engels, E., 'The Communist Manifesto', in Karl Marx, *Selected Writings*, ed. David McClellan, Oxford: Oxford University Press, 1977, pp. 221–47.

Meschonnic, H., *L'Utopie du Juif*, Paris: Desclée de Brouwer, 2001.

Mouffe, C., *On the Political*, London: Routledge, 2005.

Mukařovský, J., 'Estetická funkce, norma a hodnota jako sociální fakty', in *Studie*, ed. Miroslav Červenka and Milan Jankovič, 2 vols, Brno: Host, 2000, Vol. 1, pp. 81–148.

——., 'Záměrnost a nezáměrnost v umění', in *Studie*, ed. Miroslav Červenka and Milan Jankovič, 2 vols, Brno: Host, 2000, Vol. 1, pp. 353–88.

Nietzsche, F., *The Will to Power*, trans. Walter Kaufmann and R. J. Hollingdale, New York: Vintage, 1968.

——., 'The Genealogy of Morals', in *Basic Writings of Nietzsche*, ed. and trans. Walter Kaufmann, New York: The Modern Library, 1992, pp. 451–599.

——., *The Birth of Tragedy out of the Spirit of Music*, ed. Michael Tanner, trans. Shaun Whiteside, London: Penguin, 1993.

Osborne, P., *The Politics of Time: Modernity and Avant-Garde*, London: Verso, 1995.

Overhoff, J., 'The Theology of Thomas Hobbes's *Leviathan*', *Journal of Ecclesiastical History*, 51, 2000, 3, pp. 527–55.

Poggi, G., *Money and the Modern Mind: Georg Simmel's Philosophy of Money*, Berkeley CA: University of California Press, 1993.

Rang, F. C., 'Historische Psychologie des Karnevals', in *Karneval*, ed. Lorenz Jäger, Berlin: Brinkmann and Bose, 1983, pp. 7–45.

Rousseau, J.-J., 'A Discourse on the Origin of Inequality', in *The Social Contract and Discourses*, ed. P. D. Jimack, trans. G. D. H. Cole, London: Everyman, 1993, pp. 31–126.

——., 'A Discourse on the Moral Effects of the Arts and Sciences' , in *The Social Contract and Discourses*, ed. P. D. Jimack, trans. G. D. H. Cole, London: Everyman, 1993, pp. 1–29.

Sartre, J.-P., *Being and Nothingness: An Essay on Phenomenological Ontology*, trans. Hazel Barnes, New York: Citadel, 1954.

de Saussure, F., *Course in General Linguistics*, trans. by Roy Harris, London: Duckworth, 1983.

Schact, R., *Nietzsche*, London: Routledge, 1983.

Scheler, M., 'Love and Knowledge', in *On Feeling, Knowing and Valuing*, ed. and trans. Harold Bershady, Chicago: University of Chicago Press, 1992, pp. 147–65.

Schiller, F., *On the Aesthetic Education of Man*, ed. and trans. E. M. Wilkinson and L. A. Willoughby, Oxford: Clarendon Press, 1967.

Schleifer, R., *Modernism and Time: The Logic of Abundance in Literature, Science and Culture 1880–1930*, Cambridge: Cambridge University Press, 2000.

Schmitt, C., *Political Theology*, trans. George Schwab, Cambridge MA: MIT Press, 1985.

Scholem, G., *The Messianic Idea in Judaism*, New York: Schocken Books, 1971.

Simmel, G., *Philosophie des Geldes*, ed. David Frisby and Klaus Christian Köhnke, Frankfurt/Main: Suhrkamp, 1989.

——., 'Die Gross-Städte und das Geistesleben', in *Das Individuum und die Freiheit*, ed. Michael Landmann and Margarete Susman, Frankfurt/Main: Fischer, 1993, pp. 192–204.

——., 'Der Begriff und die Tragödie der Kultur', in *Aufsätze und Abhandlungen 1909–1918*, Gesamtausgabe Vol. 12, ed. Ottthein Rammstedt, Frankfurt/ Main, 2001, pp. 194–223.

——., 'Das individuelle Gesetz: Ein Versuch über das Prinzip der Ethik', in *Aufsätze und Abhandlungen 1909–1918*, Gesamtausgabe Vol. 12, ed. Ottthein Rammstedt, Frankfurt/Main, 2001, pp. 417–70.

Sommerville, J. P., *Thomas Hobbes: Political Ideas in Historical Contexts*, London: Macmillan, 1992.

Spengler, O., *Der Untergang des Abendlandes*, 2 vols, Munich: C. H. Beck, 1923.

Steiner, G., *Heidegger*, London: Fontana, 1992.

Taussig, M., *Mimesis and Alterity: A Particular History of the Senses*, London: Routledge, 1993.

Thibault, P. J., *Re-reading Saussure: The Dynamics of Signs in Social Life*, London: Routledge, 1997.

Thucydides, *History of the Peloponnesian War*, ed. M. I. Finley, trans. Rex Warner, London: Penguin, 1972.

Tönnies, F., *Community and Association*, trans. Charles P. Loomis, London: Routledge, 1955.

Trotsky, L., *Literature and Revolution*, trans. Rose Strunsky, London: RedWords, 1991.

Türcke, C., and Bolte, G., *Einführung in die kritische Theorie*, Darmstadt: Wissenschaftliche Buchgesellschaft, 1994.

Tynjanov, J. N., 'On Literary Evolution', in Ladislav Matejka and Krystyna Pomorska (eds), *Readings in Russian Poetics: Formalist and Structuralist Views*, Cambridge MA: MIT Press, 1971, pp. 66–78.

Weber, M., 'Science as Vocation', in *From Max Weber: Essays in Sociology*, ed. and trans. H. H. Gerth and C. Wright Mills, London: Routledge, 1991, pp. 129–45.

Weber, S., *Return to Freud: Jacques Lacan's Dislocation of Psychoanalysis*, Cambridge: Cambridge University Press, 1991.

Williams, R., *Marxism and Literature*, Oxford: Oxford University Press, 1977.

Wittgenstein, L., *Tractatus Logico-philosophicus*, German text with an English translation *en regard* by C. K. Ogden, London: Routledge, 1999.

Young, J. M., 'Functions of Thought and the Synthesis of Intuitions', in Paul Guyer (ed.), *The Cambridge Companion to Kant*, Cambridge: Cambridge University Press, 1992, pp. 101–22.

Zach, N., 'Imagism and Vorticism', in Malcolm Bradbury and James McFarlane (eds), *Modernism: A Guide to European Literature 1890–1930*, Harmondsworth: Penguin, 1991, pp. 228–42.

Zahavi, D., *Husserl's Phenomenology*, Stanford CA: Stanford University Press, 2003.

Žižek, S., *Did somebody say Totalitarianism?: Five Interventions in the (Mis)use of a Notion*, London: Verso, 2001.

——., 'A Plea for Leninist Intolerance', *Critical Inquiry*, 28, 2002, 2, pp. 542–66.

Web page

Page of Sheffield University's Bakhtin Centre's project: 'The rise of sociological linguistics in the Soviet Union, 1917–1938: Institutions, Ideas and Agendas': <http://shef.ac.uk/uni/academic/A-C/bakh/sociolinguistics.html>, accessed 4 January 2007.

Index

abstraction, 26, 50, 54–5, 59, 105, 117, 124, 176
Adorno, Theodor W., 8, 22–3, 50, 157, 168–9, 188
alibi ('non-alibi-in-Being'), 16, 61–2, 136
alienation, 50, 51, 57–8, 119, 120, 121
allegory, 128–9, 133, 141
and dialogue, 131–2
apophasis, 192, 193
Arendt, Hannah, 158, 165, 173, 176
Aristotle, 14, 144, 173
art, 119, 123–5, 144–52
aura, 26, 30, 36, 38, 55, 111, 151, 163
and dialogue, 106–7
author, position in Bakhtin's thought of, 115–16, 140–2
authority
authoritarian tradition, 30, 34, 35–41, 75, 137
authoritative discourse, 35–6, 37–8, 137
avant-garde, 6, 125, 166, 187–8

Bakhtin, Mikhail Mikhailovich
smoking, 19, 160
thought, development of, 25–6, 115–17, 148–9
works: 'Author and Hero in Aesthetic Activity', 20–2, 47, 144–5; 'Discourse in the Novel', 22, 37–9, 40–1, 102–3, 150; 'Epic and Novel', 26–7, 35–6, 195; 'Notes from 1970–1971', 108–9; 'The Problem of the Text in Linguistics, Philosophy and the Human Sciences', 34, 122; *Problems of Dostoevsky's Poetics*, 12–13, 27, 107–8, 110,

126–7, 131–2, 141–3, 150–2, 158; *Rabelais and his World*, 11–12, 158; 'Response to a Question from the *Novyi Mir* Editorial Staff', 44–5; 'Towards a Methodology of the Human Sciences', 149; *Towards a Philosophy of the Act*, 20, 56–71, 88–9, 116, 124
Barthes, Roland, 155, 167
Baudelaire, Charles, 7, 124, 129–30, 188
'À une Passante', 147–8
Baudrillard, Jean, 2
Beck, Ulrich, 3
Benjamin, Andrew, 152
Benjamin, Walter
smoking, 161
suicide, cult of, 9
thought, development of, 25–6
works: *Arcades Project*, 23, 108, 110, 111; 'The Author as Producer', 10; 'Berlin Chronicle', 23; *The Concept of Criticism in German Romanticism*, 10, 43, 44; 'On the Concept of History', 9, 15, 43, 85–6, 123, 148; 'The Crisis of the Novel', 111–14; 'The Destructive Character', 24; 'Erfahrung', 73–4; 'Experience and Poverty', 29, 163, 165; 'Franz Kafka: on the Tenth Anniversary of his Death', 47; 'Goethe's *Elective Affinities*', 43, 165; 'On Language as Such and on the Language of Man', 12, 97–101, 117–19, 121, 125; 'Moscow Diary', 5; *The Origin of German Tragic Drama*, 23, 125–9, 191; 'Problems in the Sociology of Language', 97–8;

Benjamin, Walter – *continued*
  'On the Programme of the
  Coming Philosophy', 81–4,
  88–9, 96, 120; 'A Short History
  of Photography', 106; 'On Some
  Motifs in Baudelaire', 28–9, 79,
  106–7; 'The Storyteller', 1, 25,
  46–7, 78–80, 84, 145–6;
  'Surrealism: Last Snapshot of
  the European Intelligentsia',
  135; 'The Task of the
  Translator', 45–6, 101–2, 104–5;
  'Theological-Political
  Fragment', 132–3; 'Theories of
  German Fascism', 75–8;
  'Translation – For or Against',
  102, 105; 'The Work of Art in
  the Age of its Technological
  Reproducibility', 23–4, 29–32,
  35, 101, 111, 161–2, 179
Benveniste, Émile, 94
Bergson, Henri, 54–5, 60, 129
Bernstein, J. M., 119–20
Bildung, 125, 191
biology, 65–6, 76
Bloch, Ernst, 187
body, *see* experience, bodily
Brandist, Craig, 118, 155, 159, 189
Brecht, Bertolt, 3, 7, 10, 25–6, 42–3,
  112–13, 134, 155
  epic theatre, 10, 14, 112, 151, 163,
  188
Buber, Martin, 114
Buck-Morss, Susan, 26, 110
Bürger, Peter, 187, 188

capitalism, 13, 26, 50, 64, 77, 110, 135
carnival, 11–13, 157
catastrophe, 134–5, 143, 148, 192, 193
Caygill, Howard, 24, 107
childhood, 23, 74, 178
Christ, 71, 134, 140–1, 143
cinema, 23–4, 31, 39–40, 80, 109
city, *see* experience, urban
civilization, 56, 66
Clark, Katerina, 11
closedness, 17–18, 37–8, 46–7, 113,
  137, 141, 142–3, 152, 191

  see also totalization ; *compare*
  openness
Coates, Ruth, 12, 117–18, 140, 144,
  189
Cohen, Hermann, 180
Cohen, Tom, 154
collecting, 23, 24
commodity form, 26, 50, 64, 77, 135,
  162, 174, 193
contemporaneity, 38–9, 150–2
  see also simultaneity
criticism, 6, 10, 44–7, 103

Dada, 109, 110, 111
death, 66, 68–9, 86, 145–6, 148–9, 194
Decadence, 74, 75, 178
Deconstruction, 6, 192
Deleuze, Gilles, 92, 164–5
Derrida, Jacques, 6, 94, 115–16, 182,
  192
Descartes, René, 119–20
destruction, 35, 133
  destructive character, 24, 133, 134
dialectical image, 151–2
dialogue, 26, 38, 91–2, 93, 107–8, 110,
  118, 122, 124, 136–7, 138
  and allegory, 131–2
  and aura, 106–7
  see also novel, polyphonic
Dilthey, Wilhelm, 53, 72, 172–3
distraction, 31–3
Döblin, Alfred, 111–14, 189
Dostoevsky, Fyodor, 3, 7, 37, 39, 93–4,
  107, 109, 111, 112, 118, 126–7
  Brothers Karamazov, 142
Düttmann, Alexander Garcia, 165

Eagleton, Terry, 3, 155, 159, 164, 191
Emerson, Caryl, 139, 177
epic, 2, 20, 35–6
epic theatre, *see* Brecht, Bertolt
Erasmus, Desiderius, 164
Erfahrung, *see* experience
Erlebnis, *see* experience
ethics, 21–2, 70, 77–8, 84–7, 172,
  180–1
  and politics, 84–7, 180–1
experience
  bodily, 28–9, 32–3, 38, 79–80, 83,
  120, 162, 164

Erfahrung, 74–5
Erfahrung and *Erlebnis*, 53–4, 55–6,
    57, 62–3, 71–2, 79–81, 124,
    129–30, 177–8
and form, 1–2, 7, 17–18, 35, 50,
    51–2, 55
'higher', 72, 82–4, 89, 94, 100, 124,
    125
mathematical conception of, 81–4,
    88–9, 120, 180
urban, 7, 50, 79, 129–30, 179
see also Kant, Immanuel, experience

Fall, the, 12, 117–19, 189
fascism, 8, 56, 75–6, 84–5, 178
fear, 2, 14, 153, 157
Fichte, Johann Gottlieb, 95, 171
film, *see* cinema
'final word', 130, 139–40, 143,
    144, 152
finalization, 122, 125, 136
    see also totalization
form, 1–2, 7, 17–18, 25, 35, 50, 51–2,
    55, 123, 136, 144–5, 149
closed, 17–18, 47, 112–13, 141
and experience, 1–2, 7, 17–18, 35,
    50, 51–2, 55
open, 17–18, 125, 136, 138, 142,
    150
see also art; closedness; genre; habit;
    language; openness; tradition
Foucault, Michel, 99
fragmentation, 109, 122–3, 125, 126,
    128, 191
    see also openness; *compare* totality
freedom, 11, 21–2, 24, 48–9, 135, 139
Freud, Sigmund, 79, 193
Futurism, Italian, 55–6

genre, 7, 25, 162
    see also novel; poetry; story
George, Stefan, 100, 133, 185
Giddens, Anthony, 3
Gilloch, Graeme, 157
God, 98–9, 117–18, 133, 140, 152
Goethe, Johann Wolfgang, 6
Goldmann, Lucien, 10
Great Soviet Encyclopaedia, 5
Guattari, Félix, 92, 164–5

Habermas, Jürgen, 3, 190
habit, 19–34, 55, 113
and art, 123–4
Bakhtin and, 19–22
Benjamin and, 22–4
Hegel and, 48–50
Hamann, Friedrich, 186
Hegel, Georg Wilhelm Friedrich, 2, 8,
    48–50, 138, 156
Heidegger, Martin, 94, 97, 183
heteroglossia, 104–5, 113–14
hierarchy, 2, 13, 17–18, 30, 36, 40, 137
    see also authority
Hirschkop, Ken, 19, 25, 130–1, 136,
    153, 173
historicism, 44–5, 85–6
Hobbes, Thomas, 70–1, 177
Hofmannsthal, Hugo von, 100, 185
Hölderlin, Friedrich, 95–7, 99, 117
Holquist, Michael, 11
Horkheimer, Max, 8, 190
Humboldt, Wilhelm von, 91, 182
Hume, David, 21
Husserl, Edmund, 53, 72, 171

Idealism, 77–8
    see also Kant, Immanuel
incarnation, 70, 141, 177
indirect discourse, 92–4, 97, 101, 114,
    139, 186
and allegory, 131–2
intersubjectivity, 58, 69–70, 90–5, 98,
    99, 100, 106, 116
intoxication, 13, 14, 60

Jameson, Frederic, 153
Jay, Martin, 72, 95
Jewish tradition, *see* theology
Joyce, James, 7, 156
judgement, 95–6, 117–18, 122
Jünger, Ernst, 56, 75–7, 178

Kant, Immanuel, 21, 26, 59, 67, 78,
    174, 179
aesthetics, 124–5
ethics, 78, 172
experience, 52–4, 79–80, 81–4, 170–1
freedom, 48, 160–1

Kästner, Erich, 9, 157
kenosis, 140–1, 142, 193
Kraus, Karl, 115, 133
Kristeva, Julia, 6, 155

l'art pour l'art, 75, 186
Lacan, Jacques, 164, 181–2
Lacis, Asja, 5
language, 83–4, 88–121, 124
   instrumentalization of, 100, 101,
      115, 117, 185–6
   and the messiah, 133–4
laughter, 132, 157–8
   and melancholy, 8–14
Lebensphilosophie, 5, 52, 53, 55, 65,
      75–6, 80
   see also Bergson, Henri; Simmel,
      Georg
Lenin, Vladimir Ilyich, 3
Leslie, Esther, 16, 159, 179
linguistics, 97–8, 181, 184–5
'loophole', 144, 152
   see also space, clearing of
love, 67–70, 85, 86–7, 124, 175–6
   'at last sight', 148, 194–5
Lukács, Georg, 5–6, 162, 179
   see also reification
Lyotard, Jean-François, 2

McCole, John, 191–2
Mallarmé, Stéphane, 100
Marx, Karl, 13, 64, 77, 135
   Communist Manifesto, 13, 137
   see also commodity form
Marxism, 15–16, 134–5
materialism, 7, 37, 39, 90, 165, 166
mechanical reproduction, 29, 30, 32,
      34, 38, 134, 151
Medvedev, Pavel Nikolaevich, 6
melancholy, 119, 120–1, 146
   and laughter, 8–14
memory, *see* remembrance
Meschonnic, Henri, 192
messiah, 132–4, 152
   see also Christ
Messianism, 18, 144, 194
Metropolis, 162
Mihailovic, Alexandar, 159
mimesis, 14, 110, 118, 188, 190

Modernism, 156
   see also avant-garde
modernity, 2, 6–8, 25, 26–34, 63–7,
      84, 116–17, 118, 121, 122, 135,
      138
money, 64–5, 174
monologue, 26, 27, 55, 93, 107–8,
      112–13, 116–17, 118, 121, 130–2,
      137–8
montage, 24, 31, 39, 108–13, 115,
      124, 126, 152, 166
Morson, Gary Saul, 139, 177
Mouffe, Chantal, 3
Mukařovský, Jan, 167, 168
Münster, Arno, 160
mysticism
   Jewish, 9
   linguistic, 97, 115
   Romantic, 120
Myth, 2, 8, 56, 75, 76, 77

narratability, 72, 79–80
   see also transmissibility
nature, 75–6, 77, 98–101, 118–21
   see also biology; experience,
      bodily
Nazism, 9
   see also fascism
neo-Kantianism, 5, 51, 72
Nietzsche, Friedrich, 60, 74, 75, 170
Nietzscheanism, 173
novel
   Benjamin on, 111–14
   and modernity, 7–8, 26–7
   monologic, 112, 121, 141
   polyphonic, 20, 25–6, 36–8, 40–1,
      93–4, 109, 111–14, 117, 141–4,
      150, 151
   see also Dostoevsky

openness, 17–18, 26–7, 37–8, 58,
      59, 125, 136, 138, 142–3, 150,
      152, 191
   see also fragmentation; *compare*
      closedness

photography, 80, 106
plagiarism, 187
Plate, S. Brent, 178

poetry
Bakhtin and, 40–1, 102–3
Benjamin and, 118–19
Hölderlin and, 96–7, 183
politics
depoliticization of Bakhtin and
Benjamin by critics, 8–11
'end of', 3
and ethics, 84–7, 180–1
of montage, 110–1
and theology, 14–16, 18
see also Marxism
polyphony, *see* novel, polyphonic
post-Structuralism, 6, 155
postmodernism, 156
postmodernity, 2
'pretender', 67, 73, 131–2, 174, 176
see also totalization, false
progress, 3, 86, 123, 134–5
Proust, Marcel, 7, 124

quotation, 108–9, 111, 114, 115,
186–7

Rabelais, François, 11–12, 131–2
Rang, Florens Christian, 157
reification, 22, 162, 179
religion, *see* theology
remembrance, 46, 86–7, 124, 144–6,
149–50, 157
repetition, 26, 28, 29, 30, 33–4, 101–2,
164–5
responsibility, 67, 73, 175
responsible participation, 61–3, 83–4,
88–9, 116, 124
revolution, 18, 133, 135, 138, 193
rhythm, 20–2, 32
ritual, 27–30, 32, 174
Rochlitz, Rainer, 98
Rolland, Romain, 186
Romantics, German, 43, 119–20,
127–8
Rousseau, Jean-Jacques, 99, 171, 174
Russian Formalism, 6, 20, 155, 167
Russian philosophical tradition, 171,
193

Sandywell, Barry, 3
Sartre, Jean-Paul, 176–7

Saussure, Ferdinand de, 26, 91, 97,
154, 182, 189
Schein, 26, 127–8
Scheler, Max, 175–6
Schiller, Friedrich, 125
Schlegel, Friedrich, 44, 162, 167
Schleifer, Ronald, 154
Schmitt, Carl, 3, 15
and Benjamin, 153
Scholem, Gershom, 8–9, 157, 192
Schopenhauer, Arthur, 128
seriousness, 2, 12–14, 132, 159
official, 2
shock, 26, 79–80, 126, 148
silence, 8, 12, 105, 114–16, 119,
120–1, 132
Simmel, Georg, 50–3, 57–8, 64–5, 72,
77, 89–90, 168–70, 175
influence on Bakhtin, 51
influence on Benjamin, 50–2, 72
simultaneity, 39, 166
see also contemporaneity
Soviet culture, 5, 98
space, clearing of, 10, 13–14, 134, 136,
141–4, 151–2
see also openness
Spengler, Oswald, 60, 66
Stalinism, 8, 135, 193
stasis, 144–5, 148, 150–1, 194
story, 2, 28, 80, 84, 163
storyteller, 28, 32, 43, 84
Structuralism, 6, 155, 181–2
Czech, 167, 168
Surrealism, 10, 23, 109, 180
symbol, 26, 127–9
Symbolism, 100

Taussig, Michael, 32
technology, 2, 8, 37, 65, 69, 76–7, 79,
80
information, 153
temporality, 54, 85–7, 144–52
theology, 14–16, 18, 132–4, 140–1,
192, 193
apophatic, 192, 193
Jewish, 15, 132, 192
negative, 141, 192, 193
and politics, 14–16, 18
see also mysticism

'threshold', 142, 152
  see also space, clearing of
Thucydides, 194
Tihanov, Galin, 63, 154, 156
time, *see* temporality
Todorov, Tsvetan, 162
Tolstoy, Leo, 93
Tönnies, Friedrich, 50
totality, 119, 122–3, 125
  negative, 18, 125, 129, 130, 134,
    143–4, 191
  see also closedness; totalization;
    compare fragmentation,
    openness
totalization, 138, 143–6, 148
  false, 41, 113, 128–9, 130–2, 149
tradition, 28, 30–1, 35–44, 47, 75, 79,
    103, 137
  counter-tradition, 41–4, 47
'tragedy of culture', 51–2, 57–8, 77,
    81, 89–91, 169–70
transfiguration (*Verklärung*), 55, 75,
    172, 191–2
translation, 46, 100–8
transmissibility, 35, 41, 75
  see also narratability

Trauerspiel, 9, 43, 125–9
Trotsky, Leon, 138–9

Vienna Circle, 97, 181, 184
violence, 8, 11, 69, 131, 158
Voloshinov, Valentin Nikolaevich,
    6, 20, 26, 51, 89–93, 98,
    136–40, 177, 181–2, 185,
    189, 193
  *Marxism and the Philosophy of
    Language*, 89–93, 136–40, 181
Vossler, Karl, 91

war, 1, 2, 55–6, 63, 75–8, 175, 176,
    177
  First World, 1, 55–6, 75–8, 175
  Russian Civil, 176
  on terror, 2
Watt, Ian, 10
Weber, Max, 50
Williams, Raymond, 156, 182
Wittgenstein, Ludwig, 181

Zima, Pierre (Petr), 3–4, 154
Žižek, Slavoj, 3